Compliance and Compromise

Nijhoff Law Specials

VOLUME 76

The titles published in the series are listed at brill.nl/nlsp

Compliance and Compromise

The Jurisprudence of Gender Pay Equity

By
Cher Weixia Chen

MARTINUS
NIJHOFF
PUBLISHERS

LEIDEN • BOSTON
2011

This book is printed on acid-free paper.

Library of Congress Cataloging-in-Publication Data

Chen, Cher Weixia.
Compliance and compromise : the jurisprudence of gender pay equity / by Cher Weixia Chen.
p. cm. – (Nijhoff law specials; v. 76)
Includes bibliographical references and index.
ISBN 978-90-04-20307-5 (pbk. : alk. paper) 1. Sex discrimination in employment--Law and legislation. 2. Pay equity--Law and legislation. 3. Sex discrimination against women--Law and legislation. I. Title.
K1772.C48 2011
344.01'4133--dc23

2011025619

ISSN 0924-4549
ISBN 978-90-04-20307-5

To Shawn and Ivy

TABLE OF CONTENTS

PREFACE AND ACKNOWLEDGEMENTS

I love international law. The reality that international law has been belittled by so many for so long certainly puzzles me. My quest to understand international law started with the readings of its classics. No scholar is owed a greater debt in this regard than the late Virginia Leary, whose *International Labor and National Law* (1982) was the main inspiration for this book. The level of her legal erudition is simply insurmountable to me, which is worsened by the fact that I am a political scientist and not a lawyer. But I would like to at least try hard to follow her step and I was delighted to find myself sharing something in common with the great Virginia Leary: the passion for international law.

After the successful defense of the research proposal, I went to the International Labor Organization (ILO) at Geneva, Switzerland to collect the data. The ILO is a veritable treasure house that should be of tremendous value to both practitioners and scholars. Later the internship with the United States Department of Labor enhanced my overall understanding of labor law. With such preparation, I began writing my doctoral dissertation and then this book manuscript.

This book is an attempt to broaden the scope of the subject in the field of international legal compliance. As domestic industrial relations and labor conditions have been seriously challenged by globalization, various international labor standards have been proposed to safeguard and promote labor rights. However, an important question remains: are these rules and standards enforceable and well enforced? This manuscript hopefully contributes to the existing literature on compliance of international human rights law with its study of a fundamental human right which has not been addressed before—gender pay equity.

There are various approaches to address the issue of gender pay equity. This book chooses to frame it within the research program of "international legal compliance". So "compliance and compromise" is the theme throughout the book. In other words, this book is more about the compliance of the international law (ILO No. 100 in particular) on gender pay equity rather than the causes of gender pay equity (certainly the second chapter does review the literature on gender pay equity).

There have been plenty of ups and downs during the long journey of writing this book. When I look back, I can only be grateful for this irreplaceable experience, for all the people who cared for and supported me throughout all these years.

I would like to first express my deep gratitude to my mentors: Professor Alison Dundes Renteln, Professor Stanley Rosen and Professor Eugene Cooper at University of Southern California, for their constant guidance and insightful comments. In particular, I am indebted to Professor Alison Dundes Renteln for her invaluable encouragement throughout the course of writing. I was fortunate to have Professor Renteln as my mentor. Her passion for international law and comparative law drove me into the then newly merged Politics and International Relations program. During the five years of my graduate study at USC, she taught me how to write and teach. She, as a brilliant scholar and human being, made me realize that anything is possible (OK, almost). She read drafts of this book manuscript with rigorous comments and interest, and provided critical insights for revision. If someday I could be remotely close to what she has achieved as a scholar and woman, I would be happy enough. Professor Rosen taught me about Chinese politics and films. His kindness, sense of humor, and sincerity as a scholar are what I could only hope for. Professor Cooper, from whom I learned about the anthropological perspective, offered challenging comments for my book. His continuous support and mentoring made me a better scholar.

Special thanks are due to Dr. Jennifer Cichocki for editing some part of this book. I am always amazed by her optimistic attitude towards life and work. I would also like to thank my colleague and friend Ms. Li Wenyu for her kind help with the use of SPSS.

My family back in China, provided me unconditional support and love, no matter where I was. After my father passed away when I was in my seventh grade, it was my older sisters and brothers who raised me. Without them, I could not imagine what my life will be like now. I owe my life to them, especially to my sister Weixin. She is my hero. I worked hard in the high school and went to the best university in China, just to make her proud. And now, I am still trying to make her proud.

Finally, I wish to dedicate this book to my husband Shawn and my daughter Ivy. With Shawn, I find home. He believes in me more than

I believe in myself. His presence has been a loving part that I cannot live without. I am thankful for having him as my husband, my friend, and my partner. My daughter Ivy has changed my life drastically. I am simply grateful for all of the wonderful changes she has brought into my life. I am a proud mother and hopefully she is a proud daughter.

LIST OF TABLES

LIST OF FIGURES

CHAPTER I

INTRODUCTION

> International law is an unwanted intruder into domestic law. In much the same way that common law legal systems resisted the 'Romanist' influences of European civil law, so too do many domestic legal institutions actively repel the application of international law norms.
>
> —David J. Bederman[1]

I do not "hate" international law scholarship as Bederman does, but I do wonder whether and how domestic law so "unwants" and "resists" international law.

Does international law matter to international relations or domestic politics? The literature of "international legal compliance" asks the same question. Many scholars believe that the end of the cold war has rendered international law an independent power of constraining and shaping state behavior. Since the 1990s, this body of literature has become rather theoretically and methodologically diverse. It explores the causal process leading to the states' compliance with international law, and investigates the various aspects of this process. However, this research program on compliance leaves certain questions unanswered. Particularly, the area of international labor standards surprisingly remains almost untouched.

The related research program on international institutions and domestic politics examines the ways in which domestic institutions deal with international law and how they interact with international institutions. But its literature has largely overlooked the role of legal systems including judiciaries. To fill in the gap in the existing literature, this book aims to explore the national legal systems' compliance with one of the core international labor standards– gender pay equity, by applying the dynamic "transnational legal process" theory.

---

[1] "What's Wrong with International Law Scholarship? I Hate International Law Scholarship (Sort of)" (2000), *Chicago Journal of International Law* 1: 75, p.75.

I. Literature Review

The literature on international legal compliance explores states' willingness to comply with international instruments and the conditions necessary to sustain such compliance. Scholars inquire whether how states' compliance occurs, with a focus on the role of various actors in this process. To date, several explanatory frameworks have been invented by scholars to account for international legal compliance, while certain issues remain unexplored. Among these explanatory frameworks, the theory of "transnational legal process" is the most vibrant and complete one.

1. *Does/How does International Law Matter?*

The managerialist and legitimacy theory, liberal as well as constructivist theories assume that international law is law and that states' compliance is a rule rather than an exception. The managerial theory posits that: "The fundamental instrument for maintaining compliance with treaties at an acceptable level... is an iterative process of discourse among the parties, the treaty organization, and the wider public."[2] This essentially legal process-based theory, developed by Abram Chayes and Antonia Handler Chayes, emphasizes on intergovernmental coordination at the nation-state level. It claims that the norm of "*pacta sun t servanda*"(treaties are to be obeyed) has a profound effect on state behavior. This theory maintains that international cooperation and management are instrumental in ensuring compliance. Non-compliance results mainly from lack of state capacity and insufficient knowledge about treaty obligations.[3]

The legitimacy/reputation theory portrays states as agents concerned with their reputation and legitimacy as well as distributive justice.[4] It agrees with the managerialist and transnational process theories that states generally comply. The liberal theorists adopt a different approach. They focus on domestic political and legal structure and

---

[2] Abram Chayes & Antonia Handler Chayes (1998), *The New Sovereignty: Compliance with International Regulatory Agreements*. Cambridge: Harvard University Press, p. 25.

[3] *Ibid.*

[4] Thomas M. Franck (1995). Fairness in International Law and Institutions. Oxford: Clarendon Press. Also see Ian Hurd (1999). "Legitimacy and Authority in International Politics", International Organization 53:379. H. L. A. Hart (1994). "International Law", in *The Concept of Law*. Oxford: Clarendon Press.

argue that if a country has a "liberal" structure, namely a representative government, protection of civil and political rights together with an effective judicial system following the rule of law, it has a tendency to comply with international law.[5]

Constructivism stresses the role of ideas in persuading states to follow the international regimes such as the human rights regime and to press them on others.[6] It highlights the interaction between states and NGOs and the dissemination of ideas.[7] Risse and Sikkink have developed a five-step spiral model of the human rights change which is conducive to the understanding of the compliance with the human rights agreements. They look to both the internal and external factors.[8] Internally, the domestic NGOs act as "compliance constituencies" to pressure the government officials to adhere to their international commitments.[9] Externally, the "transnational advocacy networks", which are comprised of the concerned individuals, groups, and domestic and international government agencies and officials, work to solve the human rights problems. Connecting with these transnational networks, the domestic compliance constituencies are able to create the "boomerang effect"[10] of influence on "vulnerable"[11] states by pressuring the government officials "from above" and "from below".[12]

Risse and Sikkink's support-structure-based framework has offered a seemingly plausible explanation to account for the compliance of the international human rights regimes. However, it is not flawless, as it simply dismisses the important role of the international governing

---

[5] See Andrew Moravcsik (1997). "Taking Preferences Seriously: A Liberal Theory of International Politics", International Organization 51: 513; Anne-Marie Slaughter (1995). "International Law in a World of Liberal States", *European Journal of International Law* 6: 503; Anne-Marie Slaughter (1995). "The Liberal Agenda for Peace: International Relations Theory and the Future of the United Nations", *Transnational Law and Contemporary Problems* 4: 377.

[6] See for example, Alexander Wendt (1995). "Constructing International Politics", *International Security* 20:71. Also see Margaret Keck and Kathryn Sikkink (1998). *Activists beyond Border*. Cornell University Press.

[7] Thomas Risse & Kathryn Sikkink (1999). "The Socialization of International Human Rights Norms into Domestic Practices: Introduction", in Thomas Risse et al eds. *The Power of Human Rights: International Norms and Domestic Changes*, pp. 1–39. Cambridge, the United Kingdom: Cambridge University Press.

[8] *Ibid*. Pp. 17–35.

[9] See Miles Kahler (2000). "Conclusion: The Causes and Consequences of Legalization", *International Organization* 54:661, p. 675.

[10] See Risse & Sikkink, *supra* note 7, at p. 18. See also Keck & Sikkink, *supra* note 6, pp. 12–13.

[11] See Keck & Sikkink, *Ibid*. at p. 29.

[12] See Risse & Sikkink, *supra* note 7, at p. 26.

bodies and national governments, who are the pillar of the entire process of compliance. Moreover, as constructivism is a norm-based theory, it lacks the explanatory power to explicate such a complicated and multi-dimensional process as "compliance".[13]

In contrast to the constructivists, the realists and rational choice theorists are skeptical of the role of international law in constraining state behavior. The realists doubt the independent efficacy of international law.[14] They insist that states use international law to pursue their own national interest.[15] The rational choice theory argues that law is epiphenomenal and states comply with international law only when it converges with their national interest. The interpretation and application of customary international law by the domestic courts is only to implement their national interest.[16]

2. *Do/How do Domestic Legal Systems Support International Law?*

Domestic legal systems, as scholars generally agree, play a significant role in the compliance of international law.[17] The liberal theory in particular suggests the causal relation between a liberal domestic legal structure and the compliance with international law.[18] The recurring failure to ratify the border agreements in the legislature has been argued as one of the main domestic political conditions linked with the willingness of states to subject their disputes to international arbitration.[19]

---

[13] See Rosalyn Higgins (1994). *Problems and Process-International Law and How We Use it*. Oxford: Clarendon Press. At p. 267 she puts that "International law is a process, a system of authoritative decision-making. It is not just the neutral application of rules… The role of international law is to assist in the choice between… various alternatives… International law is a process for resolving problems."

[14] Jack Goldsmith (2000), "Sovereignty, International Relations Theory, and International Law", *Stanford Law Review* 52: 959.

[15] Francis Boyle (1985). *World Politics and International Law*. Duke University Press.

[16] Jack L. Goldsmith & Eric A. Posner (1999). "A Theory of Customary International Law", *University of Chicago Law Review* 66:1113. Also see Tom Ginsburg & Richard H. Adams (2004). "Adjudicating in Anarchy: An Expressive Theory of International Dispute Resolution", *William and Mary Law Review* 45:1229. Jack L. Goldsmith & Eric A. Posner (2003). "International Agreements: A Rational Choice Approach", *Vanderbilt Journal of International Law* 44:113. Jack L. Goldsmith & Eric A. Posner (2005). *The Limits of International Law*. Oxford University Press. Eric Posner (2003). "A Theory of the Laws of War", *University of Chicago Law Review* 70: 297.

[17] Friedrich Kratochwil (1991). Rules, Norms and Decisions: On the Conditions of Practical and Legal Reasoning in International Relations and Domestic Affairs. Cambridge University Press.

[18] Anne-Marie Slaughter, *supra* note 5.

[19] Beth A. Simmons (1998). "Compliance with International Agreements", *Annual Review of Political Science* 1: 75.

It is also suggested that the domestic courts have transformed international law because they consider international law as a persuasive authority.[20] Some national judiciaries may tend to support the application of international law because international law provides an additional resource in pursuit of their agenda.[21] As argued, if those doctrinal obstacles such as standing and sovereign immunity could be reduced, the domestic courts would be the most effective agents to ensure compliance with international environmental law.[22] However, not everyone agrees. For example, it has been suggested that the American judiciary is reluctant to invoke international law because of the "territorial-democratic" principle which means judges are more skilled in applying the law of their own territorial jurisdiction and more comfortable in applying law that has gone through the national democratic process.[23] Likewise, the principal-agent model is also proposed to explain why the American courts are unwilling to apply international law. Judges are more concerned with their own careers and therefore the policy preferences of their political principals (their constituents).[24] Some also argue that the existence of the precedents can explain the reluctance of national judges in applying international law.[25]

Iwasawa in his work on the impact of international law on the Japanese courts suggests that the Japanese courts have not yet fully become the standard-bearers for international human rights law, contrary to some common law countries.[26] He provides a critical

[20] Karen Knop (2000). "Here and There: International Law in Domestic Courts", *NYU Journal of International Law and Policy* 32: 501.

[21] Karen Alter (1996). "The European Court's Political Power", West European Politics 19: 458. Also see Benedetto Conforti (1993). *International Law and the Role of Domestic Legal Systems*. Martinus Nijhotf Publishers.

[22] Mary Ellen O'Connell (1995). "Enforcement and the Success of International Environmental Law", *Indiana Journal of Global Legal Studies* 3: 47.

[23] Saadia M. Pekkanen (2005). "International Trade Law in US courts", paper presented at a seminar of Center for International Studies, University of Southern California.

[24] See J. Mark Ramseyer (1994). "The Puzzling (In)Dependence of Courts: A Comparative Approach", *The Journal of Legal Studies* 23(2): 721, pp. 724–726. Also see J. Mark Ramseyer, and Eric B. Rasmusen (2003). "Judicial Independence in a Civil Law Regime: The Evidence From Japan", *The Journal of Law, Economics, and Organization* 13(2): 259, pp. 260–261.

[25] Yuji Iwasawa (1993), "Implementation of International Trade Agreements in Japan", in *National Constitutions and International Economic Law*, edited by Mehinhard Hilf and Ernst Ulrich Petersmann. Boston, MA: Kluwer Law and Taxation Publishers, p. 328.

[26] See M. Hunt (1997). *Using Human Rights Law in English Courts*. Oxford: Hart Publishing.

assessment of the reluctance of the Japanese judges to follow international legal standards when their domestic practice or law is inconsistent with these standards.[27] Overall, Iwasawa's work is an outstanding case study. However, as Philip Alston points out, this book is somewhat ahistorical and can benefit from providing a broader social and historical context from which the view of the Japanese society towards human rights has evolved.[28]

3. *The Theory of Transnational Legal Process*

The transnational legal process theory postulates that the frequent interaction within transnational communities which consist of the policy-makers promotes the emergence of those norms favoring cooperation and ultimately leads to the internalization of these norms into the domestic law and legal institutions.[29] Koh, the author of the theory, defines it as "the process whereby an international law rule is interpreted through the interaction of transnational actors in a variety of law-declaring fora, then internalized into a nation's domestic legal system".[30] This process is comprised of three elements: the internalization of the international norm into domestic normative systems, the interpretation of an applicable global norm, and the interaction provoked by one or more transnational actors.[31]

Compared to the managerial theory that emphasizes the horizontal legal process, the transnational legal process theory is more comprehensive as it covers both the horizontal and vertical process. It is "the complex process of institutional interaction whereby global norms are not just debated and interpreted, but ultimately internalized by domestic legal systems."[32] This theory is "dynamic" in the sense that it "transforms, mutates, and percolates up and down, from the public to the private,

[27] Yuji Iwasawa (1998). *International Law, Human Rights Law and Japanese Law: The Impact of International Law on Japanese Law*. Oxford, Clarendon Press. For other case studies of international human rights law on national courts, see Benedetto Conforti and Francesco Francioni (eds.) (1997). *Enforcing International Human Rights in Domestic Courts*. Martinus Nijhoff Publishers.

[28] Philip Alston (1999). "Transplanting Foreign Norms: Human Rights and Other International Legal Norms in Japan". *European Journal of International Law* 10(3): 625.

[29] Harold Hongju Koh (1997). "Why Do Nations Obey International Law?" *Yale Law Journal* 106: 2599. Also see Mary Ellen O'Connell (1999). "New International Legal Process", *American Journal of International Law* 93:334.

[30] Harold Hongju Koh (1998). "Bringing International Law Home", *Houston Law Review* 35: 623, p. 626.

[31] Koh, *supra* note 29, p. 2646.

[32] Koh, *supra* note 29, p. 2603.

from the domestic to the international level and back down again".[33] It is also "non-statist" as it not only includes state actors, but also non-state actors. This theory is both "descriptive" and "normative" since new rules of law emerge, but through interaction, interpretation and internalization, the process starts again.[34] During the process, law influences states and other actors' behavior and their behavior in turn reshapes law.

Such relatively new theory of "transnational legal process" has a potential to fully capture the compliance of international law. The complicated nature of the compliance of international law could be disentangled only by a sophisticated theory like "transnational legal process".

4. *Critique*

In general, the research program on international legal compliance has undergone a significant development particularly since 1990s when the literature on international legal compliance proliferated. It has grown into a more diverse realm, in terms of both its topics and methods. This program has been subject to the influence of other disciplines and a broader intellectual environment. Political scientists, law scholars and intellectuals from various disciplines such as economics have shown tremendous interest in and commitment to this program. Both quantitative and qualitative studies have been applied. Global and comparative perspectives have been attempted, although to a rather limited extent. It is fair to say this program has largely benefited from such diversity. Nonetheless, it has not yet been perfect. The following text offers an evaluation of the program in terms of its definition of the key concept "compliance", its validity and completeness, and methodology and scope.

a. *The Definition of "Compliance"*

Virginia Leary has noted the inadequacy of the definition of "compliance". She suggests that the concept of "influence" is more appropriate for the discussion of "soft law".[35] However, as she admits, it is enormously difficult to measure the "influence" of "soft law" in the field of

---

[33] See Harold Hongju Koh (1996). "Transnational Legal Process", *Nebraska Law Review* 75: 181, p. 184.

[34] *Ibid.*

[35] Virginia A. Leary (1997). "Nonbinding Accords in the Field of Labor", in Edith Brown Weiss ed. *International Compliance with Nonbinding Accords: A Challenge to International Law*. Washington, DC: American Society of International Law.

international labor law due to the narrow spread of its normative pronouncement.[36] Scholars seem to equal "effectiveness" with "compliance",[37] and "obedience" with "compliance"[38]. Therefore based on the different definitions their conclusions about "compliance" vary Compliance in this book is defined as a status of being in conformity with the established international standard. Compliance defined as a "status" appears more quantifiable than "influence" and "obedience", and less prescriptive than "effectiveness". There are three levels of compliance: high compliance, medium compliance, and low compliance. The three-level allows "compliance" to become a "process" because the "status" could change from one to another.

b. *Validity and Completeness*

The realist approach to compliance had much validity in accounting for the status of international law during the Cold War. But with the emergence of globalization and particularly the European Union, the explanatory power of this interest-based theory has been seriously challenged. The rational choice theory relies on the same assumption about national interest and fails to notice the obvious power of the human rights regime.

Most theories have acknowledged the power of international law, but have not explained the phenomenon of compliance with international law. The managerial theory has been criticized for being biased in selection and incapable of explaining "high politics".[39] Likewise, reputation may not be unitary and a state's reputation may not be consistent throughout all areas. The constructivist theory provides a new approach to the field. However it may better explain customary international law or regimes but not the treaty-based international law. While emphasizing the role of domestic politics, the liberal theory predicts that democratic states are more likely to comply with international law. But such prediction has been contested.[40]

---

[36] Virginia A. Leary (1997). "Nonbinding Accords in the Field of Labor", in Edith Brown Weiss ed. *International Compliance with Nonbinding Accords: A Challenge to International Law*. Washington, DC: American Society of International Law.

[37] See, for example, Douglass Cassel (2001). "Does International Human Rights Law Make a Difference?" *Chicago Journal of International Law* 121.

[38] Koh, *supra* note 29.

[39] George W. Downs, David M. Rocke, & Peter N. Barsoom (1996). "Is the Good News About Compliance Good News About Cooperation?" *International Organization* 50: 379.

[40] Daniel E. Ho (2002). "Compliance and International Soft Law: Why Do Countries Implement the Basle Accord?" *Journal of International Economic Law* 5: 647.

Among those five explanatory frameworks, the “transnational legal process” approach is the most plausible one, as explained above. This does not mean other variables are not factors contributing to compliance. But the “transnational legal process” is the most important variable to account for states’ compliance, particularly with the treaty-based international law. It also better captures the whole process by emphasizing the interaction of various actors in this process.

c. *Methodology*

The research program on compliance has witnessed a burgeoning diversity of methodology. The constructivist discourse-based method pictures the diffusion of “idea” and “norms”, while the rational choice theory is credited with the capability for generalization. However, the program offers more normative discussion of whether states should follow international law or not, but suffers from inadequate empirical investigation. Political scientists can contribute to the field by empirically examining the process of compliance, which this book attempts to try.

d. *Scope*

Another significant weakness of this body of literature on compliance is its exclusion of certain areas such as international labor law. The international law scholarship has long been accused of being mystified and focusing on nation states only. To examine an area that is closely related to the everyday life of working men and women, may help demystify and demarginalize international law scholarship. In addition, although scholars have examined to some extent how international institutions and international law interact with domestic politics, international relations scholars have only scarcely studied how domestic legal systems deal with international law. As a result, this book is intended to fill in this gap through the examination of a rarely explored topic: the treatment of the international labor standard of gender pay equity in domestic law.

II. Research Design

The research question is whether and how domestic legal systems comply with international labor law. Two hypotheses come from this research question: first, domestic legal systems (legislative and judiciary) comply with international labor treaty (the ILO Convention No. 100); second, compliance occurs through a "transnational legal process". In this book I intend to demonstrate that after ratification, state legal systems gradually comply with that treaty by engaging in the "transnational legal process" and that the ratification of international labor treaties improves the labor conditions in that state.[41]

Compliance is defined as a status of being in conformity with the international labor treaty- the ILO Convention No. 100 on Equal Remuneration. It consists of legislative and judicial compliance. In terms of the degree of "conformity" to the articles of the Convention, both legislative and judicial compliance have three levels: high compliance, medium compliance and low compliance.

1. *Method of Analysis*

As Robert Keohane argues, it requires legal judgment to determine whether compliance occurs and social scientific methods to analyze the causal relationship between rules and behavior.[42] This study draws on legal and political science literature and employs both quantitative and qualitative methods. Legal analysis and a comparative case study between Canada and Japan are used. As the specific issue I am addressing is gender pay equity, I also explore the literature on economics, sociology, anthropology, philosophy, and gender study.

The technique of *process-tracing*[43] was used to detect causal patterns. This method can improve the validity of the causal claim and better picture the whole phenomenon. During the process-tracing, the causal mechanism and separate alternative interpretations could be reevaluated. Moreover, other predictions and implications may be

---

[41] A scholar has indicated it but not yet tested it in the 1980s. Walter Galenson (1981). *The International Labor Organization: An American View*. The University of Wisconsin Press.

[42] Robert O. Keohane (1992). "Compliance with International Commitments: Politics Within a Framework of Law", *American Society of International Law Proceedings* 86: 176.

[43] "In process tracing, the research examines histories, archival documents, interview transcripts, and other sources to see whether the causal process a theory hypothesizes or implies in a case is in fact evident in the sequence and values of the intervening variables in that case"; "The process tracing method attempts to identify the intervening causal process-the causal chain and causal mechanism- between and independent variable (or variables) and the outcome of the dependent variable". See Alexander L. George & Timothy J. McKeown (1985), "Case Studies and Theories of Organizational Decision-making", *Advances in Information Processing in Organizations* 2: 21, pp. 6, 12, 21–41.

generated in the process-tracing to make scholarly contributions. As George and McKeown suggest, during the process-tracing, the "stimuli", the "process" and the "behavior" can be investigated.[44] As for this study, it is illuminating to learn the "stimuli" or "interest" of various actors supporting the application of international law in national judiciaries. Also, it is enlightening to reconstruct the actors' definitions of the situation.[45] This book examines how "gender pay equity" is defined and constructed over time by the actors involved in the process, seeking to make a contribution to the existing literature on law and society.

Likewise, *data triangulation* can increase the validity and avoid flawed or biased data[46], especially those data collected from diverse sources and by a mixture of methods. Additionally, this study tries to make more observations to increase the validity.[47] For example, the unit of analysis may be changed from national court level to local court level during the analysis of judicial compliance.[48]

2. *Evidence Collection*

The data for the dependent variable "domestic legal compliance" (legislative compliance and judicial compliance) consists of relevant legislations and cases heard by the courts in the ratifying states. The court records in some countries are publicly available, but the data for the developing countries are particularly difficult to obtain. The major source on which I relied was the ILO CEACR's reports on individual ratifying states from 1990 to 2007 based on which I constructed a dataset. The materials found from PAIS, Index to Foreign Legal Periodicals, Westlaw, Lexis, Philosophers' Index, Econlit and CSA Sociological Abstract were employed to verify and substantiate the data from the ILO.

The data for the primary independent variable "transnational legal process" were drawn from the documentary sources and organizational documents, the secondary legal and social science literature, as well as the interviews. The field work at the department of International

[44] *Ibid.* p. 35.
[45] *Ibid.*
[46] Joseph A. Maxwell (1996). *Qualitative Research Design*. Thousand Oaks: Sage Publication, pp.75–76.
[47] KKV (1994). *Designing Social Inquiry*. Princeton: Princeton University Press, pp. 217–228.
[48] See Julian G. Ku (2004). "The State of New York Does Exist: How the States Control Compliance with International Law", *North Carolina Law Review* 82: 457.

Labor Standards of the ILO helped me procure the needed data. More specifically, "transnational legal process" is comprised of three elements: interaction between an international institution with states, interpretation of the international legal norms to the situation and internalization of legal norms into internal system.[49] In order to explore this process, I analyzed the document exchanges between the ILO and the individual ratifying states to examine "the interaction between international institutions with states", the national legislations to understand "the interpretation of the international legal norms to the situation", and the court cases and proceedings to explore the "internalization of legal norms into internal system".

III. Arrangement of the Book

This book examines the status of one of the core international labor standards-gender pay equity in international law. It explores how domestic legislative and judicial systems respond to the core ILO Convention No. 100 on Equal Remuneration, with the hope of unraveling under what circumstances legislative and judicial compliance occurs. The "transnational legal process" theory (which consists of three elements: internalization, interpretation and interaction) is employed to explain the phenomenon of "compliance". That is, I frame my book on the question of compliance by applying the theory of "transnational legal process". "Compliance and compromise" is the theme throughout the whole book. This study also provides suggestions on how to narrow the gender pay gap through the legal reform.

The opening chapter starts with a literature review followed by an explanation of the research design. It is the need to perfect the existing research programs that motivates this study. To draw attention to an extremely important area which surprisingly has been rarely explored by the international law literature, is the major concern of this book.

Chapter II discusses the importance of the issues of the gender wage gap and gender pay equity from various aspects. An analysis and a critique of the status of gender pay equity in international law are presented. This chapter takes both international and regional treaties into account.

---

[49] Koh, *supra* note 29, pp. 2600–02.

Chapter III focuses on the process of "internalization". It examines how the domestic legislative systems respond and internalize the principle of gender pay equity after their governments ratify the ILO Convention No. 100 on Equal Remuneration, the only convention specifically targeting the issue of pay equity. This chapter attempts to discover whether high compliance occurs after ratification and the causes of low compliance. A model legislative package is presented at the end of the chapter.

Chapter IV shares a similar structure with the previous one. It analyzes how the principle of gender pay equity is "interpreted" in domestic courts and explores the extent to which domestic judiciaries comply with the ILO Convention No. 100 on Equal Remuneration. The analysis is primarily based on the examination of the court cases in the ratifying states.

Chapter V offers a survey study analyzing how the relevant institutions "interact" horizontally with each other when dealing with the principle of gender pay equity, through a close examination of the ILO CEACR's reports and the secondary literature. Then, a comparative analysis of two case studies between Japan and China is provided, with the attempt to better delineate the vertical aspect of the process of "interaction".

Chapter VI presents a comparative case study between Canada and Japan. Among those highly industrialized countries, Canada and Japan have the best and worst records of complying with the ILO Convention No. 100. A detailed comparative analysis of both countries sheds insight on what causes compliance/non-compliance.

The concluding chapter summarizes the major findings of the book and suggests the directions for further research. It attempts to stimulate some normative discussion of the interdisciplinary collaboration between international relations and international law in the field of compliance. Several policy recommendations are suggested for those activists concerned with improving the labor standards.

CHAPTER II

GENDER PAY EQUITY AND THE INTERNATIONAL INSTRUMENTS

In the year of 2007, women around the world earned about 83% of what men earned.[1] The ratio was even lower in some parts of the world.[2] The gender pay[3] gap ironically is still one major feature of the modern labor market.[4] Scholars have been constantly making efforts to explore the potential solutions to the gender pay differentials. During the 1980s there was an explosion of economic research (particularly in the United States) on the wage determination and sociological analysis of the marketplace and occupational structure.[5] In the past two decades, the gendered perspective has permeated into the workplace policy analysis in the industrialized states.[6] As a result, both national governments and international organizations have for the most part adopted a relatively modern approach to mainstreaming gender into their

---

[1] See UNIFEM, *Progress of the World's Women 2008*. http://www.unifem.org/progress/2008/media/POWW08_Report_Full_Text.pdf (accessed on Sep 30, 2009).

[2] In Georgia, women were paid 51% less than men.The ILO has documented the gap between women and men's incomes: the ratio "appears to be especially low in east and Southeast Asian countries as well as in some European countries (with Japan, the Republic of Korea, Malaysia, Singapore, Luxemberg and Cyprus the only countries having a ratio below 0.60). Ratios appear to be relatively high in Scandinavian countries, as well as in some other OECD and Third World countries (with Denmark, Iceland, Norway, Sweden, Australia, Sri Lanka, Turkey and Swaziland the only countries with a ratio clearly above 0.80)." See Richard Anker (1997). "Theories of Occupational Segregation by Sex: An Overview." *International Labor Review* 136: 315–339, p. 330.

[3] "Pay" here refers to "include the remuneration, profit or income which women receive for their work (including benefits and pensions) whether from employment or self-employment." See Mary Cornish (2006). "Closing Global Gender Pay Gap: Securing Justice for Women's Work", *Comparative Labor Law & Policy* 28(2), footnote 1.

[4] Mary Cornish, Fay Faraday & Veena Verma (2006). "Securing Gender Justice: challenges Facing International Labor Law", in John D. R. Craig & S. Michael Lynk (eds.), *Globalization and the Future of Labor Law* 377.

[5] For example, in 1985 in the United States the Committee on Women's Employment and Related Social Issues established the Panel on Pay Equity Research. See National Research Council (1989). *Pay Equity: Empirical Inquiries*. Washington DC: national Academy Press, p. vii.

[6] See Heidi Gottfried & Laura Reese (2004). *Equity in the Workplace: Gendering Workplace Policy Analysis*. New York: Lexington Books, pp. 1–28. Feminist movement contributed a great deal to discovering the issue and campaigning for equal pay. For example, during as early as 1930s, there was a feminist movement campaigning for equal pay in the United Kingdom. See Harold L. Smith (1996). "British Feminism and the Equal Pay Issue in the 1930s", *Women's History Review* 5: 97–110.

policy-making.[7] This chapter examines the various aspects of gender pay equity and its status under international law, seeking to draw attention to this important issue that the literature on international legal compliance has largely overlooked for so long.

I. Causes

The gender wage gap has been an issue existing in both the developed and developing economies. Closing the gender wage gap is essential to solving the poverty worldwide as women constitute a hefty portion of the world's poverty population.[8] The causes of the gender wage gap may vary in different states, but they are always complex and multi-dimensional.

Some economists[9] have argued that the gender pay gap may have resulted from the differences in the productivity characteristics of men and women,[10] the characteristics of the enterprises and sectors employing men and women, the jobs held by women and men, the number of hours devoted to paid work,[11] the work experience and education women have,[12] the wage structure,[13] the decentralization in

---

[7] See Diane Perrons (2005). "Gender Mainstreaming and Gender Equality in the New (Market) Economy: An Analysis of Contradictions", *Social Politics* 12(3): 389–411, pp. 389–390.

[8] See http://www.unfpa.org/intercenter/beijing/poverty.htm (accessed on Oct 30, 2007). 60% of the world's 550 million working poor are women. See ILO (2004). *Global Employment Trends for Women*. Geneva.

[9] For a general discussion on the economics' view on the issue, see Jane Friesen (1993). "Alternative Economic Perspectives on the Use of Labor Market Policies to Redress the Gender Gap in Compensation", *Georgetown Law Journal* 82:31. For a critique of Friesen's analysis, see Richard A Epstein (1993). "Some Reflections on the Gender Gap in Employment", *Georgetown Law Journal*, 82:75. Also see Miller, Paul W. "Gender Differences in Observed and Offered Wages in Canada, 1980", *The Canadian Journal of Economics* 20(2): 225–244, pp. 226–227.

[10] See for example, Warren F Schwartz (1993). "Foreword: The Gender Gap in Compensation", *Georgetown Law Journal* 82: 27, p. 27.

[11] See for example, Lois Joy (2003). "Salaries of Recent Male and Female College Graduates: Educational and Labor Market Effects", *Industrial & Labor Relations Review* 56(4): 606–621. Also see Sarah Rummery (1992). "The Contribution of Intermittent Labor Force Participation to the Gender Wage Differential", *The Economic Record* 68 (202): 351–364.

[12] See Claudia Goldin (1985). "Understanding the Gender Gap", *New Perspectives* 9–13; Dorothe Bonjour & Michael Gerfin (2001). "The Unequal Distribution of Unequal Pay- An Empirical Analysis of the Gender Wage Gap in Switzerland", *Empirical Economics* 26: 407–427.

[13] Francine D. Blau & Lawrence M. Kahn (1999). "Analyzing the Gender Pay Gap", *Quarterly Review of Economics and Finance* 39: 625–46. For the economic analysis of

the wage determination,[14] the segregation of occupation[15], and the discrimination in remuneration.[16] That is to say, there is an inherent problem in employment. The jobs that women do, how jobs are valued, and how jobs are organized, may all have a profound effect on women's wage.[17] In this regard, collective bargaining, minimum wage setting, the development of a gender-neutral job evaluation, equal pay audits and the establishment of a process for remedial settlements of pay equity claims, are the areas where reforms should take place to battle the gender pay gap.[18]

In addition to the economic factors, there are also non-economic causes of the stubborn gender pay gap. Three major sociological theories have been proposed to explain the gender wage gap: the human capital theory, the dual market theory and the reserve army theory.[19] In terms of legal factors, women workers, as argued, may lack legal protection, or the law on equal pay may be inadequate. Sometimes the access to justice is limited and the judiciary is not receptive to women workers. Therefore the relevant law does not achieve its intended purpose of addressing grievance and redressing wage discrimination.[20]

Culturally, the predominant religion within a country may affect the level of women's economic participation in general. Certain religious practices reinforce gender inequality in society.[21] As Fareda

---

the causes of the gender wage gap within and between firms, see Erling Barth-Arne mastekaasa (1996). "Decomposing the Male/Female Wage Gap: Within and Between Establishment Differences", *Labor* 10: 339–356.

[14] See Jill Rubery (1994). "Decentralisation and Individualisation: the Implications for Equal Pay", *Economies et Societies* 18: 79–97.

[15] This is argued as the main reason for the gender wage gap in Norway. See Eva M. Meyersson Milgrom et al (2001). "Equal Pay for Equal Work? Evidence from Sweden and a Comparison with Norway and the U. S", *Scandinavian Journal of Economics* 103(4): 559–583.

[16] ILO (2007). *Equality at Work: Tackling the Challenges: Global Report under the Follow-up to the ILO Declaration on Fundamental Principles and Rights at Work (Part B)*, p. 73.

[17] See *Taskforce on Pay and Employment Equity in the Public Service and Public Health and Education Sector*, from http://www.beehive.govt.nz/Documents/Files/Pay%20Equity%20Q%20and%20A.pdf (accessed on Sep 10, 2007).

[18] See the CEACR, *Individual Observation, New Zealand*, 2006.

[19] See Catherine J Fillmore (1990). "Gender Differences in Earnings: A Re-Analysis and Prognosis for Canadian Women", *Canadian Journal of Sociology* 15(3): 275–299

[20] Women and Work Commission (WWC) of United Kingdom, "*Shaping a Fairer Future*", from http://www.womenandequalityunit.gov.uk/publications/wwc_shaping_fairer_future06.pdf (accessed on Oct 30, 2007).

[21] See for example, H. V. Brasted (2000). "Piecing Together the Jigsaw: Indian Women in the Urban Wage Labour Force", *Asian Studies Review* 24(2): 195–211, pp. 206–207.

Banda argues, women experience discrimination not only as a result of law but also social and cultural practice.[22] Colonialism perpetuated the inferior status of women in the sub-Saharan areas and undervalued women's work.[23] The dominant gender ideology that the role of women is to nurture the family leaves little scope for women to actively participate in the economic life and to reach those higher-paid jobs.[24] For example, even in the twenty-first century, in those countries, like Italy and Spain, less than 45 percent of women participate in the labor market.[25] In other countries like China, although the official ideology greatly promotes gender equality, women find it hard to escape the patriarchal dominance.[26]

However, the systemic gender discrimination is the ultimate and most difficult barrier to close the gender wage gap.[27] The existing job categories and job evaluation methods tend to undervalue those lines of work dominated by women workers, which significantly impacts women's wage. History has not been kind to women's work or women's skills. The skills required to perform those repetitive movements from a fixed position as in some "light" manufacturing industries have not been valued as much as the skills required to lift heavy objects.[28] Child care or nursing is undervalued compared to those "dirty" jobs performed by men.[29] The value of household work had been largely

---

[22] Fareda Banda (2006). "Blazing a Trail: the African Protocol on Women's Rights Comes into Force", *Journal of African Law* 50: 72, p. 75.

[23] See Jane Dwasi (1999). "Kenya: A Study in International Labor Standards and Their Effect on Working Women in Developing Countries: The Case for Integration of Enforcement Issues in the World Bank's Policies", *Wisconsin International Law Journal* 17: 347, p. 367.

[24] See Faye J Crosby, Joan C Williams & Monica Biernat (2004). "The Maternal Wall", *Journal of Social Issues* 60(4): 675–682. This is also the case in Japan, see Johanna Kumlin(2007). "The Sex Wage Gap in Japan and Sweden: The Role of Human Capital, Workplace Sex Composition, and Family Responsibility", *European Sociological Review* 23(2): 203–221, p. 214.

[25] *Eurostate 2002*. Percentages of women who are employed for more than one hour a week in the age range of 15–64.

[26] See Margaret Maurer-Fazio, Thomas G. Rawski & Wei Zhang (1999). "Inequality in the Rewards for Holding up Half the Sky: Gender Wage Gaps in China's Urban Labor Market, 1988–1994", *The China Journal* 41: 55–88.

[27] See Sara L Zeigler (2006). "Litigating Equality: The Limits of the Equal Pay Act", *Review of Public Personnel Administration* 26(3): 199–215, pp. 211–212.

[28] Nancy S. Barrett (1979), "Women in the Job Market: Occupations, Earnings, and Career Opportunities, in Ralph E. Smith (ed.), *The Subtle Revolution: Women at Work*, Washington, D. C.: The Urban Institute, pp. 46–54.

[29] Mary C. Corley & Hans O. Mauksch (1987). "Registered Nurses, Gender and Commitment", in Anne Statham and et al. (eds.), *The Worth of Women's Work*, Albany: State University of New York Press, pp. 135–149.

overlooked until the "pay for housework" movement in the 1960s.[30] It is these various forms of systemic discrimination against women inherent in our society that ultimately impedes the advancement of women in the workplace.

II. Gender Pay Equity

One common solution proposed to close the gender pay differential is gender "pay equity" that employs some objective criteria for determining wages excluding the use of gender as one of the determinants.[31] To clarify the concept, equal pay does not necessarily mean pay equity. Pay equity specifically refers to equal pay between men and women for equal work and work of equal value or comparable worth.[32] It consists of two parts: equal pay for equal work or identical work, and equal pay for work of equal value or comparable worth.[33] However, to avoid misunderstanding, this book uses the term "gender pay equity" to emphasize its gendered nature, considering in the future other types (for example, race) of pay gap may become the central issue.[34]

---

[30] See Gillian K. Hadfield (1993). "Households at Work: Beyond Labor Market Policies to Remedy the Gender Gap", *Georgetown Law Journal* 82: 89.

[31] The most common methods for job evaluation include rating, job classifications and paired comparisons. For example, the "points method" of factor analysis breaks down each job into factors such as skill, responsibility, working conditions and physical and mental demands. Then points are assigned to each factor in a certain job and an aggregate number of points is totaled to determine the comparative value of the job. See Christopher McCrudden (1986), "Comparable Worth: A Common Dilemma, 11 *Yale Journal of International Law* 396.

[32] CEACR, *Individual Observation, New Zealand*, 2004.

[33] "Equal work" means "jobs, performance of which requires equal or substantially equal skills, efforts, responsibility and working conditions"; "Work of comparable worth" "measures the worth of jobs to the employer, regardless of the differences in their qualifications. Between "equal work" and "work of comparable worth" is "similar work", which means "a classification of positions or individuals who are similarly situated for the purpose of compensation, e.g. college professors of different disciplines". See Lee, Young S (1989). "Shaping Judicial Response to Gender Discrimination in Employment Compensation", *Public Administration Review* 49: 420–430, p. 420.

[34] See Clarence Thomas (1983). "Pay Equity and Comparable Worth", *Labor Law Journal* 34(1): 3–12, p. 3. Also see Carol A Kates (1994). "Pay Equity and Wage Justice", *Review of Radical Political Economics* 26: 1–23. Kates employs the theory of "pay equity" to address the class wage gap. Also see Peter S. Li (1992). "Race and Gender as Bases of Class Fractions and Their Effect", *The Canadian Review of Sociology and Anthropology* 29(4): 488–510; Peggy A. Lovell(2006). "Race, Gender, and Work in Sao Paulo, Brazil, 1960–2000", *Latin American Research Review* 41(3): 63–87. The intricate relation between gender and class on the wage gap is also a concern. See Rosemary Warskett (1990). "Wage Solidarity and Equal Value: or Gender and Class in the Structuring of

How to define "wage" may affect one's attitude towards gender pay equity. Wage has been argued as a means to provide a "living" for workers,[35] as a "price" to allocate resources, and as a "social practice" which reveals the complex relation between gender, race and class.[36] Wage can be all of these, hence "wage" is "valuable". So the question remains on how to measure the "value" of work. Generally speaking, job evaluation is the central part of determining the "value" of work.[37] There are two main systems used to evaluate jobs. One is the priori method and the other is the policy-capturing method.[38] The fundamental element of a job evaluation method lies in the fact it should be gender-neutral. Only if we reexamine the value of those traditionally feminine jobs and realize and accept that jobs such as nursing and childcare involve very "valuable" and complex skills,[39] can we claim a milestone in promoting gender pay equity.[40]

Gender pay equity is a concept closely intertwined with human dignity. Whether it should be referred to as "a guiding principle", "right", or "standard" is not simply a matter of vocabulary preference, but a matter of how we fundamentally view this issue.

The ILO has long considered the right to gender pay equity as part of its four "core labor standards", which in agreement with the ILO official interpretation, should be regarded as part of fundamental human

---

Work Place Hierarchies", *Studies in Political Economy* 55–83. In Northern Ireland, the wage gap among different religious believers was on the center of the debate. See Norma Heaton et al (1997). "'The Differences between Women are More Marginal'… Catholic and Protestant Women in the Northern Ireland Labor Market", *Work, Employment and Society* 11: 237–261.

[35] Kahn and Figart argue that wage as a living should be emphasized as the new strategy to fight for gender pay equity. See Peggy Kahn & Deborah M Figart (1998). "Reviving Pay Equity: New Strategies for Attacking the Wage Gap", *Working USA* 2(2): 8–17.

[36] See Ellen Mutari, Deborah Figart & Marilyn Power (2001). "Implicit Wage Theories in Equal Pay Debates in the United States", 7(2) *Feminist Economics* 23–52, pp. 23, 26.

[37] For a discussion on the rise of job evaluation in the United States, see Deborah M Figart (2001). "Wage-Setting under Fordism: The Rise of Job Evaluation and the Idealogy of Equal Pay", *Review of Political Economy* 13(4): 405–25.

[38] For a more complete description of job evaluation process and methods, see Paula England (1999). "The Case for Comparable Worth", *Quarterly Review of Economics and Finance* 39: 743–755, pp. 745–747.

[39] See Natasha Cortis (2000). "Gender, Pay Equity and Human Service Work: A New South Wales Case Study", *Australian Journal of Political Science* 35(1): 49–62.

[40] It is certainly extremely challenging for a society to change the perception of the value of some lines of work, see for example, Margaret Thornton (1981). "(Un)equal Pay for Work of Equal Value", *The Journal of Industrial Relations* 23(4): 466–481, p. 477.

rights as well.[41] If so, it appears that the word "standards" may be confusing. I will propose "core labor rights" as an alternative. Although part of these "core labor rights", some contend that gender pay equity does not deserve to be implemented, because of its high cost and the difficulties associated with its implementation.[42] Other scholars believe that gender pay equity is a fundamental human right and is essential to achieving general equality in the whole world.[43] The plea to integrate the right to gender pay equity into international human rights law is legitimate. As a matter of fact, the right to equal pay for equal work and work of equal value is one of the founding principles recognized by the 1945 ILO constitution amendment. The ILO Convention No. 100 on Equal Remuneration has also been able to enjoy wide ratification (168 ratifying states as of the year 2011), which demonstrates a general acceptance of the norm. Therefore this norm of gender pay equity the potential to be considered as customary international law.

The right to gender pay equity is not only a fundamental human right, but an issue of justice. No matter how many factors may contribute to the gender pay gap, discrimination is always one of them.[44]

---

[41] See ILO. *Protecting Labor Rights as Human Rights: Present and Future of International Supervision*. From http://www.ilo.org/public/english/standards/norm/download/resources/colloquium80ceacr.pdf. (accessed on Sep 10, 2007).

[42] See Judy Fudge & Patricia MdDermott (eds.) (1991). *Just Wages: A Feminist Assessment of Pay Equity*. Toronto: University of Toronto Press. Margaret Hallock (1999). "Pay equity: The Promise and Practice in North America", *Labor. & Industry* 10: 53. Nitya Iyer (2002). *Working Through the Wage Gap: Report of the Task Force on Pay equity* (Commissioned by the British Columbia Government), from http://www.ag.gov.bc.ca/public/working_through_the_wage_gap.pdf (Accessed on Sep 10, 2007).

[43] See Mary Cornish (2007). "Closing the Global Gender Pay Gap: Securing Justice for Women's Work". *Comparative Labor Law & Policy Journal* 28(2), p. 220. Pat Armstrong, Mary Cornish & Elizabeth Millar (2003). "Pay equity: Complexity and contradiction in Legal Rights and Social Processes", in *Changing Canada: Political Economy as Transformation*, ch. 7 (Wallace Clement & Leah F. Vosko ed.). Canada: McGill-Queen's University Press; *Pay equity, A New Approach to a Fundamental Right: Pay Equity Task Force Final Report* (2004), from http://justice.gc.ca/en/payeqsal/6000.html (Accessed on Sep 10, 2007); Jill Rubery, Damian Grimshaw & Hugo Figueiredo (2005). "How to Close the Gender Pay Gap in Europe: Towards the Gender Mainstreaming of Pay Policy", *Industrial Relation Journal* 36: 184; ILO, Director-General (2003). *Time For Equality at Work: Global Report Under the Follow-up to the ILO Declaration on Fundamental Principles and Rights at Work* (International Labor Conference, 91st Sess., Report I(b)). ILO, Director-General (2007). *Equality at Work: Tackling the Challenge: Global Report Under the Follow-up to the ILO Declaration on Fundamental Principles and Rights at Work* (International Labor Conference, 96th Sess., Report I(b)).

[44] Discrimination has been proven to be the main reason causing the gender wage gap in non public sector in those late transition economies. See Stephan Jurajda (203). "Gender Wage Gap and Segregation in Enterprises and the Public Sector in Late

In many countries, as the subsequent chapters suggest, women suffer from discrimination in compensation even for identical work. "Equals should be treated equally".[45] It appears no one could convincingly argue otherwise. Even though some may argue that women are simply willing to work for less pay,[46] it is hardly sufficient to use women's willingness to justify the differential treatment for equal work performed by men and women workers.[47]

Nevertheless, in contrast to the right to equal pay for equal work that has been widely agreed upon, the right to equal pay for work of comparable worth has been surrounded by controversy and disagreement since its inception. As the conventional equal pay law was not able to address comparisons among different occupations, the comparable worth theory was therefore proposed to enable such comparison.[48] This theory is based on the premise that "women's jobs" should be valued as much as those "men's jobs". Teachers and nurses, for instance, should be paid as much as truck drivers.[49] Opponents of comparable worth first argue that it is unrealistic and costly to ensure

---

Transition Countries". *Journal of Comparative Economics* 31: 1999–222. Also see Carole A. Green & Marianne A. Ferber (2005). "Do Detailed Work Histories Help to Explain Gender and Race/Ethnic Wage Differentials?" *Review of Social Economy* LXIII: 55–85.

[45] Wil Waluchow (1988). "Pay Equity: Equal Value to Whom?" *Journal of Business Ethics* 7: 185–189, 185.

[46] See Neil Millward & Stephen Woodland 1995). "Gender Segregation and Male/Female Wage Differences", *Gender, Work and Organization* 2(3): 125–139; Rosemary Hunter (1993). "A Feminist Response to the Gender gap in Compensation Symposium", Georgetown Law Journal 82: 147, pp.148–149. Also see Benson Rosen, Sara Rynes and Thomas A. Mahoney (1983). "Compensation, Jobs, and Gender", *Harvard Business Review* 61: 170, p. 170; Robert Cherry (1988). Discrimination by Gender: Economic Theories and Policy Implications, in Vroman, Georgine M etc (eds.) *Women at Work: Socialization toward Inequality*. New York: Gordian Press. Louise Marie Roth (2004). "Engendering Inequality: Processes of Sex-Segregation on Wall Street", *Sociological Forum* 19: 203–228. But scholars such as P J Sloanne disagrees and argues that job segregation is not the main cause of the gender wage gap. See Sloane, Peter J (1988). "Gender, Pay Equity and Equal Value: A Solution in Search of a Rationale?" *Managerial and Decision Economics* 45–50. For the discussion on the process leading to sex segregation and gender pay gap, see Don Tomaskovic-Devey & Sheryl Skaggs(2002). "Sex Segregation, Labor Process Organization, and Gender Earnings Inequality", *The American Journal of Sociology* 108(1): 102–128.

[47] See Judith M Hill (1987). "Pay Equity", *International Journal of Applied Philosophy* 3: 1–9, p. 2.

[48] See Kenneth A. Kovach (1996). "Comparable Worth: the Canadian Legislation", *Business Horizon* 41–46, p. 42.

[49] See Rita Mae Kelly & Jane Bayes (1986). "Symposium: Implementing Comparable Worth in the Public Sector: Theory and Practice at the State and Local Level", *Policy Studies Review* 5: 769- 870, pp. 769–770.

the right to equal pay for work of comparable worth.[50] No doubt it is very difficult to measure "work of equal value".[51] The implementation of this principle would have to convince governments, employers, unions, or male workers.[52] However, no matter how difficult it might be, it is not impossible, as the following chapter shows, to objectively evaluate jobs.

Opponents of comparable worth also argue that the value of work should be determined by the market rather than anything else.[53] Nevertheless, the market is itself discriminatory. As scholars have suggested, the segregation of the labor market is one of the main causes of the gender wage gap.[54] Moreover, this type of segregation for the most part results from the historical discrimination against women in the job market.[55] Therefore, without a better alternative,[56] to reevaluate women's work and to pay women workers what they deserve is indispensable to redress historical discrimination women have long suffered from.[57] In a sense, to reevaluate women's work is just to right the past wrong.

---

[50] To grasp the debate about comparable worth in the United States in 1980s, see the following literature: Christopher McCrudden (1986). "Comparable Worth: A Common Dilemma", The Yale Journal of International Law 11: 396–436; Philip E Devine (1987). "Comparable Worth", *International Journal of Applied Philosophy* 3: 11–19. Also see Gail C Kaplan (1987–1988). "Pay Equity or Pay Up", *Los Angeles Law Review* 21:305, pp. 317–318.

[51] Donald P Schwab (1985). "Determining the Worth of Work", *Society* 22: 61–67.

[52] See for example, Keith Grint argues that "men were the primary inhibitors of equal pay", see Keith Grint (1988). "Women and Equality: The Acquisition of Equal Pay in the Post Office 1870–1961", *Sociology* 22(1): 87–108.

[53] For a more detailed discussion on the market defense, see Helena Kaminski (1986). "Comparable Worth and the Market Defense: A National Debate", *Golden Gate University Law Review* 16: 475.

[54] See F. L Jones (1983). "Sources of Gender Inequality in Income: What the Australian Census Says", *Social Forces* 62(1): 134–152. Also see Nabanita Datta Gupta & Donna Rothstein (2005). "The Impact of Worker and Establishment-level Characteristics on Male-Female Wage Differentials: Evidence from Danish Matched Employee-Employer Data", *Labor* 19(1): 1–34.

[55] See A Cheung (1995). "Pay Equity for Hong Kong: A Preliminary Exploration", *Hong Kong Law Journal* 33(25): 383–400, p. 386.

[56] Barbara Mackey Carlson and Mary Pat McEnrue proposed an alternative called "realignment". However, this strategy requires an overhaul of the value system as well as the whole structure. "Comparable worth" essentially is a reform of wage determination system. See Barbara Mackey Carlson and Mary Pat McEnrue (1985). "Comparable Worth and Realignment are two Strategies Proposed to Reduce the Gap in Earnings between Men and Women", *Business Horizons* 76–81.

[57] Paula England argues that job evaluation can be used to correct the discrimination women workers suffer from. See Paula England(1999). "The Case for Comparable Worth", *Quarterly Review of Economics and Finance* 39: 743–755, p. 743.

To narrow down the gender wage gap, as Gregory has argued, we have to battle with both vertical and horizontal job segregation.[58] Anti-discrimination legislation[59] aims to redress vertical job segregation through providing women with more opportunities at various levels of their career. As to horizontal job segregation, "comparable worth" could be a feasible strategy. Those female dominated jobs are traditionally undervalued compared to those jobs predominated by men.[60]

However, gender pay equity is more than an economic strategy. It is also a matter of "economic necessity". In some countries such as Australia women have constituted almost half of the work population.[61] Women workers are certainly an undeniable force in the economy. Gender pay equity may also enhance market's competitiveness and efficiency by "increasing the quality of work and employees' productivity".[62] Moreover, to implement gender pay equity can be instrumental in solving the issue of poverty,[63] as a larger segment of the poverty population are women.

At the same time, gender pay equity, because of its intricate connection to market, has to be part of the trade and globalization

---

[58] Jeanne Gregory (1992). "Equal Pay for Work of Equal Value: The Strengths and Weaknesses of Legislation", *Work, Employment & Society* 6: 461–473, p. 461.

[59] Anti-discrimination legislation here refers to both legislation on the right of men and women to equal pay for equal work and legislation on equal employment opportunities. However, it is important to point out that the concept of "equal pay" is different from "equal employment opportunities". They are however dependent on each other. See Jeanne Gregory (1992). "Equal Pay for Work of Equal Value: The Strengths and Weaknesses of Legislation", *Work, Employment & Society* 6: 461–473, p. 461.James P Henderson (1992). "Equal Pay vs. Equal Job Opportunity for Women: The Debate in Great Britain from 1891 to 1923", *International Journal of Social Economics* 19: 298–316. Also see Margherita Rendel(1978). "Legislating for Equal Pay and Opportunity for Women in Britain", *Signs* 3(4): 897–908, p. 897. Equal job opportunity is important to redress "allocative discrimination" (such as in the hiring process), see Petersen, Trond & Saporta, Ishak (2004). "The Opportunity Structure for Discrimination1", *The American Journal of Sociology* 109(4): 852- 901.

[60] See for example, Jeanne Gregory (1992). "Equal Pay for Work of Equal Value: The Strengths and Weaknesses of Legislation", *Work, Employment & Society* 6: 461–473, p. 461.

[61] Deirdre Lander & Graham O'Neill (1991). "Pay Equity: Apples, Oranges and a Can of Worms", *Asian Pacific Journal of Human Resources* 29: 16–28, pp. 16–17.

[62] See Revital Goldhar (2004). *Restructuring Pay Equity in the Era of the New Economy*. L.L.M Thesis. University of Toronto (Canada) 0779, abstract.

[63] See Rubery, Jill (1993). "The Economics of Equal Value", *Labor* 7(3): 117–131, p. 128. Also see Carlos Gradin et al (2006). *Poverty and Women's Labor Market Activity: the Role of Gender Wage Discrimination in the EU*. Society for the Study of Economic Inequality Working Paper Series, from http://www.ecineq.org/milano/WP/ECINEQ2006-40.pdf (accessed on Oct 30, 2007).

conversation. Globalization has been proven to have widened the gender wage gap.[64] In this regard, there raises a question concerning how to close the gender pay gap and safeguard labor rights in general in the context of free trade and globalization. Should the WTO, as the international organization responsible for advocating free trade, include a "social clause" that specifies the labor standards such as gender pay equity to be followed? Within the WTO, the concern is whether it is appropriate for the WTO to enforce labor standards and whether and how these labor standards would affect the comparative advantages of those countries that depend on labor-intensive industries. The 1996 Ministerial Declaration stated that the WTO would work with the ILO to establish and enforce core labor standards to be applied to WTO member nations. But it generally would leave the labor issues to the ILO.[65]

This interesting phenomenon of the exclusion of the ILO, an international organization committed to promoting labor rights, from the world trade system is a double-edged sword, as argued by Rorden Wilkinson.[66] The independence of the ILO provides it an opportunity to focus solely on workers' rights. But the downside of this lack of inclusion is also obvious, since the voice of workers is mostly unheard in the globalization and trade conversation.

The close relationship between gender pay equity, human rights, economy and trade suggests that there ought to be collaboration between the ILO and other UN organizations on an adequate scale. Legally speaking, Article 11 of the Convention 100 requires the ILO to report to the Secretary-General of the UN about the ratification matters of the Convention. The International Labor Conference (ILC) has long expressed its willingness to assist in ensuring the implementation of the provisions of the UN's International Covenant. The year (1967)

---

[64] See Remco H. Oostendorp (2004). *Globalization and the Gender Wage Gap*. World Bank Policy Research Working Paper Series 3256; Also see Sandra E. Black & Elizabeth Brainerd (2004). "Importing Equality? The Impact of Globalization on Gender Discrimination", *Industrial & Labor Relations Review* 57: 540–559. For a critique on the debate about globalization and gender wage gap, see Sylvia Walby (2003). "Policy Developments for Workplace Gender Equity in a Global Era: The Importance of the EU in the UK", *Review of Policy Research* 45–64, pp. 45–47.

[65] See http://www.wto.org/english/thewto_e/minist_e/min96_e/wtodec_e.htm (accessed on Sep 10, 2007).

[66] Rorden Wilkinson (2002). "Peripheralizing Labor: The ILO, WTO and the Completion of the Bretton Woods Project", in Jeffrey Harrod & Robert O'Brien (eds.) *Global Unions? Theory and Strategies of Organized Labor in the Global Political Economy*. New York: Routledge, pp. 204–220.

after the International Covenant on Economic, Social and Cultural Rights (ICESCR) was approved by the General Assembly, the ILC adopted a resolution encouraging its member states to ratify both ICESCR and relevant ILO Conventions. The Governing Body conducted a comparative study between ICESCR and the ILO Conventions ratified, in order to evaluate how the ILO could best support promoting the protection of human rights.[67] The Economic and Social Council also informed the ILO of their observations of the activities of the ratifying states of the Covenant related to the ILO Conventions.[68] The 156 states which have so far ratified or acceded to the Covenant are all members of the ILO. The former ILO Director-General Francis Blanchard expressed the view that the ILO has assisted its member states in working "towards the realization of the economic and social rights proclaimed in the Declaration", through "direct contacts with member states, regular reviews of problems of ratification and application of Conventions, the establishment of special procedures for the protection of trade union rights, and the use of constitutional complaints procedures".[69]

The above kind of interaction between the ILO and other UN organizations unfortunately is lacking between the WTO and the ILO. Some scholars therefore urge collaboration between these two organizations. Daniel Ehrenberg has even developed an innovative proposal for the ILO and WTO to devise a concrete coordinated means of enforcing labor standards through trade sanctions, while remaining sensitive to the development and sovereignty concerns.[70]

III. The Sources of International Standards on Gender Pay Equity

The importance of the issue of the gender pay gap has certainly been recognized by international law. The issue has gone "beyond borders".[71]

---

[67] See James Avery Joyce (1980). *World Labor Rights and Their Protection*. New York: St. Martin's Press, p. 39.

[68] *Ibid*. pp. 38–41.

[69] *Ibid*. p. 59.

[70] See Daniel S. Ehrenberg (1996). "From Intention to Action: An ILO- GATT / WTO Enforcement Regime for International Labor Rights", in Lance A. Compa & Stephen F. Diamond. (eds.). *Human Rights, Labor Rights, and International Trade: law and Policy Perspectives*. Philadelphia; University of Pennsylvania Press.

[71] See Patrick Macklem (2002). "Labor Law beyond Borders", *Journal of International Economic Law* 5 (3): 605–645.

As a UN specialized agency, the ILO has been dedicated to promoting gender pay equity in the workplace worldwide. The concept of gender pay equity is enshrined in the preamble of the ILO Constitution:

> And whereas conditions of labor exist involving such injustice hardship and privation to large numbers of people as to produce unrest so great that the peace and harmony of the world are imperiled; and an improvement of those conditions is urgently required; as, for example, by recognition of the principle of equal remuneration for work of equal value.[72]

The major treaty which specifically aims at the implementation of gender pay equity is the ILO Equal Remuneration Convention, 1951 (No. 100) and its Recommendation, 1951 (No. 90).[73] Article 2. 1 of the Convention 100 states that "each member shall, by means appropriate to the methods in operation for determining rates of remuneration, promote and, in so far as is consistent with such methods, ensure the application to all workers of the principle of equal remuneration for men and women workers of work of equal value". While Article 3. 3 is even more specific: "differential rates between workers which correspond, without regard to sex, to differences, as determined by such objective appraisal, in the work to be performed shall not be considered as being contrary to the principle of equal remuneration for men and women workers for work of equal value".

Article 2 of the Convention 100 provides that the ratifying states should promote the application of the principle of equal remuneration for work of equal value when their domestic methods of wage determination allow it. This Article has been repeatedly referred to as an example of the aspirational nature of this Convention, which implies the Convention may not be applied directly by a court. However, scholars like Ruiz Moreno disagree with this presumption. Moreno suggests that this Article, along with an Argentine Act which provides that

[72] The principle "equal remuneration for work of equal value' appeared in the initial text, but it was not included (Why not?) in the final text of the preamble of the 1919 ILO Constitution. It was only in the 1945 amendment, which entered into force in 1946. See http://www.ilo.org/ilolex/english/iloconst.htm (accessed on Sep 10, 2007).

[73] The following preparatory documents can be consulted as to the meaning of the Convention and its accompanying Recommendation No. 90: Equal Remuneration for Men and Women Workers for Work of Equal Value, *Reports V(1) and (2)*, ILC, 33rd Session, 1950, and *Reports VII(1) and (2)*, ILC, 34th Session, 1951: *Proceedings*, ILC, 34th Session, 1951. See also *International Labor Code*, vol. 1, arts. 233 and 234, pp. 183–189. The Committee of Experts has carried out three General Surveys of the Convention and Recommendation, in 1956, 1975 and 1986.

collective agreements should not modify a legal provision aiming at the protection of public interest, is clear and complete enough to be self-executing[74] in Argentina.[75] Even though the generality of its provisions are frequently used as a determinant for the non-self-executing nature of a Convention,[76] some scholars such as Ramirez Gronda argue that the general provisions of the Convention could be regarded as self-executing.[77]

As the Convention is drafted in general terms,[78] there is considerable misunderstanding regarding the meaning and scope of the Convention. Nonetheless, through years of work, the ILO Committee of Experts on the Application of Conventions and Recommendations[79] have step by step clarified and enriched the meaning of the provisions in the Convention and its Recommendation. It has repeatedly stressed that economic considerations should not justify exceptions[80] to the right to equal pay, and this is a right that should be guaranteed to all women and men workers.[81]

Art. 1(1)(a) defines "remuneration" to include "the ordinary, basic or minimum wage or salary and any additional emoluments whatsoever payable directly or indirectly, whether in cash or in kind, by the employer to the worker and arising out of the worker's employment". The CEACR has considered "any additional emoluments" to include

---

[74] "In principle, a treaty can be deemed self-executing when it already contains all the elements that allow for its implementation in the domestic legal system and no further integration needs to be added by state organs". See Davor Vidas (2000). *Implementing the Environmental protection Regime for the Antarctic*. London: Kluwer Academic Publishers, p. 356.

[75] In 1974 an Argentine law came into force which provided for equal remuneration for men and women for work of equal value. An editorial in La ley laboral y Previsional, 3 (1 junio 1973), pointed out that this law rendered operative both Article 14 of the argentine constitution and the ILO Equal Remuneration Convention (ratified by Argentina in 1956). In doing so it supported the contested view that the Supreme Court had held that ILO conventions could not be automatically incorporated into national law. See Virginia Leary (1982). *International Labor Conventions and National Law*. Hague: Martinus Nijhoff Publishers, p. 95.

[76] *Ibid.*

[77] *Ibid*, p. 98.

[78] Hector Bartolomei de la Cruz, Geraldo von Potobsky, and Lee Sweptston (1996). *The International Labor Organization: the International Standards System and Basic Human Rights*. New York: Westview Press, p. 240.

[79] Hereafter, it is referred to as "the CEACR".

[80] For example, in some national legislations, employees at public sector, or domestic workers, or workers in family undertakings, or agricultural workers are excluded from this principle.

[81] CEACR, *General Survey*, 1986, paras. 95–99.

seniority raises, marriage benefits, cost of living raises, use of a dwelling and family subsidies paid by employers, as well as payment for such kind as cleaning work clothing.[82] As to whether social security is included, the CEACR has concluded that a distinction must be made between social security systems financed by the employers or industries concerned, and benefits paid by those social security systems that are strictly public, with the latter not covered by the Convention.[83]

The Convention 100 lists the means of applying the principle: legislation, legally established or recognized machinery for wage determination, collective agreements between employers and workers or a combination thereof. Another key instrument, the Recommendation No. 90, suggests the manners in which government can actually promote gender pay equity, such as job analysis, vocational guidance, employment counseling, placement, welfare and social services, promoting public understanding, investigations, etc. The Convention does not specify the timetable to achieve gender pay equity. Instead it adopts the "progressive realization" approach,[84] the same as the one UN has used to other social and economic rights.

Some other ILO conventions also prescribe this important principle of gender pay equity, such as the ILO Discrimination (Employment and Occupation) Recommendation, 1958 (No. 111),[85] the ILO Social Policy (Basic Aims and Standards) Convention, 1962 (No. 117),[86] the ILO Minimum Age Recommendation, 1973 (No. 146),[87] the ILO Night Work Recommendation, 1990 (No. 178).[88] Gender pay equity is also

---

[82] CEACR, *General Survey*, 1986, para. 15.

[83] *Ibid.* para. 16.

[84] Equal Remuneration Recommendation 1951, preamble.

[85] See paragraph 2(b)(v): all persons should, without discrimination, enjoy equality of opportunity and treatment in respect of: v. remuneration for work of equal value.

[86] See article 14. 1(i) and 14.2: It shall be an aim of policy to abolish all discrimination among workers on grounds of race, color, sex, belief, tribal association or trade union affiliation in respect of: 1. wage rates, which shall be fixed according to the principle of equal pay for work of equal value in the same operation and undertaking. 2. All practicable measures shall be taken to lessen, by raising the rates applicable to the lower-paid workers, any existing differences in wage rates due to discrimination by reason of race, color, sex, belief, tribal association or trade union affiliation.

[87] See paragraph 13(1)(a): In connection with the application of the preceding Paragraph, as well as in giving effect to Article 7, paragraph 3, of the Minimum Age Convention, 1973, special attention should be given to: a. the provision of fair remuneration and its protection, bearing in mind the principle of equal pay for equal work.

[88] See paragraph 8. (1) (a). Night work should generally give rise to appropriate financial compensation. Such compensation should be additional to the remuneration paid for the same work performed to the same requirements during the day and

included as part of the equality principle in the ILO's 1996 Declaration on Fundamental Principles and Rights at Work.[89] It is fair to say the ILO standards concerning gender pay equity have achieved general consistency. Considering the wide ratification of the Convention 100 (168 states have ratified this Convention as the year of 2011), we can safely draw the conclusion that the principle of "gender pay equity" is commonly accepted throughout the globe and it has the potential to become a customary international norm.

In addition to the ILO conventions on the principle of gender pay equity described above, there are other UN instruments that prescribe this principle or a similar concept. The Universal Declaration of Human Rights refers to gender discrimination and other kinds of discrimination. Article 23.2 states that 'everyone, without any discrimination, has the right to equal pay for equal work".[90] Article 7(a) (i) of the International Covenant on Economic, Social and Cultural Rights (ICESCR) states that "the State Parties to the present Covenant recognize the right of everyone to the enjoyment of just and favorable conditions of work which ensure, in particular: a. Remuneration which provides all workers, as a minimum, with: i. Fair wages and equal remuneration for work of equal value without distinction of any kind, in particular women being guaranteed conditions of work not inferior to those enjoyed by men, with equal pay for equal work."[91] Gender discrimination in pay was highlighted right from the very beginning of the international human rights movement.[92]

Article 11.1(d) of the Convention on the Elimination of All Forms of Discrimination against Women(CEDAW) also stipulates that "states parties shall take all appropriate measures to eliminate discrimination against women in the field of employment in order to ensure, on a basis of equality of men and women, the same rights, in particular: d. the right to equal remuneration, including benefits, and to equal treatment in respect of work of equal value, as well as equality of treatment

---

a. should respect the principle of equal pay for men and women for the same work, or for work of equal value.

[89] See http://www.ilo.org/dyn/declaris/DECLARATIONWEB.static_jump?var_language=EN&var_pagename=DECLARATIONTEXT (accessed on Sep 10, 2007)

[90] http://www.un.org/Overview/rights.html (accessed on Sep 10, 2007)

[91] See http://www.unhchr.ch/html/menu3/b/a_cescr.htm (accessed on Sep 10, 2007)

[92] Brian S. Johnson (1998). "Ensuring Equality: Pursuing Implementation of the Equal Pay Principle via the Institutions of the European Union, the North American Agreement on the Labor Cooperation, and Corporate Code of Conduct", *Virginia Journal of International Law* 38: 849, p 853.

in the evaluation of the quality of work".[93] The 1995 Beijing Platform and Declaration of Action, and the Beijing +10 UN Documents both recognize the importance of the right to equal pay and require states to take actions to ensure the equality in pay for women.[94] To respect the right to equal pay is considered as an essential step to ultimately achieving gender equality worldwide.

It is noteworthy that these international instruments on gender pay equity have some remarkable and even direct impact on domestic legislations. For example, in Costa Rica, the Act of 1990 respecting the promotion of social equality for women, in sections 1 and 2 lays down general principles of equality for men and women in all areas of political, economic, social and cultural life. Notably section 2 refers to the United Nations Convention on the Elimination of all Forms of Discrimination against Women which provides for "the right to equal remuneration, including benefits, and equal treatment in respect of work of equal value, as well as equality of treatment in the evaluation of the equality of work" (Article 11(1)(d)).[95] Some other states also make explicit reference to the international instruments in their domestic legislations. For instance, Lebanon in its decree provides that "the Department of Labor Inspection, Protection and Safety of the Ministry of Labor supervise the implementation of all labor laws ... and the protection of workers in the workplace, including the provisions of ratified international labor Conventions".[96]

However, the existing international law on gender pay equity is problematic in many ways. The most serious difficulty is that the existing international legal standards, particularly the ILO conventions on equal pay, are ahead of reality and not reflected in actual practice. Whether they are advancing the ultimate goal of promoting gender equality is still debatable.[97] Another challenge is the discrepancy among the principles embodied in these international treaties. Only the Convention 100 and ICESCR use the term of "equal pay for work of equal value" which was intended to be a better defined and advanced

---

[93] http://www.un.org/womenwatch/daw/cedaw/cedaw.htm (accessed on Sep 10, 2007)

[94] United Nations (2005). *Taking Action: Achieving Gender Equality and Empowering Women*. UN Millennium Project, Task Force on Education and Gender Equality.

[95] CEACR, *Direct Request*, Costa Rica, 1993.

[96] Section 2 of Decree No. 3273. CEACR, *Direct Request*, Lebanon, 2002.

[97] F. Eyraud et al (1993). *Equal Pay Protection in Industrialized Economies: In Search of Greater Effectiveness*. Geneva: International Labor Office, p. 1.

concept for gender pay equity,[98] by selecting the word "work of equal value" rather than "equal work", "the same work" or "similar work". Other international treaties such as the Universal Declaration of Human Rights (UDHR), in contrast, employ different words ("equal work"). In this sense the general international labor standards on gender pay equity are still vague and incomprehensible to the public. The different wordings not only reflect the variation of the understanding of the issue among the international organizations, but also could be subject to different interpretation, which is very likely to generate inconsistency among the international law on gender pay equity and make it difficult to follow. This inconsistency could be easily employed to advance the argument that only the right to equal pay for equal work should be considered as a fundamental human right. Nevertheless, for those 168 ratifying countries, it is their obligation to implement "equal pay for work of equal value". Surprisingly the CEACR has concluded that the Convention 100 does not require the abolition of differences in the general level of wages between regions, sectors or even undertakings, so long as these differences apply equally to men and women.[99] The CEACR has also pointed out that "work of equal value" should also consider work performed in the different establishments, and jobs performed by single sex. That is to say, some work traditionally occupied by women should not be undervalued.[100]

Moreover, although the Convention 100 stresses that the ratifying countries should promote "equal pay for work of equal value",[101] the scope of the concept of "work of equal value" still demands a more complete and consistent interpretation in order for the ratifying states to effectively fulfill their obligation under the Convention.[102]

According to the Convention 100 and the Recommendation 90, an objective job appraisal should be implemented.[103] The major

[98] See Nicholas Valticos (1979). *International Labor Law.* Kluwer: International Law, p.176.

[99] CEACR, *General Survey*, 1986, para. 22.

[100] *Ibid.* CEACR, *General Survey*, 1986, para. 22. Also see ILO (2007). *Equality at Work: Tackling the Challenges: Global Report under the Follow-up to the ILO Declaration on Fundamental Principles and Rights at Work (B)*, p. 74.

[101] The term "remuneration" includes the ordinary basic or minimum wage or salary and any additional emoluments whatsoever payable directly or indirectly, in cash or in kind, by the employer to the worker and arising out of the worker's employment.

[102] See CEACR, *General Observation*, 2007, para. 1.

[103] See Convention 100, art 3; Recommendation 90, para 7.

requirement is that the sex of the worker who is doing or might do a certain kind of work should not be taken into consideration in wage determination. However, this raises a question of what constitutes "objectivity". It is certainly challenging to come up with a set of "objective" criteria to evaluate a job even within the same establishment. Even more technical difficulties will arise if the job comparison is extended to different establishments. For instance, the job of nursing and the job of truck-driving involve so different sets of skills that it is extremely so difficult to measure and compare them objectively.

One main difficulty regarding the application of the principle is how to ensure its implementation in private sectors. Some states do not interfere directly in the wage determination process of private sectors. Other states employ a federal political system, which decentralizes the monitoring of private sectors. Consequently, the Convention 100 adopted a more pragmatic approach, requiring that the ratifying governments implement this principle when it is compatible with their domestic wage-determination methods and where the wage-determination method is under the control of public authorities.[104] It obligates states to apply the principle in various levels of government employees and other public sectors.[105] The Convention calls for "the progressive application", which essentially allows the principle to be implemented first in public sectors and then gradually in private sectors.[106] Nonetheless, the question still remains with regard to how long it should take to achieve this "progress". The flexibility of the implementation schedule along with the vagueness of this principle provides an excuse for tardiness in complying with the Convention.

Another major criticism is that the international system lacks a compulsory enforcement mechanism to ensure that countries implement the labor standards included in the ILO conventions. However, it is fair to say that the ILO has achieved a certain level of success by combining its precise standard setting practice and a flexible enforcement machinery.[107]

---

[104] *Ibid.* art 2.

[105] Equal Remuneration Recommendation 1951. paras.1, 2.

[106] *Ibid.* preamble.

[107] James Avery Joyce (1980). *World Labor Rights and Their Protection.* New York: St. Martin's Press, p. 60. Also see E. A. Landy (1966). *The Effectiveness of International Supervision.* London: Stevens, pp. 209–210; Victor-Yves Ghebali (1989). *The International Labor Organization: a Case Study on the Evolution of U.N. Specialized Agencies.* Dordrecht, Boston & London: Martinus Nijhoff Publishers, Chapters 4 & 5.

The ILO has a supervisory system which has functioned effectively for several decades. The ratifying states have to submit their reports documenting precisely how they have implemented those ratified Conventions. These reports are then examined by the Committee of Experts which submits its own reports to the annual International Labor Conference. The Conference Committee which is uniquely composed of tripartite representatives (governments, employers and workers) examines reports from both. It sometimes invites government representatives to be present before the Conference and to answer questions raised by the experts. As the Conference is open to the public and all the documents issued are public, government representatives are usually very conscious of the image of their governments and try to avoid being criticized by the experts. This process allows for the influence of public opinion and illustrates the power of "mobilization of shame". For instance, New Zealand was not pleased when it was discussed as an individual case in the 1994 annual International Labor Conference. This is because "individual cases" typically concern states that have grossly violated the Convention 100 and New Zealand is arguably not among them.[108]

The ILO's supervisory machinery allows one government to file a complaint against another government, if one believes the other ratifying state does not live up to its obligations. Both the ILO's Governing Body and a Conference delegate can file a complaint. The Governing Body will then appoint a Commission of Inquiry. The government at issue will decide whether to accept the report issued by the Commission or to appeal to the International Court of Justice. The Governing Body may recommend further actions if the government continues its behavior of non-compliance.[109] But the ILO has rarely taken "further actions".

In general, the ILO's supervisory mechanism has achieved a certain degree of success but with limits. For example, in Jamaica, wage distinctions based on sex in the 1973 Minimum Wage (Printing Trade) Order has been essentially maintained in the 1989 Order, despite the introduction of a neutral language. After several years of communication between the ILO and Jamaica, the Jamaican government issued a 1989 Order which sets a single rate of pay for an "unskilled worker". However, the 1989 Order had simply removed the explicit reference

[108] ILLCR, *Individual Case, New Zealand*, 1994.

[109] See Joyce. *Supra* note 103, *at p.* 60.

to the sex of the worker from various categories, while maintaining both the former definitions of those categories and differentials in the respective increased minimum rates which correspond to those laid down in the 1973 Order.[110] That is to say, the substance of 1973 Order and its discriminatory nature have persisted in the 1989 Order. The 1989 Order only magnifies the government's intent to circumvent the issue of the real gender wage discrimination. The communication between the ILO and Jamaica in this case is basically a failure.

In short, the ILO has accomplished some measure of success in promoting gender pay equity during the short time it has existed for. Even though the effectiveness of its supervisory mechanism to enforce standards may from time to time be questioned, its increasing symbolic and moral power in constraining state behavior is momentous.

IV. Regional and Other Standards on Gender Pay Equity

Let me now turn to the regional instruments containing provisions on gender pay equity. The European Economic Community Treaty provides for "the application of the principle that men and women should receive equal pay for equal work" in its member states (Art. 119). It has been amended by the Amsterdam Treaty and reads: "Each member state shall ensure that the principle of equal pay for male and female workers for equal work or work of equal value is applied." Pay is defined as "the ordinary basic or minimum wage or salary and any other consideration, whether in case or in kind, which the worker receives, directly or indirectly, in respect of his employment from his employer". It adds that equal pay without discrimination on the basis of sex means: (a) that pay for the same work at piece rates shall be calculated on the basis of the same unit of measurement; and b) that pay for work at time rates shall be the same for the same job.[111] Although "equal work" was the initial formulation and appears to be a limited version of the equal remuneration principle, the interpretation given by the EEC has resulted in the jurisprudence that is very similar to what is embodied in the Convention 100.[112]

---

[110] See CEACR, *Individual Observation, Jamaica*, 1991, 1992, 1993, 1994, 1995, 1996, 1997.

[111] See Article 119 of the Rome Treaty Establishing the European Community, 1954.

[112] See Lammy Betten (1993). *International Labor Law: Selected Issues*. Deventer, the Netherlands: Kluwer Law and Taxation Publishers, pp. 266–276. Also see Evelyn Ellis (1998). *EC Sex Equality Law*. Oxford: Clarendon Press, pp. 59–149.

The European Social Charter (1961) declares that its Contracting Parties have the obligation to "recognize the right of men and women workers to equal pay for work of equal value" (Art. 4, para. 3). In the EEC Equal Pay Directive based on Article 119 of the EEC Treaty, the terms are further defined. The principle of "equal pay for equal work" means, according to the Directive, for the same work or for work to which equal value is attributed, and the elimination of all discrimination on grounds of sex with regard to all aspects and conditions of remuneration.[113] The Directive centers on the issue of job classification system used for determining wage.[114]

The Arab Labor Organization has also adopted two Conventions that include the subject of equal remuneration. Article 3 of the 1976 Convention on Female Workers (No. 5)[115] and Article 13 of the 1983 Convention on the Determination and Protection of Wages (No. 15) provide that men and women should be paid equally for "similar work".[116] The Protocol of San Salvador obligates its ratifying states to ensure "fair and equal wages for equal work, without distinction" (Art.7).[117] The 1981 African Charter on Human and People's Rights guarantees "equal pay for equal work" for every individual (Art. 15).[118] The American Declaration of the Rights and Duties of Man has a general reference to the right to fair remuneration[119] and equal rights.[120]

---

[113] See *Council Directive 75/117/EEC of 10 February 1975 on the approximation of the laws of the Member States relating to the application of the principle of equal pay for men and women*, from http://www. europa.eu/…/sga_doc?smartapi!celexapi!prod! CELEXnumdoc&lg=en&numdoc=31975L0117&model=guichett (Accessed on Sep 10, 2007), Article 1.

[114] *Ibid.* Treaty of Rome art 141 *(previously art 119)* is the "equal pay for equal work" article; EC Directive 75/117/EEC is the Equal Pay Directive; EC Directive 76/207/EEC is the Equal Treatment (employment) Directive; EC Directive 79/7/EEC is the Equal Treatment (social security) Directive.; EC Directive 2002/73/EC amends 76/207/EEC. A new Consolidating Directive 2006/54 ("on the implementation of the principle of equal opportunities and equal treatment of men and women in matters of employment and occupation – recast"), effective from 15th August 2006 was made on 5th July 2006.

[115] http://training.itcilo.it/ils/CD_Use_Int_Law_web/Additional/Library/English/ILO_S_B/general_gurveys/25882.htm (accessed on Sep 10, 2007).

[116] http://www.bah-molsa.com/english/sec2ch8.htm (accessed on Sep 10, 2007).

[117] http://www.worldpolicy.org/globalrights/treaties/achr-esc.html (accessed on Sep 10, 2007).

[118] http://www1.umn.edu/humanrts/instree/z1afchar.htm (accessed on Sep 10, 2007).

[119] Article XIV.

[120] Article II.

The World Bank in its 2006 World Development Report identifies the distinct problem of the gender pay gap as one key element of the global poverty issues which affect not only women, but children and families as well as the whole community.[121] Its 2006 Gender Action Plan urges governments to take action to solve the inherent economic inequalities women are encountering, in order to achieve a sustainable economic development.[122] Similarly, the Organization for Economic Cooperation and Development (OECD) has also incorporated closing the gender pay gap as one of its main goals to achieve gender equality.[123] It is noteworthy that the OECD has a mechanism for receiving complaints concerning labor rights violations committed by multinational corporations, although it has no sanction authority.[124] The North American Free Trade Act (NAFTA), a trade agreement, also addresses labor rights. It stipulates that "equal wages for women and men by applying the principle of equal pay for equal work in the same establishment."[125] But thus far no cases have been filed by member states citing this article. Its side agreement, the North American Agreement on Labor Cooperation (NAALC) has also been accused of failing to adequately protect labor rights including the right to equal pay.[126]

In general, regional instruments except the EU law have not advanced from the general prescription of the right to "equal pay for equal work" to "equal pay for work of equal value or comparable worth".

---

[121] World Bank (2006). *Global Monitoring Report, Millennium Development Goals: strengthening Mutual Accountability, Aid, Trade and Governance*, from http://web.worldbank.org/WBSITE/EXTERNAL/EXTDEC/EXTGLOBALMONITOR/EXTGLOBALMONITOR2006/0,,menuPK:2186472~pagePK:64218926~piPK:64218953~theSitePK:2186432,00.html (accessed on Sep 10, 2007).

[122] World Bank (2006), *World Development Report 2006: Equity and Development 2*, from http://econ.worldbank.org/external/default/main?pagePK=64165259&theSitePK=469372&piPK=64165421&menuPK=64166093&entityID=000112742_20050920110826 (Accessed on Sep 10, 2007); World Bank (2006). *Gender Equality is Smart Economics: The World Bank Gender Action Plan.* http://siteresources.worldbank.org/INTGENDER/Resources/GAPNov2.pdf. (Accessed on Sep 10, 2007).

[123] See OECD, *Declaration on Policies for the Employment of Women*, from http://webdomino1.oecd.org/horizontal/oecdacts.nsf/Display/16C0D7AF80EB0754C125729B004DB379?OpenDocument (accessed on Sep 10, 2007).

[124] Lance Compa (1995). "The First NAFTA Labor Cases: A New International Labor Rights Regime Takes Shape", *US-Mexico Labor Law Journal*, p. 160.

[125] See Article 49 of NAFTA.

[126] See Brian S. Johnson 91998). "Ensuring Equality: Pursuing Implementation of the Equal Pay Principle via the Institutions of the European Union, the North American Agreement on the Labor Cooperation, and Corporate Code of Conduct", *Virginia Journal of International Law* 38: 849, pp. 862–868.

The principle of equal pay provided in these regional instruments is narrower than the one contained in the ILO Convention 100. Both international and regional instruments have by and large addressed the issue of gender pay equity. However, are these instruments effective? Do the ratifying states (their legislative systems and judiciaries) comply with these treaties? The following two chapters are to answer these two questions.

CHAPTER III

LEGISLATIVE COMPLIANCE – THE PROCESS OF "INTERNALIZATION"

The ILO Convention No. 100 on Equal Remuneration is the only international treaty which endeavors to promote gender pay equity worldwide and to resolve the issue of the gender wage gap. It is considered as one of the core ILO conventions. This chapter is based on the analysis of a large quantity of data drawn from the reports on the implementation of this Convention issued by the ILO Committee of Experts on the Application of Conventions and Recommendations since 1990.[1] It includes 290 individual observations, 1373 direct requests, 14 individual cases, volumes of national legislation obtained from the ILO NATLEX database, as well as various secondary literatures. It consists of four parts: the first two parts survey and analyze how the major articles in the ILO Convention No. 100[2] are internalized in the policies of its ratifying states. This will allow me to see if national legislative systems are complying with the Convention; the third part examines the phenomenon of legislative compliance with the Convention through a detailed investigation of several exemplary ratifying states; the last part suggests that a comprehensive legislative approach should be adopted in order to eliminate the gender wage gap.

I. General Observation on Legislative Compliance

Many countries have adopted national legislation in accordance with the terms of the Convention. There has been an emerging understanding among the ratifying governments that the mere removal of male and female wage classification is not enough. "An analysis of the position and pay of men and women in all job categories within and between the various sectors" is repeatedly stressed by the CEACR. However, the difficulties of application persist. The CEACR's observation in 2007 concludes that the difficulties of the application of the principle result

[1] Hereafter, it is referred to as the CEACR.
[2] Throughout this chapter, it is referred to as the Convention.

from the lack of understanding of the scope and meaning of the concept of "work of equal value". That is, the ratifying states have not yet reached a consensus on what constitutes "comparable worth".

Based on the analysis of the CEACR's reports and the domestic legislation, I constructed a study (see Table 1, Table 2 and Figure 1) to delineate the status of the domestic legislation in the area of gender pay equity in the 154 ratifying states.[3] Table 2 and Figure 1 summarize the

Table 1: The Legal Status of Equal Pay in the Ratifying States

Country	Ratification Year[4]	Specific Legislation (Equal Value=1, Equal Work=0.5, General/non=0)[5]
Afghanistan	1969	0.5
Albania	1957	1.0
Algeria	1962	0.0
Angola	1976	1.0
Argentina	1956	0.5
Australia	1974	1.0
Austria	1953	1.0
Azerbaijan	1992	0.5
Bahamas	2001	0.5
Bangladesh	1998	1.0
Barbados	1974	0.5
Belarus	1956	1.0
Belgium	1962	0.5
Belize	1999	0.5
Benin	1968	1.0
Bolivia	1973	0.0

[3] There are 168 ratifying states, but only 154 are presented in this study. This is because countries like Vanuatu, Montenegro, Uganda, Antigua and Barbuda, just ratified the Convention recently and have not yet submitted their report on the implementation of the Convention.

[4] As of the year of 2007, see http://www.ilo.org/ilolex/english/newratframeE.htm (accessed on Dec 8, 2007).

[5] More specifically, as of the year of 2007, 1 means a ratifying state has a legislative enactment that prescribes equal pay for equal work or work of equal value; 0.5 means a ratifying state only has a legislative enactment which prescribes equal pay for equal work (not work of equal value); 0 means a ratifying state either has legal enactment that generally prescribes gender equality or has no legislative enactment at all in this regard.

Table 1: *(Cont.)*

Country	Ratification Year	Specific Legislation (Equal Value=1, Equal Work=0.5, General/non=0)
Bosnia and Herzegovina	1993	1.0
Botswana	1997	0.5
Brazil	1959	0.0
Bulgaria	1955	0.5
Burkina Faso	1969	0.5
Burundi	1993	0.5
Byelorussian	1956	0.5
Cambodia	1999	0.5
Cameroon	1970	0.5
Canada	1972	1.0
Ced'Ivoire	1961	1.0
Central African Republic	1964	0.5
Chad	1966	1.0
Chile	1971	0.0
China	1990	0.5
Colombia	1963	0.5
Comoros	1978	0.5
Congo	1999	0.0
Costa Rica	1951	0.5
Croatia	1991	1.0
Cuba	1954	0.5
Cyprus	1987	1.0
Czech Republic	1993	1.0
Djibouti	1978	0.5
Dominica	1983	0.5
Dominican Republic	1953	0.5
Ecuador	1957	1.0
Egypt	1960	0.5
El Salvador	2000	0.5
Equatorial Guinea	1985	1.0

(Continued)

Table 1: *(Cont.)*

Country	Ratification Year	Specific Legislation (Equal Value=1, Equal Work=0.5, General/non=0)
Eritrea	2000	0.5
Estonia	1996	0.0
Ethiopia	1999	1.0
Fiji	2002	0.5
Finland	1963	0.5
France	1953	1.0
Gabon	1961	0.5
Gambia	2000	0.0
Georgia	1993	0.5
Germany	1956	0.5
Ghana	1968	0.5
Greece	1975	0.5
Grenada	1994	1.0
Guatemala	1961	0.5
Guinea	1967	1.0
Guinea-Bissau	1977	0.5
Guyana	1975	1.0
Haiti	1958	1.0
Honduras	1956	0.5
Hungary	1959	0.5
Iceland	1958	1.0
India	1959	0.5
Indonesia	1958	0.0
Iran	1972	0.5
Iraq	1963	1.0
Ireland	1974	1.0
Israel	1965	1.0
Italy	1956	1.0
Jamaica	1975	0.5
Japan	1967	0.0
Jordan	1966	0.5
Kazakhstan	2001	0.5
Kenya	2001	0.0
Kyrgyzstan	1992	0.5

Table 1: *(Cont.)*

Country	Ratification Year	Specific Legislation (Equal Value=1, Equal Work=0.5, General/non=0)
Latvia	1992	1.0
Lebanon	1977	0.5
Libyan Arab Jamahiriya	1962	0.5
Lithuania	1994	1.0
Luxembourg	1967	0.5
Madagascar	1962	0.5
Malawi	1965	1.0
Malawi	1965	0.5
Malaysia	1997	0.0
Mali	1968	0.5
Malta	1988	1.0
Mauritania	2001	0.5
Mauritius	2002	0.0
Mexico	1952	0.5
Mongolia	1969	0.5
Morocco	1979	1.0
Mozambique	1977	1.0
Nepal	1976	0.5
Netherlands	1971	0.5
New Zealand	1983	0.5
Nicaragua	1967	0.5
Niger	1966	0.5
Nigeria	1974	0.5
Norway	1959	1.0
Pakistan	2001	1.0
Panama	1958	0.5
Papua New Guinea	2000	0.5
Paraguay	1964	1.0
Peru	1960	0.0
Philippines	1953	1.0
Poland	1954	1.0

(Continued)

Table 1: *(Cont.)*

Country	Ratification Year	Specific Legislation (Equal Value=1, Equal Work=0.5, General/non=0)
Portugal	1967	1.0
Republic of Korea	1997	1.0
Republic of Moldova	2000	0.5
Romania	1957	0.5
Russian Federation	1956	0.5
Rwanda	1980	0.5
Saint Lucia	1983	1.0
Saint Vincent and the Grenadines	2001	0.5
San Marino	1985	0.5
Sao tome and Principle	1982	0.5
Saudi Arabia	1978	0.5
Senegal	1962	0.5
Servia and Montenegro	2000	0.0
Seychelles	1999	1.0
Sierra leone	1968	0.0
Singapore	2002	0.0
Slovakia	1993	0.5
Slovenia	1992	1.0
South Africa	2000	1.0
Spain	1967	1.0
Sri Lanka	1993	0.0
Sudan	1970	0.5
Swaziland	1981	0.5
Sweden	1962	1.0
Switzerland	1972	1.0
Syrian	1957	0.5
Tajikistan	1993	1.0
Tanzania	2002	1.0
Thailand	1999	0.5
Togo	1983	0.5
Trinidad and Tobago	1997	0.5

Table 1: *(Cont.)*

Country	Ratification Year	Specific Legislation (Equal Value=1, Equal Work=0.5, General/non=0)
Tunisia	1968	0.0
Turkey	1967	1.0
UK	1971	1.0
Ukraine	1956	0.5
United Arab Emirates	1997	0.5
Uruguay	1989	0.5
Uzbekistan	1992	0.5
Venezuela	1982	0.5
Vietnam	1997	0.5
Yemen	1976	0.5
Zambia	1972	0.5
Zimbabwe	1989	1.0

Table 2: Frequency – Specific Legislation (Equal Value=1, Equal Work=0.5, General/non=0)

Specific Legislation	Number of Countries	Percentage
Equal Value (1)	52	33.8%
Equal Work (.5)	84	54.5%
General/Non (0)	18	11.7%
Total	154	100%

number of countries that have specific legislations on "equal pay for equal work", or "equal pay for work of equal value". Among the 154 ratifying states, 54 ratifying states have legal enactments on "equal pay for work of equal value" and 84 have legal enactments on "equal pay for equal work". Thus in total, 88% of the states investigated have some form of legal enactment on "equal pay for equal work" or "equal pay for work of equal value" or the equivalent. This high percentage is no doubt remarkable. It at the very least suggests a positive sign of general legislative compliance.

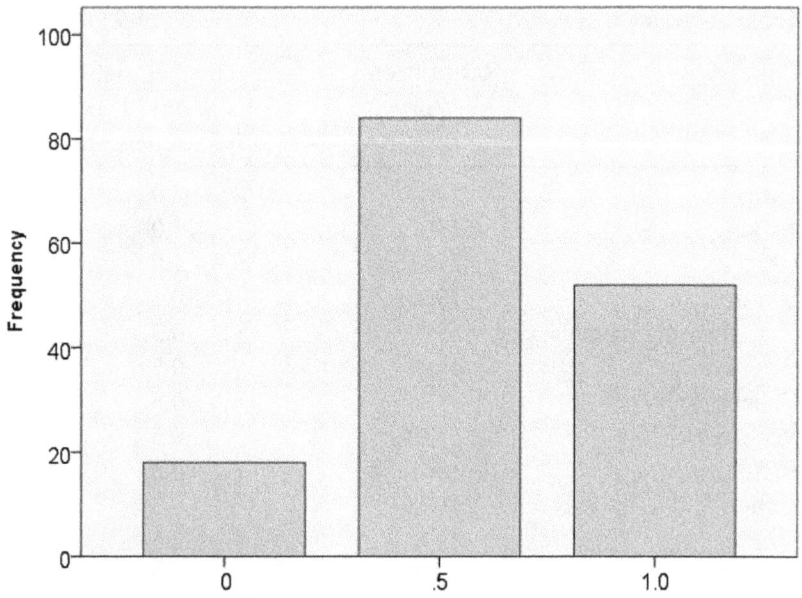

Figure 1: Frequency – Specific Legislation (Equal Value=1, Equal Work=0.5, General/non=0)

The following text provides a detailed analysis of how each key article of the Convention (namely Article 1, 2, 3)[6] is implemented in the ratifying states.

[6] Article 1:….a) the term remuneration includes the ordinary, basic or minimum wage or salary and any additional emoluments whatsoever payable directly or indirectly, whether in case or in kind, by the employer to the worker and arising out of the worker's employment; b) the term equal remuneration for men and women workers for work of equal value refers to rates of remuneration established without discrimination based on sex. Article 2: Each member shall, by means appropriate to the methods in operation for determining rates of remuneration, promote and, in so far as is consistent with such methods, ensure the application to all workers of the principle of equal remuneration for men and women workers for work of equal value….. Article 3:1. where such action will assist in giving effect to the provisions of this Convention measures shall be taken to promote objective appraisal of jobs on the basis of the work to be performed. 2.… 3. Differential rates between workers which correspond, without regard to sex, to differences, as determined by such objective appraisal, in the work to be performed shall not be considered as being contrary to the principle of equal remuneration for men and women workers for work of equal value. See the ILO Convention No. 100 on Equal Remuneration, 1951, from http://www.ilo.org/ilolex/cgi-lex/convde.pl?C100 (accessed on Oct 30, 2007)

1. *The Concept of "Work of Equal Value"*

It appears that since the early twenty-first century, the CEACR has expected the ratifying states to take legislative actions to implement the right to equal pay for "work of equal value" (or comparable worth) in addition to just "equal work" or "similar work". Those reports have since repeatedly emphasized the importance of "work of equal value". Eventually the CEACR was no longer satisfied if a ratifying state only has a legal provision on "equal pay for equal work". That is, the CEACR has determined that the ratifying state should have progressed to implement the right to "equal pay for comparable worth" rather than just "equal pay for equal work".

However, not all ratifying states are progressing from "equal pay for equal work" to "equal pay for work of equal value". In some states the legislation has even gone backwards with the passage of time. For example, in Indonesia, its Government Regulation No. 8 of 1981 provides in its section 3 that in determining wages employers shall be prohibited for discriminating against women workers for work of equal value. The section 11392 of the former Manpower Act of 1997 also provides that "in determining wages the employers shall be prohibited to practice discrimination on whatever basis with respect to jobs of the same value", but the new Act of 2003 does not include a specific provision guaranteeing that men and women workers shall receive equal remuneration for work of equal value.[7] Going from "equal pay for work of equal value" to "equal pay for equal work" is essentially going regressively rather than progressively. Therefore it is a violation of the "progressive realization"[8] principle set out in the Convention.

The right to equal pay for equal work and work of equal value has been elevated to become a constitutional principle in some ratifying states. For example, in 1999, Venezuela made a significant step towards the implementation of "equal pay for work of equal value" by establishing the principle of equal pay for equal work and work of equal value in its new Constitution.[9]

Nevertheless, many ratifying states still struggle with implementing the principle of gender pay equity. As the CEACR has pointed out in

[7] CEACR, *Individual Observation, Indonesia*, 2004.

[8] Equal Remuneration Recommendation 1951, preamble.

[9] See Art 91. Also see Comprehensive Labor Act 1997 (Art 135), from http://www.ilo.org/public/english/employment/gems/eeo/law/venezuel/l_cla.htm (accessed on Oct 30, 2007).

its general observation several times, the difficulties of implementing the Convention No. 100 mainly stem from the lack of understanding of the concept of "work of equal value".[10] The ratifying states have proposed various criteria to define "work of equal value". In the 1990s, many countries such as Bulgaria and Byelorussia[11] adopted the criteria of "quantity and quality" for the job evaluation. Nonetheless, these criteria only allow the job comparison for workers in the establishment of the same nature. Therefore it merely provides "equal pay for equal work", rather than "equal pay for work of equal value" as defined in the Convention. Occasionally, even though the grand concept of "work of equal value" is placed in some domestic legislation, the ensuing guidelines restrict the scope of the principle to equal work only. In other states such as the Netherlands, the job comparison for "work of equal value" has been extended to comparison between different enterprises. The Netherlands in its 1989 Act provides the basis for comparing remuneration that is restricted to the wage normally received by a worker of the other sex in the same undertaking for work of equal value, instead of work of virtually equal value. But through the interpretation of the Supreme Court, it has been made possible to compare jobs for the purpose of "work of equal value" between different industries.[12]

Another puzzle is whether "work of equal value" is only applied to domestic female workers and whether foreign female workers should be included. For example, Libya establishes a unified wage system for workers employed in public services and in state enterprises, institutions and bodies. But this system applies solely to nationals.[13] The CEACR has raised the concern on whether foreign female workers working in Libya are included in this system. The government indicates that even though this system specifically targets its nationals, in practice the salaries and indemnities of foreign laborers remain essentially higher than those of national workers provided for in law.[14] If the right to gender pay equity is a fundamental human right, there is no reason to exclude foreign women workers from the application. Every working woman regardless of her nationality should be guaranteed such right.

---

[10] CEACR, *General Observation*, 1990, 1999, 2007.

[11] CEACR, *Direct Request, Bulgaria, Byelorussian*, 1990.

[12] CEACR, *Direct Request, Netherlands*, 1994. Section 3(2) of equal pay legislation also allowed for this possibility. See CEACR, *Direct Request, Netherlands*, 1992.

[13] Act No. 15 of 1981.

[14] Law No. 15 of 1981. CEACR, *Direct Request, Libyan*, 1990.

2. *The Concept of Pay*

According to Article 1 of the Convention, "remuneration" includes "the ordinary, basic or minimum wage or salary and any additional emoluments whatsoever payable directly or indirectly, whether in cash or in kind, by the employer to the worker and arising out of the worker's employment".[15] It appears most countries have no problem in including a broad definition of "remuneration" in their legislation. For instance, in Israel, the 1996 new law provides for equal remuneration for "work of equal value" and defines "remuneration" as all forms of payment to a worker "in connection with employment".[16] However, as the following text indicates, whether wage above the "minimum wage", family allowance, maternity leave, and working hours should be incorporated into the concept of "pay" has been frequently subject to debate.

Most countries have passed legislation in which the "minimum wage" is to be given equally to both men and women.[17] However, when it comes to the wage or salary above "minimum wage", the manner in which domestic legislations have dealt with this component of pay differ significantly. In Slovakia, the Labor Code excludes from the definition of wages certain payments such as those "provided in relation to employment pursuant to other provisions of the Act, or special regulations".[18] Revenues from capital shares or bonds or payments made by the employer from profits after taxation do not appear to be considered as part of remuneration. The Slovakian government explains that the definition of "wage" is used only for legal purposes. For the sake of correctly ascertaining the average earning of an employee, the legal system differentiates payments arising out of the employment relationship that are directly dependent on the work performed from those that are not, such as traveling expenses and revenues from capital shares and bonds. The government further indicates

---

[15] ILO Convention No. 100, Art 1.

[16] See Male and Female Equal Pay Law, 1996, from http://www.ilo.org/public/english/employment/gems/eeo/law/israel/mfwe.htm (accessed on Oct 30, 2007)

[17] For the discussion on the impact of National minimum wage policy on closing gender wage gap, see Helen Robinson (2005). "Regional Evidence on the Effect of the National Minimum Wage on the Gender Pay Gap", *Regional Studies* 39: 855–872. Also see Robinson, Helen (2002). "Wrong Side of the Track? The Impact of the Minimum Wage on Gender Pay Gaps in Britain", *Oxford Bulletin of Economics and Statistics* 64(5): 417–448.

[18] Section 118(2).

that there are "special regulations" governing payments which prescribe that the employer is obligated or entitled to provide to employees, for example, the compensation for income in the case of temporary inability to work[19] or sickness benefits[20]. Based on such explanation, the CEACR concludes that the above-mentioned Slovakian method of defining "pay"is in conformity with the concept of remuneration as outlined in Article 1(a) of the Convention.[21]

In general, The CEACR has been pushing for a broader definition of "remuneration".[22] If "remuneration" does not cover payments that are paid by the employer for certain occasions and out of generosity (such as occasional premiums, bonuses or rewards), or the allowances in cash or in kind that are paid to workers to carry out their jobs(such as the costs of representation, means of transport or other similar expenses), and certain social benefits or customary or occasional benefits (such as food, housing or clothing, holiday bonuses above the legal minimum and holidays for service or Christmas), as in Colombia,[23] this kind of concept is not in accord with the Convention, as insisted by the CEACR.

A dilemma arises with regard to whether benefits such as those related to social security should be included in the principle.[24] For example, in Argentina, family allowances are not considered as part of the definition of "wages" or "remuneration".[25] They are not part of the annual supplementary wage nor compensation for arbitrary dismissal.[26] However, according to the CEACR, "the Convention covers all components of remuneration-direct and indirect-which arise out of the employment relationship" and that "allowances paid under social security schemes financed by the undertaking or industry concerned were part of the system of remuneration… in respect of which there should be no discrimination based on sex".[27] Therefore,

---

[19] Act No. 462/2003.

[20] Act No. 461/2003.

[21] CEACR, *Direct Request, Slovakia*, 2006.

[22] *Ibid.*

[23] Section 128 of the Substantive Labor Code, as amended by Act No. 50 of 1990. CEACR, *Direct Request, Colombia*, 1992.

[24] For a discussion on the relevant law of European Court of Justice on social security, see Ingeborg Heide (2004). "Sex Equality and Social Security: Selected Rulings of the European Court of Justice", *International Labor Review* 143(4): 299–339.

[25] The Legislative Decree No. 18017/68.

[26] Section 12 of Act No. 18037. CEACR, *Direct Request, Argentina*, 1990.

[27] CEACR, *General Survey*, 1986, paras 15–17, 88–89.

the exclusion of family allowance is not in accordance with the principle of the Convention. The CEACR states that allowances made under a public system of social security are not to be considered as part of remuneration and are not therefore covered by the Convention.[28] Nevertheless those allowances paid under social security provided by employers may fall under "discrimination in employment" under Convention No. 111[29].

Women with children often suffer double discrimination (that is, the "family gap" and the "gender gap") in pay. As a result, whether maternity leave should be part of the notion of gender pay equity is another important issue.[30] In some country legislative actions have been taken to protect pregnant women. For instance, in the Czech Republic, workers with diminished working capacity are legally guaranteed working conditions taking into consideration the state of their health. During the periods when workers are unable to work due to illness, pregnancy or motherhood, "their labor law relations shall be protected by law to a heightened extent".[31]

The discrimination women have long endured partly results from their inferior social and legal status. In Lebanon, for example, under current national legislation it would be difficult to consider the possibility of allowing both spouses to choose who would be the beneficiary of family allowances, as both the legislature and judiciary[32] still presume that a father has the legal responsibility for his children and therefore is the primary beneficiary of family allowances. As the CEACR suggests, social security legislation is often based on the premise that the man is the head of the family and therefore the woman benefits from protection derived only from her husband's entitlements. It is exceptionally challenging to break with this paternalistic mentality. Therefore national policies on social security would have to take the initiative to guarantee equal rights to men and women, which may empower women and expedite the ultimate realization of gender equality.[33]

---

[28] *Ibid.* para. 17.

[29] *ILO Convention (No. 111) concerning Discrimination in Respect of Employment and Occupation*, 1958.

[30] See Jane Waldfogel (1998). "Understanding the 'Family Gap' in Pay for Women with Children", *The Journal of Economic Perspectives* 12(1): 137–156.

[31] Section IX of the Labor Code, CEACR, *Direct Request, Czech*, 1995.

[32] Cassation Court Decision No. 6/2000.

[33] CEACR, *Direct Request, Lebanon*, 2006.

Another intriguing question concerns part-time workers.[34] Many more women work part time than men.[35] Most of these women workers choose to work part time in order to balance their career and family.[36] Scholars such as Rosenfeld and Kalleberg have found that part-time work has a significant effect on the gender wage gap in some countries.[37] Certain ratifying states have therefore taken proactive actions in protecting part-time workers from discrimination because of their different working hours. In Netherlands, the Parliament enacted legislation to prohibit discrimination between employees on the basis of their working hours.[38] The Dutch government hoped that this law would improve the legal status of part-time workers. The improvement in the legal status of part-time workers might attract more men to take on part-time jobs. Hence it may help balance the distribution of paid and unpaid work between men and women.[39] By the same token, it may alleviate the discrimination faced by part-time workers and women workers through regulating the conditions including remuneration and promotion of women working under the part-time system, and providing child-care facilities for mothers working in the administrative, service and production services. Libya has promulgated this sort of regulation.[40] This kind of law may contribute to improving the conditions of employment of women working part-time and to promoting equality of opportunity and treatment of women in general.[41]

3. *Job Evaluation*[42]

The explicit expression "work of equal value" in national legislation is of great significance. In addition to its symbolic value, it serves to

[34] See Diane Perrons(2000). "Living with Risk: Labor Market Transformation, Employment Policies and Social Reproduction in the UK", *Economic and Industrial Democracy* 21: 283–310.

[35] Helen Hughes (1998). "Equal Pay for Work of Equal Value: Moving toward, or Away from, Wage Justice for Women?" *Policy* 14: 29–34, p. 30.

[36] Janet Smithson and et al. (2004). "Flexible Working and the Gender Pay Gap in the Accountancy Profession", *Work, Employment and Society* 18: 115–135.

[37] Rachel A. Rosenfeld & Arne L. Kalleberg (1990). "A Cross-national Comparison of the Gender Gap in Income", *American Journal of Sociology* 96: 69–106.

[38] effective from Nov 1996.

[39] CEACR, *Individual Observation, Netherlands*, 1997.

[40] Decision of the People's Congress, No. 164 of 1985.

[41] CEACR, *Direct Request, Libyan Arab Jamahiriya*, 2004.

[42] For a more detailed analysis of the importance of job evaluation to equal pay principle, see Deborah M. Figart (2000). "Equal Pay for Equal Work: The Role of Job Evaluation in an Evolving Social Norm", *Journal of Economic Issues* 34: 1–19.

raise public awareness. Moreover, the broader comparison is vital in addressing sex-based discrimination with regard to remuneration in situations where the job market is sex segregated. It also helps the public appreciate those historically undervalued lines of work dominated by women.

However, what constitutes "work of equal value"? How to determine the value of the jobs performed by men and women is a complicated and intricate challenge for the ratifying states. The common problem employers raise is whether there is an objective method of evaluating different kinds of jobs and assessing the concept of "work of equal value". The states that have tried to define the concept sometimes find their definitions problematic. For example, Jamaica and Germany have created a concept of "light work". But as the CEACR has pointed out, even in the absence of any direct and explicit reference to sex, "light work" is usually paid at a lower rate and is typically feminine, which may lead to a systematic underestimation of female-dominated type of work and to the reinforcement of indirect discrimination.[43]

Some states do not base their job evaluation on types of work performed. Instead they use a set of "objective factors" to determine the value of work. For example, in Poland, the Labor Code does require that remuneration be determined not only in accordance with equality, but also with "objectivity" and based on seemingly more objective factors such as the kind of work performed, the skills required for its performance and the quality and quantity of work. In practice, public and private enterprises employ different methods of job evaluation to determine minimum rates of remuneration. The criteria they use include the factors of complexity of the work,[44] the level of responsibility,[45] the strenuousness of the work[46] and the working conditions. This greater reliance on the objective job assessment, as pointed out by the CEACR, has resulted in a more positive and balanced relationship among positions and among industries and has facilitated a more

---

[43] Light work "typically cover jobs which demand little physical effort on the part of the worker", see http://www.eurofound.europa.eu/emire/GERMANY/LIGHTWORKPAYGRADES-DE.htm (accessed on Sep 30, 2007). Also see CEACR, *Direct Request, Jamaica, Germany*, from 1990–2007.

[44] Such as educational and professional qualifications and the need for innovation.

[45] Such as responsibility for the safety of other workers and contacts with external units.

[46] Such as physical, mental, psychoneurotic effort, including monotony.

equalized wage relation between industrial and service enterprises. Nonetheless, the wage differential persists in Poland. Considering women usually take physically lighter jobs than men in manual work, the elements used in this job evaluation schemes still disadvantage women. Those factors such as skills required for caring of patients or children, organizational skills or manual dexterousness, are usually overlooked and hence undervalued.[47] That is to say, even though those factors may be seemingly objective, we may subjectively omit other objective factors that may favor women workers.

Although the legislation in some states establishes an objective job appraisal method, the scope of comparison it allows for is typically restrictive. For example, in Ireland, the 1997 Act was intended to design an objective appraisal of jobs based on the work performed. A comparison between jobs is required to be conducted "on the basis of skill, physical or mental requirements, responsibilities and working conditions"[48] The Act establishes that, in order for a female worker to be entitled to receive the same rate of remuneration as a male worker employed by the same or an associated employer, both employees must be engaged in "like work". The term "like work" is defined to include three concepts: (1) work performed under the same or similar conditions; (2) work of a similar nature; and (3) work performed by one employee which is equal in value to the work performed by the other, having regard to such matters as skill, physical or mental requirements, responsibility and working conditions.[49] Additionally, the Act provides that, if the comparison is to be made between employees in associated employers, it is not considered as "like work" if the conditions of employment of both employees are not the same or "reasonably comparable".[50] This scope of comparison is, at best, similar to the concept of "equal pay for similar work". It is still more restrictive than "equal pay for work of comparable worth". As a result it is not in conformity with the Convention. As the CEACR explicates in its general survey, "the scope of the comparison contemplated by the Convention should be "as wide as allowed at the level at which wage policies, systems and structures are coordinated".[51]

[47] CEACR, *Direct Request, Poland*, 1997.
[48] Section 7(1)(c)).
[49] Section 7(1)(a)–(c) of the Act.
[50] Section 19(3). CEACR, *Direct Request, Ireland*, 2000.
[51] See CEACR, *General Survey*, 1986, para. 22.

4. *Collective Agreement*

Article 2 of the Convention provides that collective agreements are instrumental in implementing gender pay equity.[52] These agreements usually cover a large number of female workers represented by unions and therefore directly affect the interest of women workers. In certain countries such as Austria[53], the provisions of individual employment contracts or collective agreements that run counter to the principle of equal remuneration might be deemed null and void.

Some governments, however, have been found hesitant to invalidate such collective agreements despite the fact that the law prescribes so. In Slovakia, all higher level collective agreements must be formulated in a gender neutral manner, and work activities must be classified into equal categories. Any violations of the principle would result in the invalidity of that clause.[54] Under section 7 of the Slovakian Collective Bargaining Act, the government can extend a higher level collective agreement, including wage conditions, to employers with a similar economic activity. But the government has rarely done so. The Confederation of Trade Unions of the Slovak Republic (KOZSR) maintains that the government has been unwilling to extend collective agreements to the lower level. The reluctance of the Government comes partly from the resistance of employers.[55]

---

[52] See Article 2 of the Convention.

[53] See section 879 of the Austrian Civil Code, and section 2 of the Equality of Treatment Act of 1979. Similarly, in Guinea-Bissau, collective agreements may not contain standards that are contrary to those set forth in the ILO Conventions. See Section 166 of the Labor Code 1986. CEACR, *Direct Request, Guinea-Bissau*, 1990. In France-New Caledonia, any clauses of agreements, or contracts made by an employer or group of employers, which provide lower remuneration for one sex than the other for the same work of equal value, are automatically annulled. See Section 166 of the Labor Code 1986. CEACR, *Direct Request, Guinea-Bissau*, 1990. A similar policy exists in Zambia. The collective agreement between the Zambia Bankers (Employers) Association and the Zambia Union of Financial Institutions and Allied Workers abolished a clause 19, which had provided that a "married male employee in group 1 shall receive a marriage allowance of K20 a month upon production of a satisfactory documentary proof of marriage". This Clause 19 violated both section 108 of the Industrial and Labor Relations Act, 1993, and the principle of gender pay equity enshrined in the Convention. This positive policy development, according to the Government, ensures that no collective agreements award marriage allowances or any other benefits that are differentiated on the basis of sex. CEACR, *Direct Request, Zambia*, 1997.

[54] Section 4(2)(a) of the Collective Bargaining Act (Act No. 2/1991).

[55] CEACR, *Individual Observation, Slovakia*, 2006.

5. *Burden of Proof*

More and more countries have adopted legislation that places the burden of proof on employers, in order to further protect employees. Norway, for instance, mandates that if differential treatment regarding wages can be established between men and women performing work of equal value, the employer at issue must prove that this is not due to the gender of the employees.[56] Norway also amended its law to reverse the burden of proof in cases concerning recruitment, promotion, notice to leave or temporary lay-offs.[57] Similar policies are also found in France.[58]

In addition to the burden of proof, some states have also imposed more responsibilities on employers to tackle the issue of discrimination. In Latvia, the Labor Code of 2001 provides that an employer has a duty to pay equal remuneration for men and women for the same kind of work or work of equal value.[59] Other states go even further and impose specific legal responsibilities on employers. For example, Finland places a duty on employers to promote equality and to include measures for equality in their annual staff plans.[60] According to the Finnish law,[61] private and public enterprises with more than 30 employees are

---

[56] Section 5 of The Gender Equality Act 1978 (This Act was amended in 1995).

[57] Section 4 of The Gender Equality Act 1978 (This Act was amended in 1995). CEACR, *Individual Observation, Norway*, 1996.

[58] The Labor Code of France was amended to combat discrimination, by virtue of Act No. 2001–1066. The amendments impose the burden of proof on employers in equal remuneration cases. When a worker presents facts from which it may be presumed that discrimination has occurred, the defendant must prove that there has been no breach of the principle of equal remuneration for men and women workers for work of equal value. See CEACR, *Individual Observation, France*, 2003. Likewise, in Lithuania, the Act on Equal Opportunities establishes a presumption of discrimination on the part of the employer if, the employer applies to an employee less (more) favorable terms of employment or payment for work on the basis of his or her sex, see CEACR, *Individual Observation, Lithuania*, 2001. Also in Greece, the burden of proof is also placed on employers (section 6(2) of the Employment Act No.6 of 2000, see CEACR, *Individual Observation, Greece*, 2002. In Slovenia, the Labor Relations Act of 2002 shifts the burden of proof in sex discrimination case, see CEACR, *Individual Observation, Slovenia*, 2003. In the case of Italy: Act No. 125/91 stipulating that the burden of proof should be shifted in some cases, when the complainant alleges indirect discrimination based on sex and supports her claim with statistical evidence. See CEACR, *Direct Request, Italy*, 1995.

[59] Section 60(1). CEACR, *Individual Observation, Latvia*, 2004.

[60] Section 5 of the Act concerning equality between men and women amended in 1995. CEACR, *Individual Observation, Finland*, 1998.

[61] The Act amending the Act on Equality between Men and Women (Act No. 232/2005).

obligated to have equality plans, which ought to include information necessary for workers and employers to monitor the equality situation in the enterprise concerned, i.e., details concerning the employment of men and women in different jobs and a survey of the grade of jobs performed by men and women, the remuneration for those jobs and the impact of measures previously taken to this end. Employers are also obligated to promote equality in regards to recruitment and career advancement.[62]

Employers in other states are required to have an action plan in addition to equality plans. Sweden, for example, in its 2000 Amendments to the Equal Opportunities requires enterprises of more than ten employees to prepare wage mapping annually to identify any gender wage differentials. Employers have to prepare an action plan to remedy any detected pay discrimination and to provide the remedy within a designated timeline. The preparation of wage mapping is supposed to focus on any wage gap between men and women workers performing work of equal value. The Amendments appear to contemplate the issue of the under evaluation of those types of work traditionally dominated by women by obligating employers to compare employees in these fields and employees performing work that is not customarily dominated by women.[63]

This new legal practice in Sweden is a timely response to the CEACR's plea for more attention to the historically undervalued work dominated by women. The impact of this legal requirement on closing the gender wage gap remains to be seen.

Employers are forced legally to take more responsibilities for implementing gender pay equity. But there is another way by which employers can be actively involved in applying gender pay equity: code of practice which is mostly voluntary. Codes of practice have witnessed a surging popularity. In the United Kingdom, the Equal Opportunities Commission has developed a Code of Practice on Equal Pay. It is designed to assist employers in bridging the pay gap by offering practical advice on other means of implementing pay systems free of gender bias. It is noteworthy that this Code can even be quoted as evidence in any proceedings before the industrial tribunals. The Code provides information about the implications of the law for employers, and about some of the causes leading to the gender pay gap. For example,

[62] *Ibid*, section 6(2). CEACR, *Individual Observation, Finland*, 2007.

[63] CEACR, *Individual Observation*, Sweden, 2004.

Paragraph 21 states that undervaluation of work performed by women workers may partly result from the fact that men and women tend to perform different jobs or have different work patterns. The segregation is commonly reinforced by discriminatory recruitment, training, selection and promotion procedures.[64] The Code also encloses various recommendations for implementing a review of pay systems on possible existing gender bias, and suggestions for employers on how to develop an equal pay policy.[65] In general, the Code seeks to implement the principle of equal pay for work of equal value contained in the relevant legislation by taking a pragmatic approach. However, the voluntary nature may limit its impact on eliminating the discriminatory practice of employers.

6. *Penalty and Dispute Resolution*

Sometimes employers are unwilling to implement gender pay equity and they may violate the law on gender pay equity. The violation of the equal pay principle by natural and legal persons has been commonly defined as an administrative offence subject to fines. The Czech Republic,[66] Turkey[67] and Italy[68] have all adopted this approach. In other states, the violation of the principle could even be subject to penal sanctions, as in Philippines.[69] The violation of the principle is also punishable under the law in Nepal, but exceptions are set for economic development.[70] The exception of "economic development" is untenable.

---

[64] Paragraph 21. Equal Opportunities Commission of UK, *Code of Practice on Equal Pay*, from http://www.equalityhumanrights.com/Documents/Welsh%20language%20publications/Comisiwn%20Cyfle%20Cyfartal/Gender%20Code%20of%20practice%20on%20equal%20pay.pdf (accessed on Oct 30, 2007).

[65] *Ibid.*

[66] Section 13 and 26 of the Labor Inspection Act of 2005. Also see CEACR, *Individual Observation, Czech*, 2007.

[67] The approach adopted by the Czech Republic is similar to the one in Turkey in which violation of section 5 of the new Labor Act of 2003 constitutes an administrative offence punishable with a fine of 50 million Turkish liras. See CEACR, *Individual Observation, Turkey*, 2006.

[68] In Italy, the violation of the principle of equal pay for work of equal value is sanctioned with a fine from £200,000 to £1,000,000. See Article 2(1) and (2) of Act 903/77. CEACR, *Direct Request, Italy*, 2004.

[69] According to Republic Act No. 6725 of 12 May 1989 which amends section 135 of the Labor Code, it is unlawful and liable to penal sanctions to pay a lesser compensation to a female employee as against a male employee, for work of equal value. See CEACR, *Individual Observation, Philippines*, 1990.

[70] CEACR, *Individual Observation, Nepal*, 1997. In the United States and the province of Ontario of Canada, exceptions to gender pay equity requirement include the

As the CEACR has pointed out, gender pay equity is a fundamental human right and should be implemented without any exception.[71]

India even increased the penalty against the violation of the principle in its Equal Remuneration Amendment Act 1987. Section 10 of the Act had been amended to provide enhanced penalties. In cases of serious violation of the law, fines up to 20,000 rupees or imprisonment up to one year, and up to two years' imprisonment for a subsequent offence could be imposed. This has produced an increased number of cases brought before the court. Remarkably, the Act 1987 also empowers the court to try any offence punishable under the Act upon its own knowledge or upon a complaint lodged by the appropriate government or authorized officer, an aggrieved person or any recognized welfare institution or organization.[72] Trade unions have also been authorized to submit equal remuneration claims to the court on behalf of alleged victims in France.[73]

A proper mechanism should be made available for women workers when their equal pay rights are violated. Most ratifying states leave the dispute over equal pay to labor tribunals. A few states have a special agency that is responsible for dealing with the issue of promoting gender pay equity. In Austria, for instance, the "Ombud for Gender Equality in Employment" provides information about the Equal

---

seniority system, the merit system and etc. See Ellen M. Bowden (1994). "Closing the Pay Gap: Redefining the Equal Pay Act's Fourth Affirmative Defense", *Columbia Journal of Legal and Social Problems* 27: 225, p. 227. Also see Kathleen Weaver (1991). "Comparable Worth in the United States and the Canadian Province of Ontario", *British Columbia International & Comparative Law Review* 14: 137, p. 152.

[71] *Ibid.*

[72] For the Equal Remuneration Act, see http://nrcw.nic.in/shared/sublinkimages/26.htm (accessed on Oct 30, 2007). Also see CEACR, *Individual Case, India*, 1991. At least four organizations have been recognized to be able to file the lawsuit in the court: Development Studies, New Dehli; the Self-Employed Women's Association, Ahmedabad; the Working Women's Forum (INDIA), Madras, and the Institute of Social Studies Trust, New Delhi.

[73] Sections L. 122–45 and L. 122–45–2, the Labor Code adopted on Nov 16, 2001 by Act No. 2001–1066 to Combat Discrimination. Spain has also combined both fine and imprisonment as the penalty to the violation of the principle. Act No. 8 of 1988 sanctions discrimination as regards remuneration on the grounds including sex. Royal Legislative Decree No. 5/2000 categorizes pay discrimination as a very serious offence and establishes fines to discourage such practices. In accordance with section 40(1)(c) of the Act respecting offences and sanctions in the social domain, serious offences are punishable by fines ranging from euros 3,005.70 to euros 90,151.81. This deterrent effect of penalties is reinforced by Organic Act No. 10 of 23 November 1995, which provides for the sanction of imprisonment. See CEACR, *Direct Request, Spain*, 1990.

Treatment Act in the private sector and support victims of discrimination.[74] There is another unit- the Equal Treatment Committee. It is responsible for investigating on a case-by-case basis if a violation of the equal treatment principle has occurred.[75] The agency commits its expertise and resources solely to handling the issue of equal pay.

The protection of victims is particularly important as the victim's job security may be endangered once she files a complaint or lawsuit. Some states have therefore taken legislative efforts to legally protect these victims. In Malta, a worker alleging unequal payment for work of equal value may, within four months of the alleged discrimination, lodge a complaint with the Industrial Tribunal and should be protected against victimization.[76]

In some states, the established mechanism appears to be flawed. For example, in Croatia, violations of the equal pay provisions contained in section 89 of the Labor Act[77] are not subject to fines and the State Labor Inspection Services lack authority to enforce these provisions.[78] In other words, there is no enforcement mechanism. Even with various institutional mechanisms, women workers do not always benefit from legal protection. In Hungary, there are laws that allow women to seek remedy for pay discrimination. But according to the government itself, most women workers do not "take advantage of the possibility of labor inspection, nor do they turn to a court of justice to seek redress".[79] Lack of awareness of the relevant law is the main reason why women do not use the administrative or judicial assistance to address their grievance.[80] Therefore, more proactive non-legal measures are needed to encourage women to come forward to utilize judicial assistance when their rights are violated. Consciousness-raising is thus crucial.

II. Specific Observation on Legislative Compliance

In general, the ratifying states have mostly adopted necessary legislation and some of them have also established a gender neutral wage

---

[74] See http://www.equineteurope.org/infopages/2194.html (accessed on Sep 30, 2007).

[75] *Ibid.*

[76] According to section 28 & 30(1) of Employment and Industrial Relations Act. CEACR, *Individual Observation, Malta*, 2005.

[77] No. 137/2004 (former section 82).

[78] CEACR, *Direct Request, Croatia*, 2007.

[79] CEACR, *Direct Request, Hungary*, 2000.

[80] *Ibid.*

system. The CEACR has maintained over the years that equality legislations, including equal pay legislations and the use of gender neutral salary scales, are essential conditions for the application of the principle of the Convention, but are not by themselves sufficient to ensure the enforcement of the Convention.[81] After the above general discussion of the status of the application of the major articles of the Convention in the ratifying states, several interesting phenomena such as the impact of regional international law, and inconsistencies within domestic policies warrant further analysis.

1. *The Impact of Regional International Law*

The European Union law on gender pay equity in particular has been playing a major role in the development of the jurisprudence of gender pay equity in its member states.[82] Legally the EU law[83] on gender pay equity applies to all workers in all member states and even to the employment outside the Union if the parties inhabit in the Union and the discriminatory act occurs in the Union.[84] In 1975 the EEC passed its first major directive on equal pay,[85] despite the strong opposition from several member states and trade unions. This directive largely results from the strong and creative political will as well as the increasingly pressing women's movement.[86] Even though several member

---

[81] CEACR, *Individual Observation, Morocco*, 2004.

[82] For a more detailed analysis of the EU law on gender pay equity and gender equality in general, see Angelika Von Wahl (2005). "Liberal, Conservative, Social Democratic, or...European? The European Union as Equal Employment Regime", *Social Politics* 12(1): 67–95.

[83] The EU law on gender pay equity includes the Treaty of Amsterdam of 1994 (Article 141), Council Directive 75/117EEC on Approximation of the Members States Laws on Application of the Principle of Equal Remuneration for Men and Women, Council Directive 76/20 EEC on the Implementation of the Principle of Equal Treatment for Men and Women, Directive of the European Parliament and the European Council 2002/73/EC amending Council Directive 76/207/EEC on the Implementation of the Principle of Equal Treatment for Men and Women as regards access to employment, vocation training and promotion, and working conditions, Council Directive 97/80/EC concerning the Burden of Proof in Cases of Discrimination bases on Sex, and various rulings of the European Court of Justice. The most important cases of the ECJ are: the case "Rummler" of 1986, Case 237/85; "Danfoss" of 1989, Case 109/88; "Enderby" of 1993, Case C-127/92; "Barber" of 1990, Case C-262/88; "Royal Copenhagen" of 1995, Case C-400/93.

[84] See Ingeborg Heide (1999). "Supranational Action against Sex Discrimination: Equal Pay and Equal Treatment in the European Union", *International Labor Review* 138(4): 381–410, p. 381.

[85] EEC Equal Pay Directive of 1975.

[86] Tiziano Treu (1986). "Equal Pay and Comparable Worth: A View from Europe", *Comparative Labor Law and Policy Journal* 8:1, pp. 9–10.

states have opposed to the directive, they have repeatedly acknowledged the importance of the European Union law in their reports to the CEACR. The government of Slovakia in its report to the CEACR indicates that, in order to harmonize the legislation with the Directive No. 75/117/EEC, the Bill of the new Labor Code provides that the wage conditions must be equal for men and women without discrimination based on sex. By the same token, to comply with the Directive No. 97/80/EC, the Labor Code Bill provides that the burden of proof rests with the employer.[87] In this case it is the legal requirement to comply with the EU law that ultimately forces Slovakia to reform its policy on gender pay equity.

The Court of Justice of the European Community decided in 1993 that the pre-pension indemnities granted under the National Labor Council's Collective Agreement No. 17of Belgium (December 19, 1974) constituted remuneration within the meaning of Article 119 of the Treaty of Rome.[88] Following this decision, the government of Belgium indicated its intention to eliminate pre-pension discrimination and its commitment to reform and modernize its social security system in order to achieve equal treatment between men and women with regard to pensionable age and methods of calculation.[89] Act of 7 May 1999 has thus brought the legislation into conformity with article 119 of the Treaty of Rome.[90]

The respect for the EU law of equal pay on social security is also evident in the Netherlands. Following the enactment of the Barber

[87] CEACR, *Direct Request, Slovakia*, 2002. Similarly, in Ireland, the Pensions Act has been amended to reflect the principle laid down by the European Court of Justice.[87] Hungary also adopted the Act XVI of 2001, in order to harmonize Hungarian legislation with European Council Directive No. 75/117/EEC on the Approximation of the Laws of the Member States relating to the Application of the Principle of Equal Pay for Men and Women, and Directive No. 97/80/EC on the Burden of Proof in Cases of Discrimination Based on Sex. Following the adoption of this Act, the Labor Code expressly spells out the principle of equal pay for work of equal value and establishes a broad definition of "wage" which is considered to be in conformity the EU law. See CEACR, *Direct Request, Ireland*, 2004; CEACR, *Direct Request, Hungary*, 2002.

[88] For the direct legal effect of Article 119, see Anthony Arnull (1986). "Article 119 and Equal Pay for Work of Equal Value", *European Law Review* 11: 63.

[89] CEACR, *Direct Request, Belgium*, 1997.

[90] Since June 29, 1999, Article 4, paragraph 2(b), of the Collective Labor Agreement No. 25 of 15 October 1975 on the equality of remuneration between male and female workers, which provides that the notion of remuneration encompasses the benefits paid by non-statutory supplementary social security schemes covered by the principle of equality of remuneration, has been applied to all non-statutory supplementary social benefits, including those linked to statutory benefits. CEACR, *Direct Request, Belgium*, 2002.

Directive (96/97/EC of the Council of the European Union) which amends the Directive 86/378/EEC of the Council of the European Communities on the implementation of the principle of equal treatment for men and women in occupational social security schemes, Netherlands amended the Equal Opportunities Act in 1998 to prohibit discrimination between men and women with regard to the pension eligibility.[91] The government also amended its Civil Code to include payments and entitlements under pension schemes as terms of employment.[92]

Similarly, to execute the European Commission Directive for the incorporation of equal opportunities for men and women in every policy and activity, in May 2000 the Council of Ministers of Bulgaria adopted a regulation and designated functions concerning the application of equal opportunities for men and women to the Minister of Labor and Social Policy (MOLSP).[93]

Not only has EU law had a tremendous impact on the legislation of its member states, other regional treaties have also achieved a significant impact. The Government of Saint Lucia has passed the Windward Islands Constituent Assembly Act,[94] in order to fulfill its obligations under Article 3 of the Organization of East Caribbean States' Treaty (OECS Treaty) which concerns its member states' obligation to the international community. The member states of the OECS are expected to review and harmonize their labor legislation, with assistance from the International Labor Office, to ensure full compliance with the provisions of the ratified Conventions.[95]

2. *The Inconsistency within the Domestic Legislation*

The inconsistency within the domestic legislation is another problem present in a number of ratifying states, particularly the developing countries. The concept of "equal pay" encompasses three stages: "equal pay for equal work", "equal pay for similar work", and "equal pay for work of equal value". Regarding which one of these three should be

[91] Section 12(b) of the Equal Opportunities Act.

[92] Section 7:646 of the Civil Code. CEACR, *Direct Request, Netherlands*, 1999.[92] In order to implement the Council Directive 98/52/EC of the Council of the European Union on the implementation of the burden of proof in cases of sexual discrimination, the Equal Opportunities Act and the Civil Code were also amended, to ensure that they are in conformity with the EU law.

[93] CEACR, *Direct Request, Bulgaria*, 2002.

[94] The Windward Islands Constituent Assembly Act, No. 6 of 1991.

[95] CEACR, *Direct Request, Saint Lucia*, 1992.

used in their law, several countries exhibit inconsistency in their domestic legislations. This in part reflects the complicated nature of the principle and the Convention. The three stages are not interchangeable. They are not merely choices of wordings. They stand for the ascending requirements of the concept provided in the Convention. The choice of the wording in its legislation at the very least represents the legal status of gender pay equity in that state. The incoherent use of the concept lends the possibility that for the same violation of the principle, individuals going to the court may get different outcomes, by using different laws. As a result, the fairness of law may be questioned. For example, in Ecuador, Article 36 of the new Political Constitution of 1998 provides that women are guaranteed "equal remuneration for work of equal value". This is consistent with the principle set forth in Article 1 of the Convention. But the other domestic laws such as section 79 of the Labor Code that essentially provides only the right to "equal pay for equal work", are more restricted than those reflected in the Convention.[96]

Some states have an advanced version of the principle that is "equal pay for work of equal value" in legislation adopted even though their earlier legislation which is still in force has a different version of the principle. For instance, in Guyana, the Prevention of Discrimination Act No. 26 of 1997 imposes the obligation on every employer to pay equal remuneration to men and women performing work of equal value,[97] while Act No. 19 of 1990 provides for equal remuneration for the same work or work of the same nature, which is a narrower concept than the one required by the Convention.[98] According to the government's statement, the Prevention of Discrimination Act No. 26 of 1997 takes precedence over the latter one. Nevertheless, it will certainly

[96] CEACR, *Individual Observation, Ecuador*, 1999. This is also the case with Panama. Executive Decree No. 53 of 2002 of Panama establishes equality of opportunity for women. Section 43 of the Decree provides that mechanisms and procedures for the appraisal of tasks to ensure the application of the principle of equal remuneration for men and women workers for work of equal value. In contrast, the existing Labor Code which is still in force provides in Section 10 that "equal wages shall be paid for equal work in the service of the same employer, performed in the same job, working day, conditions of efficiency and seniority". See CEACR, *Individual Observation, Panama*, 2004.

[97] Section 9 of the Prevention of Discrimination Act No. 26 of 1997.

[98] Section 2(3) of Equal Rights Act No. 19 of 1990. CEACR, *Individual Observation, Guyana*, 2007.

be less bewildering if there is an explicit legal enactment to clarify the issue.[99]

It is even more confusing that within a certain code the principle is stated inconsistently. In Equatorial Guinea, for instance, the Labor Code in its sections 13, 28 and 53 words the principle differently.[100] This may essentially lead to misunderstanding and interpretation of the principle that usually is not in the favor to the principle of "equal pay for work of equal value". Likewise, In Gabon, Section 7 of the Labor Code provides that "equal wages for the same work or for work of equal value", but Section 84 specifies that given equal conditions such as work, skill and output, the same wages are payable to all workers irrespective of their sex, which appears to be a narrower concept than what is defined in the Convention.[101]

Not only the concept of "equal work and work of equal value" is stated inconsistently in some ratifying states, but also the scope of "pay" is presented differently. In Jamaica, the Employment Act includes in its scope any additional emoluments with respect to work or services performed. But the minimum wage orders generally exclude any ancillary benefits.[102] The disagreement over the meaning of "pay" of the principle may cause some difficulties in practice.

Similarly, in Romania, the adoption of a new Labor Code[103] has not been taken as an opportunity to give full legislative expression to the principle of equal remuneration for men and women for work of equal value. The Labor Code continues to refer to the narrower notion of equal pay for "equal work",[104] while prohibiting any discrimination based on gender in respect of establishing and granting wages defined as comprising the basic wage, allowances, benefits, as well as other additional payments.[105] In contrast, its Act. No. 202/2002 on equality of opportunity for men and women requires employers to ensure equal pay for "work of equal value" in accordance with the Convention. Therefore it appears necessary to harmonize the Labor Code with the provisions of the Act No. 202/2002, in order to fully

[99] CEACR, *Direct Request, Guyana*, 2002.
[100] CEACR, *Direct Request, Equatorial Guinea*, 1990.
[101] CEACR, *Direct Request, Gabon*, 1990.
[102] CEACR, *Individual Observation, Jamaica*, 1992.
[103] Act No. 53/2003.
[104] Section 6(2) of the Labor Code.
[105] Section 154(3) and Section 155. *Ibid.*

comply with the Convention. The Labor Code should be amended by referring to equal remuneration for men and women for "work of equal value" other than just "equal work".[106]

Obviously, the contradiction within the domestic legislation can generate both confusion and uncertainty. The process of recognizing the problem and thus formulating the laws in a consistent manner could not only maintain the integrity of law, but achieve universal understanding about the principle.

3. *The Function of Legislation*

Even with flaws, legislation is the main means of implementing gender pay equity. The CEACR for years has maintained the position that to achieve gender pay equity there ought to be a comprehensive approach that includes formal prescriptive legislative measures.[107] The CEACR apparently prefers legislative action as one main measure to implement the Convention as it has expressed this opinion multiple times in its observations of Saudi Arabia.[108] However, the value and effectiveness of these policies have been questioned in several states. For example, in the United Kingdom, despite the fact that the Equal Pay Act made a significant impact on the increase of women workers' wages in the early 1970s,[109] the Equal Opportunities Commission drew a conclusion in its report that the Equal Pay Act had reached the limit of its usefulness and a radical new action should be taken.[110] The Act has not yet achieved its intended impact on closing the gender wage gap. The new emerging job evaluation method and the increasingly popular merit system both have challenged the existing Act.[111] Therefore it is fair to say that in order to be effective, legislation has to be flexible enough to be able adjust to the new social context.

---

[106] CEACR, *Direct Request, Romania*, 2006.

[107] CEACR, *Individual Observation, New Zealand*, 1997.

[108] CEACR, *Direct Request, Saudi Arabia*, 1999.

[109] See Alan Manning (1996). "The Equal Pay Act as an Experiment to Test Theories of the Labor Market", *Economica* 63: 191–212, p. 191.

[110] CEACR, *Individual Observation, UK*, 2006. Scholars like Giapponi and McEvoy hold a different view. They argue that it is better to implement the current Equal Pay Act. See Catherine Giapponi & Sharlene A. McEvoy 92005). "The Legal, Ethical and Strategic Implications of Gender Discrimination in Compensation: Can The Fair Pay Act Succeed Where the Equal Pay Act Has Failed?" *Journal of Individual Employment Rights* 12: 137–150.

[111] See Jeanne Gregory (1996). "Dynamite or Damp Squib?-An Assessment of Equal Value Law", *International Journal of Discrimination and the Law* 1: 313–333.

From the economic point of view, the adoption of legislation on equal pay was arguably insufficient to reduce the pay differentials and therefore active measures were required, such as the introduction of effective equality programs.[112] Nevertheless, legislation provides governments with certain leverage. According to the CEACR, a ratifying state's obligation to ensure implementation of the principle is limited to those areas where the government is in a position to exert direct or indirect influence on the wage-fixing process; in all other cases, the government must promote the application of the Convention.[113] While the Convention does not require that legislation to be enacted, legislative action does, however, extend the government's competence to intervene in the field of wages and hence to ensure the application of the principle. For example, in New Zealand where the labor market is deregulated, the government is obligated, by virtue of the provisions of the 1972 Equal Pay Act and of the 1977 Human Rights Commission Act, to ensure that the provisions of those texts comply with in all employment contracts concluded pursuant to the Employment Contracts Act, 1991.[114] This is to say that legislation may give governments the legitimacy, the leverage as well as the obligation to implement the principle. In this sense, a legal enactment is indispensable in enforcing gender pay equity.

The CEACR has urged governments to adopt more proactive legislation that explicitly prescribes the principle of "equal pay for work of equal value" set out in the Convention. For example, in Jordan, the Constitution generally provides that all workers shall receive wages appropriate to the quantity and quality of the work achieved.[115] The government argues that the definition of wages in the Labor Code and the fact that the Labor Code defines worker as any person male or female, who performs work for remuneration, reiterate the principle. But the CEACR in its observation underscores the importance of an explicitly stated principle in the national legislation, out of the concern that those objective criteria such as quality and quantity of work may result in the neglect of other criteria such as responsibility, skill, effort and working conditions.[116]

---

[112] According to a study commissioned by the Equality Ombudsman in Finland. See CEACR, *Individual Observation, Finland*, 1999.

[113] Article 2. 1 of the Convention.

[114] CEACR, *Individual Observation, New Zealand*, 1992.

[115] Section 23(ii) (a) of the Constitution.

[116] CEACR, *Individual Observation, Jordan*, 2007.

As a matter of fact, Afghanistan has adopted a similar approach to Jordan. Its Labor Code provides for the determination of wages on the basis of quantity and quality of work according to rank, grades or specific posts[117] and includes occupation, working period, practical work and other conditions as additional criteria.[118] Furthermore, it provides that men and women have equal rights and shall receive equal pay for "equal work".[119] Interestingly, the comments made by the CEACR exhibit two different attitudes: in the case of Afghanistan, the CEACR did not indicate any dissatisfaction, but in the case of Jordan, the CEACR explicitly expressed its disappointment. The reason may rest with the different time these two observations were published: the one with Jordan was in the year of 2007, while the other one with Afghanistan was in the year of 1990. This suggests that with the passage of time, the CEACR requires the ratifying states to progressively realize the principle: from "equal pay for equal work" to "equal pay for work of equal value", as defined in the Convention.

III. Typology of Legislative Compliance

Having considered how the domestic legislation have internalized those key articles in the Convention, I now turn to a review of legislative compliance. In general, the domestic legislatures comply with the ILO Convention No. 100 once it is ratified by their governments. However, the degree of compliance varies. I employ a tripartite typology of legislative compliance (high, medium and low) in terms of their response to the ILO Convention No. 100 and their corresponding legislative actions on gender pay equity to characterize legislative compliance.

1. *High Compliance*

This category encompasses those states (such as Canada, Sweden, Netherlands, France, Switzerland, United Kingdom, Norway) that have a legal enactment prescribing equal pay for work of equal value, and in practice have made substantial progress in narrowing the gender wage gap. More specifically, in such states legislative compliance may consist of most of the following elements: a) Legally, they have

---

[117] Art 7 of the Labor Code 1988.

[118] Art 75, *Ibid.*

[119] Article 9, *Ibid.* CEACR, *Direct Request, Afghanistan*, 1990.

explicit enactments on the principle of "equal pay for equal work or work of equal value" and detailed guidelines to implement the principle; b) Institutionally, by virtue of certain legislation they have a judicial or semi-judicial special agency handling the issue of equal pay. c) In terms of real monetary impact, attributed to some legislation, women workers can be awarded a significant amount of monetary compensation.

2. *Medium Compliance*

This category includes those states which have promulgated legislation on "equal pay for equal work" and have achieved a certain level of success in closing the gender wage gap. It has the following characteristics: a) Their legislatures started dealing with the issue of equal pay for a short while; b) Their legislation on equal pay stays general and only covers the principle of "equal pay for equal work" instead of "equal pay for equal work and work of equal value"; c) There lacks a powerful agency whose sole purpose is to promote gender pay equity; d) the legislation on equal pay has not yet yielded significant social impact. Most developing countries such as China and Guatemala and some developed countries such as Japan belong to this category.

The legislature of Guatemala has achieved medium compliance with the Convention No. 100. Its law provides for equal pay for equal work performed under equal conditions, efficiency and seniority.[120] However, this limited version of the equal pay principle to a great extent is merely a symbol. It has no other supplemental legislative and policy guidelines. Guatemala has not established an objective job appraisal method. There also lacks a special agency on equal pay. Guatemala has not yet passed formal legislation to ensure women enjoy equal "wage above the minimum wage". More importantly, over the years the government has not taken any positive steps to address the issue, despite the constant plea for the attention from the CEACR.[121]

It should be noted that Rwanda, a country whose history has been marked by conflicts and civil wars, in 2001, by law[122] provides that

[120] Article 102(c) of the 1985 Constitution and section 89 of the 1961 Labor Code. CEACR, *Direct Request, Guatemala*, 1990.

[121] CEACR, *Direct Request, Guatemala*, 1992, 1993, 1994, 1995, 1997, 1999, 2001, 2002, 2003, 2004, 2007.

[122] Through the section 84 of the new Labor Code (Act. No. 51/2001), which replaces 82 of the former Labor Code.

equally competent workers carrying out the same type of work under the same condition must be equally remunerated, regardless of their origin, sex, or age.[123]

Compared to those states with high legislative compliance, the states with medium legislative compliance have not paid enough attention to the issue of gender pay equity. Because of the insufficient attention to the matter, they are generally slow in taking prompt legislative actions to deal with institutional aspects of gender gap equity. Therefore, without a strong and detailed legal enactment and a supplemental agency to implement the principle, law on gender pay equity in these states has not yet become an entrenched and influential force that could significantly impact women workers' life.

3. *Low Compliance*

This group consists of those countries, despite the ratification, that have made little legislative progress in implementing the Convention No. 100 they ratified. In spite of the rampant gender wage gap, their legislators have not yet responded to the issue. Even though they have ratified the Convention No. 100, their legislation are far from being in conformity with the principle set out in the Convention. The ratifying states such as Sri Lanka, Malaysia, and Tunisia have low legislative compliance. They commonly make no reference to the principle of equal pay whatsoever in their legislation. Their legislation usually just provides a very general prohibition against discrimination. The definition of "wage" is typically limited and does not encompass benefits in kind and excludes certain elements of remuneration defined in the Convention. The notion of "work of equal value" is simply dismissed by the governments.[124] To develop a wage system free from gender bias is not on the governments' agenda.

According to the CEACR, most ratifying countries have serious difficulties in applying the Convention. Various factors contribute to the low compliance: the lack of knowledge and information of the real situation; the inadequate data and research; the limited comprehension of the concept of equal value as it is set out in the Convention; the lack of knowledge of the principles of job appraisal which is instrumental in determining the relative value of jobs; and the shortage of

---

[123] CEACR, *Individual Observation, Rwanda*, 2004.
[124] See for example, CEACR, *Direct Request, Malaysia*, 2005.

the financial resources necessary to collect and analyze data and to institute systems of job evaluation.[125]

In addition to these common factors, culture plays a role in a number of ratifying states. There are some cultural practices that do not favor women and may more or less adversely affect the gender wage gap. These practices are so ingrained in the daily life that it is extremely challenging to reexamine their impact on women's life critically. For example, according to the law in Swaziland,[126] widows are entitled to 30 days of compassionate leave, while widowers receive only seven days' leave. The government argues that this legal requirement would allow companies to accommodate the cultural practice that widows were supposed to be indoors for at least 30 days following the death of their husbands. However, this culturally driven practice may have an adverse effect on women's pay.[127] Some other governments did realize certain cultural practice may have contributed to the existing gender wage gap. In Bolivia, women's main access to land is via inheritance, but inheritance as a right has been limited by tradition. The law favors male offspring, particularly in the case of indigenous peoples. Under this circumstance only a culturally sensitive approach could effectively address the issue of the gender pay gap. As such, the 2004-07 National Public Policies Plan designed to ensure the full exercise of women's rights has incorporated gender equity into public land distribution, and inheritance systems.[128]

Compared to certain cultural practices that may hinder the governments from recognizing the gender wage gap as an issue and hence from adopting the appropriate legislative actions to comply with the Convention, the systemic gender discrimination is even more covert thus difficult to deal with. The historical and structural discrimination against women is the fundamental barrier to realizing gender equality. Many female predominated job classes are customarily undervalued, which is the main factor causing the gender wage gap. This systemic gender discrimination is so entrenched in the daily life that many policymakers may not be even aware of it. Even if policymakers have good

[125] CEACR, *General Observation*, 1990.

[126] For a more complete discussion of the challenges the Swazi women face, see John L. Daly (2001). "Gender Equality Rights versus Traditional Practices: Struggles for Control and Change in Swaziland", *Development Southern Africa* 18(1): 45–56.

[127] CEACR, *Direct Request, Swaziland*, 2006.

[128] CEACR, *Direct Request, Bolivia*, 2007.

faith and are willing to tackle the issue, it is a daunting task to change the status quo and eliminate such deeply ingrained discrimination against women. But as the CEACR has emphasized several times, it is also the objective of the Convention to eradicate differences in remuneration in sectors in which jobs are considered to be traditionally "feminine" and may be undervalued as a result of stereotypes based on gender, and in sectors where the access of women to higher skilled and better paid jobs is not encouraged.[129] To eliminate this systemic gender discrimination thus should be considered as a key component of compliance. It is unlikely to achieve "high compliance" if ratifying states do not address the issue of the systemic gender discrimination.

IV. A Comprehensive Legislative Approach

Many ratifying states more or less are doing their jobs in trying to close the gender wage gap. A two-sample t-test was conducted to examine the gender wage gap in the two time periods. The test shows that "women's wage from 2000–2005" is significantly higher than "women's wage in 1990" (t=. 678, p <.000). It indicates a positive trend in those 29 ratifying states of the ILO Convention No. 100 on narrowing down the gender wage differentials (see Table 3–7). However, there is still a long way to go to fully realize the goal set out in the Convention and completely eliminate the gender wage gap.

Ideally, to achieve high compliance and ensure the implementation of the Convention, a comprehensive legislative package is needed. This legislative package should encompass the whole industrial relations regulations and not be limited to the area of the equal pay policies.[130] It[131] should at the very least include the ratification of the relevant international treaties (ILO Convention No. 100 in particular). Engaging in dialogue with the ILO and other international governing bodies will assist government in obtaining updated information, seeking possible international assistance including the ILO's technical support, and

[129] CEACR, *Direct Request, Costa Rica*, 2004.

[130] Jill Rubery argues that the equal pay directives themselves have a very limited effect on closing the gender wage gap. See Jill Rubery (1992). "Pay, Gender and the Social Dimension to Europe", *British Journal of Industrial Relations* 30(4): 605–621.

[131] Scholars usually recommend a multi-dimensional package to solve the issue of the gender wage gap, see for example, Amy Y. C. Liu (2004). "Sectoral Gender Wage Gap in Vietnam", *Oxford Development Studies* 32: 225–239, p. 236.

Table 3: Gender Pay Equity and Gender Wage Gap in 29 States

State	Ratification Year[132]	Specific Legislation (Equal Value=1, Equal Work=0.5, General/non=0	Women's Wage in1990[133]	Women's Wage@ 2000–2005[134]	Improvement of Women's Wage from 1990 to 2005
Australia	1974	1.0	82	85	3
Belgium	1962	0.5	76	78	2
Costa Rica	1951	0.5	74	78	4
Cyprus	1987	1.0	58	57	−1
Czech Republic	1993	1.0	68	65	−3
Denmark	1983	1.0	85	87	2
Egypt	1960	0.5	68	66	−2
El Salvador	2000	0.5	94	84	−10

132 The source of the information on "ratification year" and "Specific legislation"(which means the status of the current legislation of each state on equal pay) is from the ILO CEACR's reports(individual observations and direct requests) on the application of the ILO Convention No. 100 in individual states from 1990–2007.

133 See United Nations (1995). The *World's Women 1995: Trends and Statistics*. UN: New York. At p. 128, Chart 5. 20 women's average wages in manufacturing as percentage of men's, 1970, 1980, and 1990.

134 See http://unstats.un.org/unsd/demographic/products/indwm/ww2005/tab5g.htm (Accessed on Oct 30, 2007). Note: The indicator presented in this table is the ratio of the female wages to the male wages in the manufacturing industries, expressed as a percentage. The statistics of wages from which the ratio is computed are, in general, average earnings per wage-earner (regardless of age) or in some cases wage rates. The data on average earnings are usually derived from payroll data supplied by a sample of establishments often also furnishing data on hours of work and on employment. In a few cases, average earnings are compiled from social insurance statistics or labor force surveys. International comparisons of wage ratios presented here must be made with great caution. The coverage, definitions and methods of compiling wage statistics differ significantly from country to country. Disaggregation of statistics by sex is available for only a few countries and may be based on a narrow segment of the population. Furthermore, earnings are very much dependent on the number of hours worked, and where female workers generally work a much smaller number of hours than male workers, this factor must be kept in mind when interpreting the wage ratio.

Table 3: (*Cont.*)

State	Ratification Year	Specific Legislation (Equal Value=1, Equal Work=0.5, General/non=0	Women's Wage in1990	Women's Wage@ 2000–2005	Improvement of Women's Wage from 1990 to 2005
Finland	1963	0.5	77	84	7
France	1953	1.0	79	78	−1
Germany	1956	0.5	73	74	1
Greece	1975	0.5	76	82	6
Hungary	1959	0.5	72	73	1
Iceland	1958	1.0	69	81	12
Japan	1967	0.0	41	60	19
Kenya	2001	0.0	74	123	49
Luxembourg	1967	0.5	65	72	7
Netherlands	1971	0.5	77	83	6
New Zealand	1983	0.5	75	82	7
Norway	1959	1.0	86	89	3
Paraguay	1964	1.0	66	53	−13
Portugal	1967	1.0	72	68	−4
Republic of Korea	1997	1.0	50	56	6
Singapore	2002	0.0	55	61	6
Sri Lanka	1993	0.0	88	87	−1
Swaziland	1981	0.5	54	63	9
Sweden	1962	1.0	89	91	2
Switzerland	1972	1.0	68	75	7
UK	1971	1.0	68	75	7

Table 4: Frequency – Specific Legislation (Equal Value=1, Equal Work=0.5, General/non=0) in 29 States

Specific Legislation	Number of Countries	Percentage
Equal Value (1)	13	44.8%
Equal Work (.5)	12	41.4%
General/Non (0)	4	13.8%
Total	29	100%

Table 5: Two Sample T-Test – Paired Samples Statistics

Paired Samples Statistics					
		Mean	N	Std. Deviation	Std. Error Mean
Pair 1	Women's Wage in 1990 & 2000–2005	71.69	29	12.030	2.234
		76.21	29	13.973	2.595

Table 6: Two Sample T-Test – Paired Samples Correlations

Paired Samples Correlations				
		N	Correlation	Sig.
Pair 1	Women's Wage in 1990 & 2000–2005	29	.678	.000

Table 7: Two Sample T-Test – Paired Samples Test

Paired Samples Test									
		Paired Difference					t	df	Sig. (2-tailed)
					95% Confidence Interval of the Difference				
		Mean	Std. Deviation	Std. Error Mean	Lower	Upper			
Pair 1	Women's Wage in 1990 & 2000–2005	−4.517	10.578	1.964	−8.541	−.493	−2.300	28	.029

continuously adjusting their domestic policies so that they conform to the ILO standards. Therefore, ratifying international treaties is not only a symbolic action, but an international obligation which in the end will benefit states as well.

Similarly, to respect gender pay equity as a fundamental human right may expedite the process of narrowing the gender wage gap. This rights-based approach will elevate the entire spectrum of gender pay equity and give it a place as a fundamental value of society, to a level equal to other rights and superior to ordinary legislation. Some ratifying states have treated gender pay equity as a human rights issue in their domestic practice. For example, in Canada, "equal pay for work of equal value" is part of the human rights legislation of the federal jurisdiction.[135]And in New Zealand, within the Human Rights Commission, an Equal Employment Opportunities Commissioner has just been appointed and entrusted with certain responsibilities with respect to equity in remuneration.[136]

The legislative and policy package towards eliminating the gender wage differentials ought to include those basic elements provided in the Convention: an explicit expression of the principle of "equal pay for equal work or work of equal value", a broad definition of "remuneration", and an objective appraisal of jobs based on the work to be performed. In many ratifying states, there is an urgent need for an overhaul of their job evaluation systems. For the ratifying states who struggle to establish an objective job appraisal system, the Canadian federal job classification and evaluation system may be a model to follow. Furthermore, a gendered perspective should be reflected in all wage legislation.[137] An appropriate legal measure to encourage women workers to use judicial assistance is also crucial. Women typically face difficulties and barriers in lodging equal pay claims and the solution may lie in the introduction of generic or representative equal pay claims.[138] If unions or other organizations are allowed to bring equal pay claims on behalf of women workers, it may largely increase the likelihood to achieve a successful outcome for women workers and to have a long-term lasting impact on advancing women workers' interest.[139]

---

[135] CEACR, *Direct Request, Canada*, 1990.

[136] See http://www.hrc.co.nz/index.php?p=44860 (accessed on Oct 30, 2007).

[137] Jill Rubery and Colette Fagan(1994). "Equal Pay Policy and Wage Regulation Systems in Europe", *Industrial Relations Journal* 25: 281–294, p. 289.

[138] See the CEACR, *Individual Observation, UK*, 2007.

[139] See for example, Christine Short (1986). "Equal Pay – What Happened?" *The Journal of Industrial Relations* 28(3): 315–335. Also see Cunnison (1991). "Equal Value

In many countries, employers are one of major sources of opposition towards implementing the principle of gender pay equity.[140] Therefore, to narrow the gender wage gap, it is vital to cooperate with employers. Code of conduct, as an emerging concept, is gaining a certain level of support among both employers and governments. The European Union published a "Code of Practice on the Implementation of Equal Pay for Work of Equal Value for Men and Women" after consultation with the users and social partners, aiming at fewer barriers of obtaining more concrete results of closing the gender wage gap.[141] The causes of the gender wage gap are multi-dimensional, therefore its solutions ought to be diverse as well. One way is to combine legal obligations with voluntary codes of conduct mentioned above.

Affirmative action is another strategy that may encourage women's participation in the higher-paid job classes.[142] It has been proven that affirmative action has a positive effect on narrowing the gender pay gap.[143] In Israel, the Women's Equal Rights Law was amended to provide affirmative action in the appointment of women at all grades within public institutions.[144] Similarly, Section 15 of the Civil Service Law has been revised to obligate government offices to promote the representation of women by setting aside or giving preference to certain positions for qualified female applicants.[145] The government demonstrated that in addition to the abovementioned amendments, a proposal that establishes target percentages concerning the representation of women in specified ranks and positions has been drafted.

Legislation and the Unions: A Case Study from the UK", *Journal of Gender Studies* 1(1): 12–28, pp. 14–22; Edmund Heery (2006). "Equality Bargaining: Where, Who, Why?" *Gender, Work and Organization* 13(6): 522–542. Also see Kates, Carol A (1994). "Pay Equity in Local Government: A Case Study", *Labor Studies Journal* 48–66 (arguing for an active role of unions in wage negotiations.)

[140] See Jeanne Gregory (1992). "Equal Pay for Work of Equal Value: The Strengths and Weaknesses of Legislation", *Work, Employment & Society* 6: 461–473, pp. 463–465.

[141] See European Commission (1996). *A Code of Practice on the Implementation of Equal Pay for Work of Equal Value for Men and Women*. Brussels: Office for Office Publications of the European Communities.

[142] Some scholar argues for "female quotas" system which essentially is the same as "affirmative action". See Myra Strober (1972). "Lower Pay for Women: A Case of Economic Discrimination", *Industrial Relations* 11(2): 279–284, p. 284.

[143] James Albrecht & Susan Vroman (1993). "Evaluating Policies to Reduce the Gender Gap: An Economic Approach", *Georgetown Law Journal* 82: 69. Also see Jane Friesen (1993). "Alternative Economic Perspectives on the Use of Labor Market Policies to Redress the Gender Gap in Compensation", *Georgetown Law Journal* 82:31.

[144] No. 5711–1951.

[145] No. 5719–1959.

This proposal sets the goals of employing women in 25 per cent of the specified positions in three years, and 30 per cent of the positions in five years. The adoption of such affirmative action measures is expected to result in the narrowing of the remuneration gap between men and women.[146]

Another major component of this comprehensive legislative approach is awareness raising and capacity building. Brazil provides an excellent example in this regard. The government initiated the campaign "Brazil Gender and Race – United for Equal Opportunity". It seeks to disseminate information in regional seminars on the principles of the Conventions Nos. 100 and 111 to workers' and employers' organizations, non-governmental organizations and public institutions.[147] The campaign includes the training events for various agencies and institutions who, in turn organize the presentations and seminars on equality issues. The Brazilian government also launched Volunteer Civil Service, with the attempt to train the Brazilian youngsters to act as multipliers to promote the equality policies in the labor market. The guidelines for the National Occupational Qualification Plan (PLANFOR) for 1999–2002 provide a preferential access to those training programs for the economically and socially vulnerable persons such as the female heads of household. Social partners also play a significant part in this campaign. The Central Unitario de Trabalhadores (CUT) organized a seminar in April 2001 on equal remuneration for men and women workers for work of equal value.[148] Similarly in Iceland, there is a renewed emphasis on the reconciliation of work and family responsibilities. On the center are awareness raising activities established to ensure equal educational opportunities and to promote women's participation in the higher status jobs. It is particularly noteworthy that a two-year multilateral agreement has been signed to enhance women in leadership in the labor market, which is intended "to eradicate stereotyped gender roles in education and to diminish the gender wage gap in knowledge society of the future".[149]

In general, the international governing bodies such as the ILO, the governments and the social partners are equally important to the

[146] CEACR, *Direct Request, Israel*, 2003.
[147] CEACR, *Direct Request, Brazil*, 1999.
[148] CEACR, *Direct Request, Brazil*, 2002.
[149] CEACR, *Direct Request, Iceland*, 2004.

success of eliminating the gender wage differentials. Both compulsory legal policies and voluntary self-disciplinary practice are crucial. As Whitehouse has argued, a legislative action can achieve its "emancipatory potential" by working with other measures.[150] The full realization of gender pay equity demands efforts from the institutions at all levels and the actions from all actors. Policymakers should be open-minded to the new developments with regard to gender pay equity in other countries such as Canada and to see if they can learn from others' experience.[151]

As this chapter suggests, domestic legislative compliance occurs, but with compromise in most cases. The ratifying states internalize the principle of gender pay equity provided in the Convention, into their own domestic policies, through more detailed and tailored legislation. However, these policies vary a great deal among the ratifying states. Sometimes a state may do little to implement what is prescribed in the Convention, which leads to a "low compliance". It is certainly possible to achieve a "high compliance" among all ratifying states, if a comprehensive legislative approach is adopted. In addition to domestic legislatures, domestic judiciaries could also play a significant role in promoting gender pay equity. How did the domestic judiciaries react after their governments ratified the Convention? This is the focus of the discussion in the next chapter.

---

[150] See Gillian Whitehouse (1992). "Legislation and Labor Market Gender Inequality: An Analysis of OECD Countries", *Work, Employment & Society* 6: 65–86.

[151] For a criticism on the "insularity of the United States" on the issue of gender pay equity, see Steven L. Willborn(1986). "Equal Pay for Work of Equal Value: Comparable Worth in the United Kingdom", *the American Journal of Comparative Law* 34: 415–457, p. 416.

CHAPTER IV

JUDICIAL COMPLIANCE- THE PROCESS OF "INTERPRETATION"

If there is any hope that the principle of the Convention will be protected, the ratifying states should have enforceable legislation that expressly guarantees the right to gender pay equity. But that is not enough. Judicial decisions offer another crucial means of applying the principle. This chapter investigates the extent to which the domestic judiciaries comply with the Convention. The first part of the chapter provides a comprehensive analysis of how the concept enshrined in the Convention is interpreted in the domestic courts. The second part examines the role of the judiciary in implementing the right to equal pay for equal work or work of equal value and seeks to provide a typology of judicial compliance. For this analysis I draw the data (mostly the court cases) from the CEACR's reports.[1]

I. Judicial Compliance- The "Interpretation" of the Convention in National Judiciaries

As the articles of the Convention are phrased in general language, the interpretation of these terms is therefore particularly important. Through the national judiciaries' interpretation on the controversial issues such as the concept of "work of equal value", the principle provided in the Convention is substantiated and fulfilled, to a varying degree in each ratifying state. The following text analyzes how the national judiciaries in their judgment interpret three key issues which correspond to the Articles 1 and 3 in the Convention: the concept of "equal pay for equal work and work of equal value", the scope of "remuneration", and what constitutes an objective job analysis method. It also discusses the issue of the low number of equal pay cases in many ratifying states and suggests legal adjustments be made accordingly.

[1] The CEACR reports sometimes mentioned very briefly the cases related to equal pay in those ratifying states. I started from this brief information and used the other database such as the ILO NATLEX database to get more information.

1. *The Concept of Equal Pay for Equal Work and Work of Equal Value*

In general, the high courts in the ratifying states over the years have more or less endorsed the principle of equal pay. They usually had no problem in granting equal pay for "equal work", as the violation of "equal pay for equal work" is typically a case of "discrimination". The following case in Japan is a case in point.

Nineteen female employees of Uchiyama Manufacturing Corporation were responsible for molding rubber products and conducting tests. But their basic pay level was set lower than the one of their male counterparts with the same number of years of experience and similar qualifications. Moreover, bonus and retirement payments were calculated in a way discriminatory towards these female employees by multiplying lower coefficients than the one for their male counterparts. The chief judge in his decision said that there was no apparent difference between the jobs performed by the female employees and their male counterparts. The wage differential was therefore an "irrational discrimination". The Hiroshima High Court ordered the company to pay about 230 million yen to compensate the wage differential (covering 14 years) to these women workers.[2]

As the above case indicates, if a case concerns unequal pay for equal work, it is relatively easy for the court to rule against the employer. "Unequal pay for equal work" is an apparent act of discrimination and violates the basic principle of equality. Based on the existing national law on discrimination, several judiciaries have found the violation of the equal pay principle in their cases. The Federal Labor Court of Germany in 1992 decided that there was a violation of the equal pay principle. The male and female employees performed the same work in the warehouse of the defendant. Even though the work performed was substantially equal, the defendant paid half of the male employees and only one tenth of the female employees a higher salary above the standard rate. The Court found that it constituted an infringement of section 612(3) of the Federal Civil Code, if the higher remuneration paid to men was not justified by the factors unrelated to sex.[3] Also in 1994,

[2] See http://www.jil.go.jp/foreign/emm/bi/27.htm) (accessed on Sep 30, 2007).

[3] 4 AZ R 30/92, September 23, 1992. Also see CEACR, *Direct Request, Germany*, 1995. See also http://www.ilo.org/public/english/employment/gems/eeo/law/germany/cl_lc.htm (accessed on Oct 30, 2007).

the Supreme Court of Austria declared a group classification (which uses the criterion "physical capability") within a wage scheme was excessively favorable to men and discriminatory against women and therefore violated the Labor Court Act and was invalid.[4]

Other ratifying states have also ruled against employers in the cases of equal pay. For instance, in 2000 the Helsinki District Court of Finland by its ruling required the Federation of Special Service and Clerical Employees (ERTO) to pay compensation to a female employee who experienced the wage discrimination.[5] Also in Israel, in a 1998 equal remuneration case, the Labor Court ruled in favor of a female plaintiff who had been earning a lower salary than her male counterparts in light of the Equal Employment Opportunities Law.[6]

The right to gender pay equity has also been incorporated into the existing labor law. The South African Supreme Court has regarded the principle of equal pay for equal work and work of equal value as part of the "fair labor practice". In the 1999 case *Louw v. Golden Arrow Bus Services* it stated that although the principle of equal pay for equal work and work of equal value was not prescribed in the unfair labor practice definition, it was a principle of "justice, equity and logic" that could be taken into consideration to determine if there is a violation of the fair labor practice.[7]

Gender pay equity has not only been an issue of the "fair labor practice", but also a matter of "human rights". In addition to the existing labor law, the principle of gender pay equity has been incorporated into the domestic human rights law. Canada included the principle of equal pay in its Human Rights Act in 1978.[8] In 1999, the Supreme Court of

---

[4] 14.9. 194, ObA 801/94. Also see Directorate-General for Employment, Social Affairs and Equal Opportunities, European Commission. *Report on Equal Pay*, April 2006, see http://www.retepariopportunita.it/Rete_Pari_Opportunita/UserFiles/news/equal_pay_report.pdf, (accessed on Oct 30, 2007), p. 10.

[5] CEACR, *Direct Request, Finland*, 2004.

[6] L.A. 300880/98 *Orit Goren v. Home Centers Int.* CEACR, *Direct Request, Israel*, 2006.

[7] (2000) 3 BLLR 311 (LC). For the judgment, see http://www.saflii.org/za/cases/ZALC/1999/12.html (accessed on Sep 30, 2007). Also see CEACR, *Individual Observation, South Africa*, 2005. It should be noted that the expert witness testimony which explicated "Peromnes job evaluation system" played a significant role in determining whether two jobs are of "work of equal value". The Peromnes method, which is commonly used, is a point-assessment technique employing eight factors, each of which is weighted to determine the position of the job in the grade ranking: "problem solving; consequences of judgment; pressure of work; knowledge; job impact; comprehension; educational qualification; and training experience".

[8] Section 11.

Canada issued a ruling on how to apply the human rights legislation in the workplace.[9] It established a "Meiorin test" to unify the conventional "direct" and "adverse effect" approaches to discrimination.

> First, the employer must show that it adopted the standard for a purpose rationally connected to the performance of the job. The focus at the first step is not on the validity of the particular standard, but rather on the validity of its more general purpose.
>
> Second, the employer must establish that it adopted the particular standard in an honest and good faith belief that it was necessary to the fulfillment of that legitimate work-related purpose.
>
> Third, the employer must establish that the standard is reasonably necessary to the accomplishment of that legitimate work-related purpose. To show that the standard is reasonably necessary, it must be demonstrated that it is impossible to accommodate individual employees sharing the characteristics of the claimant without imposing undue hardship upon the employer.

This Meiorin test was an attempt to ensure the principle of equality is implemented through daily practice and workforce standard in the federal public sectors. In a sense the Court sought to shift the focus on the case-by-case discrimination to the systemic discrimination.[10] The Human Rights tribunals in other ratifying states, such as the New Zealand, have also started to deal with the issue of equal pay. During 2004–2005, two complaints involving gender pay discrimination were made to the Human Rights Commission of New Zealand under the Human Rights Act, one of which was heard by the Human Rights Review Tribunal.[11] As addressed above, equal pay is not only a labor issue, but also a human right. Applying human rights legislation to equal pay cases reflects a positive change of mindset towards the principle of equal pay, although it may be too early to say there occurs a shift of "paradigm" from viewing equal pay as a labor issue to a human right. The use of human rights legislation certainly helps raise the awareness of the issue among both labor lawyers and human rights practitioners. Moreover, human rights legislation could provide a viable channel to redress the pay discrimination.

---

[9] *British Columbia (Public Service Employee Relations Commission) v. British Columbia Government Service Employees' Union* [1999] 3 S.C.R. 3, 1999 SCC 48.

[10] See http://www.chrc-ccdp.ca/publications/1999_lr/introduction-en.asp (accessed on Sep 10, 2007).

[11] CEACR, *Direct Request, New Zealand*, 2006.

Some national judiciaries have exhibited their willingness to interpret the concept of equal pay to encompass "the right to work of equal value or comparable worth", as provided in the Convention. For example, in Spain, the Constitutional Court in 1984 gave the interpretation to Article 14 of the Constitution, holding that equal pay as prescribed in Article 14 must be applied not only to the same work but also to work of equal value.[12] The Spanish Constitutional Court reaffirmed that section 28 of the Workers' Charter should be interpreted in conformity with the Convention, to provide for equal remuneration for work of equal value. The ruling also states that job evaluation criteria should not include the sex of the workers and those factors associated with the inferior status of women or reflecting social or economic under valuation of women's work.[13] It is noteworthy that the ruling specifically refers to the ILO Conventions as supplementary sources of law.[14]

It is important to point out the direct reference to the Convention in several European Court of Justice (ECJ) cases. Even though the ILO has not yet referred any case to the International Court of Justice under the Convention,[15] the Convention has been used as a source for interpretation in the equal pay cases. One example is *Gabrielle Defrenne v. Sabena*:

> Article 119 (of the Treaty of Rome) is the extension, the 'European Translation', of Convention 100 adopted by the International Labor Organization on 29 June 1951 'concerning equal remuneration for men and women workers for work of equal value'...The Convention, which came into force a year later, on 23 May 1953, is accordingly applicable in all the member-states although not with effect from the same date. The question whether it is or is not 'self executing' has no bearing on the interpretation to be placed in Community law on the provisions of Article 119 of the EEC Treaty which is, essentially, its counterpart.[16]

---

[12] Decision No. 31/84 of Mar 7, 1984. Also see CEACR, *Direct Request, Spain*, 1990.

[13] *Constitutional Court Judgment STC 145/1991* (Spanish Constitutional Court). Section 28 only provides equal remuneration for "equal work".

CEACR, *Direct Request, Spain*, 1992.

[14] CEACR, *Direct Request, Spain*, 1994.

[15] According to Article 29(2) of the ILO Constitution, if the member state does not accept the recommendation contained in the report of the Commission of Inquiry, the Governing Body can refer the complaint to the ICJ.

[16] Case 43/75, Gabrielle Defrenne v. Sabena (Case #2), (1976) 2 *C. M. L.R.* 98, 110.

The ECJ essentially endorsed the broader concept of equal pay enshrined in the Convention:

> This view is all the more essential in the light of the fact that the Community measures on this question…implement Article 119 from the point of view of extending the narrow criterion of 'equal work', in accordance in particular with the provisions of Convention 100 on equal pay concluded by the International Labor Organization in 1951, Article 2 of which establishes the principle of equal pay for work of 'equal value'.[17]

The Convention has also been referred to as the source for interpretation in Israel. The National Labor Court held that the principle of equal pay for the "same or substantially the same work" should be understood as intended to be in accordance with the Convention No. 100 Israel has ratified.[18]

Some national legislation use very vague terms without specifying "work of equal value". This is where the Court can work to its full capacity. The case *D'Costa v. MacKinnon, MacKenzie and Company* in India represents a calculated effort made by the judiciary in terms of balancing its domestic law and international obligations. In this case, the Supreme Court of India dismissed an appeal by the employer who claimed that a collective agreement that fixed the wages of female stenographers at a rate significantly lower than that of male counterparts, was outside the scope of the Equal Remuneration Act of 1976.[19] The Supreme Court stated that discrimination arose only where men and women performed the same kinds of work or similar work, but was of the opinion that a flexible approach should be taken in deciding whether the work is the same or broadly similar.[20] The government argued that this case broadened the scope of the section 4 of the Equal Remuneration Act that has been narrower than that of the Convention.[21] The Court stated that the concept of similar work implies variation in details, but emphasized that these details should not defeat a claim for equality on trivial grounds. Accordingly, the Court proposed that job evaluations should be conducted and that jobs should be compared

[17] *Ibid.*

[18] See *"Elite" Israel Sweets and Chocolate Industry ltd. v. Lederman*, March 5, 1978; RCE, 1980, p. 143 (Israel).

[19] *Supreme Court Cases* (1987) 2 SCC pp. 469–482.

[20] *Ibid*, p. 478.

[21] See Equal Remuneration Act of 1976, Article 4, from http://labour.delhigovt.nic.in/act/details_acts/equalremuneration/intro/chapter2.html (accessed on Oct 30, 2007).

based on the duties actually performed.[22] The Court's ruling could be interpreted as expanding the scope of the legislation which was narrower than the one set out in the Convention. However, it certainly did not go as far as formally accepting the concept of "work of equal value or comparable worth".

Other judiciaries have been more conservative in their interpretation of the concept of equal pay. In New Zealand, the High Court in the case of *Clerical Workers' Union 1986*, interpreted the Equal Pay Act 1972 (EPA) narrowly, so that rates of pay under the Clerical Workers' Award could not be compared with rates under the Building Trades Award. Afterwards, section 28 of the Employment Contract Act 1991 codified the principle established in the *Clerical Workers Union case* that employees must hold "substantially similar" employment as a condition precedent to making an equal pay claim. The subsequent Human Rights Act 1993 also reflects a "substantially similar" employment requirement in its definition of discrimination.[23]

2. *The Scope of Remuneration*

The Convention adopted a very expansive definition of remuneration. But this concept has been compromised in many ratifying states. The Canadian judiciaries, in contrast, have gradually accepted a broad interpretation of the concept of "remuneration" over time. In 1998, the Human Rights Tribunal of Canada held that the government employees in several primarily female occupational groups such as secretaries, clerks, hospital workers, librarians were under paid for work of equal value. The Tribunal ordered the Treasury Board and the PSAC to make arrangements to pay the wage adjustments.[24] The Treasury Board and the PSAC worked out an agreement in Oct, 1999 and the Tribunal endorsed it in Nov, 1999. Under the terms of the agreement, about 230, 000 employees would receive between 3.3 and 3.6 billion Canadian dollars. It is noteworthy that the payments under this agreement include not only the pay equity adjustments but the lump-sum payments,

---

[22] CEACR, *Individual Observation, India*, 1999.

[23] CEACR, *Individual Observation, New Zealand*, 1999.

[24] *PSAC v. Treasury Board*, for the decisions see http://www.chrt-tcdp.gc.ca/search/view_html.asp?doid=166&lg=_e&isruling=0 and http://www.chrt-tcdp.gc.ca/search/view_html.asp?doid=58&lg=_e&isruling=0. Also see http://www.psac-afpc.org/issues/ucs/special-edition-may01-e.shtml (accessed on Oct 30, 2007). http://www.crtfp-pslrb.gc.ca/decisions/fulltext/2001-81_e.asp (accessed on Oct 30, 2007)

interest, maternity benefits, severance pay, invalidity benefits, promotions and overtime, and old-age pension.[25] This case vividly signifies the trend in Canada to expand the definition of "remuneration".

In some other states, even though the applicable legislation may exclude a certain element of "remuneration", the judiciary tends to include it as a part of the equal pay principle. For example, in Chile, remuneration did not include sums paid to a worker by an employer on occasional basis and out of generosity (bonuses, premiums or awards) or allowances paid to workers to carry out their jobs (costs of representation, transport or other similar expenses) or certain social benefits or customary or occasional benefits when the parties have explicitly provided that they do not constitute remuneration (food, housing or clothing, certain bonuses above the legal minimum).[26] However, according to the interpretation given by the Supreme Court of Justice in 1993, premiums, bonuses or awards, reimbursement of costs and allowances do not constitute wages in the legal sense, but are nevertheless benefits arising out of employment.[27]

Whether "retirement age" should be included in the concept of "remuneration" is controversial. Early retirement certainly would affect one's earnings. Therefore, it is justifiable to incorporate retirement age into the concept. According to the ruling of the European Court of Justice in the case of *Barber v. Guardian Royal Exchange Assurance Group*,[28] benefits paid from occupational pension schemes are "pay" within the meaning of Article 119 of the Treaty of Rome.[29] Following this decision, the British government announced its commitment to achieving equal treatment for women and men in the state pension scheme as well as in the occupational pension schemes including those concerning the unequal pension ages.[30] Subsequently, the UK passed Pensions Act 1995 s.62 to provide an occupational pension

[25] CEACR, *Individual Observation, Canada*, 2002.

[26] Section 128 of the Labor Code, amended by section 15 of Act No. 50 of 1990.

[27] CEACR, *Direct Request, Chile*, 1994.

[28] See *European Court reports 1990 Page I-01889, also see* http://eur-lex.europa.eu/Notice.do?val=165320:cs&lang=en&list=165320:cs,165245:cs,&pos=1&page=1&nbl=2&pgs=10&hwords=Barber%20v.%20Guardian%20Royal%20Exchange%20Assurance%20Group~ (accessed on Oct 30, 2007).

[29] For a more complete discussion over the EU's policy on pension scheme, see Sarah Moore (1995). "'Justice Doesn't Mean a Free Lunch': The Application of the Principle of Equal Pay to Occupational Pension Schemes", *European Law Review* 19–20: 159–177.

[30] CEACR, *Individual Observation, United Kingdom*, 1992.

scheme which includes an equal treatment rule. There are also a series of cases following *Barber*, including *Coloroll Pension Trustees Ltd. V. Russell, Mangham & Others*, which throw further light on the retroactive scope of the *Barber* decision.[31]

The pay difference related to the retirement age has led to an interesting case in Madagascar. Air Madagascar paid an unequal remuneration because of the difference in their retirement ages for the male and female on-board staff, which is set at 50 years for men and 45 for women. According to Air Madagascar, the age limitation on the age of female on-board staff had been adopted out of the concern of the early aging and nervous fatigue caused by the specific nature of their work. Air Madagascar also stated that the age to stop flying is different from the retirement age, since on-board staff can be transferred to a ground job according to the section 12 of the "conditions of work and remuneration of commercial on-board staff" approved by the trade union, the labor inspector and the labor tribunal. The ILO Convention was referred to several times in the case. According to Air Madagascar, the concept of "equal remuneration", whether under the terms of the Convention No. 100 or Act No. 94-029, does not include retirement age that concerns physiological characteristics. The CEACR states that although the determination of different retirement ages for men and women constitutes a difference of treatment which is covered primarily by Convention No. 111, it has an indirect impact on equal remuneration considering the fact that remuneration is directly linked to employment. The same outcome applies to the determination of a different age for ceasing to work as on-board staff. The Arbitration Council of the Court of First Instance of Antananarivo ruled on this issue on Nov 18, 1997, and declared section 12 of the "conditions of work and remuneration of commercial on-board staff" inapplicable because it constituted sex discrimination. This decision was applauded by the CEACR.[32] In 2003, the Supreme Court of the Republic of Madagascar ruled in the case of *Dugain and others v. Air Madagascar* that the courts may annul provisions of collective agreements when they were against public order or international conventions such as the Convention No. 111.[33]

---

[31] See http://eur-lex.europa.eu/LexUriServ/LexUriServ.do?uri=CELEX:61991J0200:en:NOT (accessed on Oct 30, 2007).

[32] CEACR, *Individual Observation, Madagascar*, 2001.

[33] CEACR, *Individual Observation, Madagascar*, 2005. The case had then been sent back to the lower court. The lower court, in its interlocutory judgment No. 01 of

Like retirement age, pension is a contentious issue. Between June 1, 1998 and April 13, 2000, the Equal Treatment Commission of the Netherlands decided in seven cases on discrimination between men and women in relation to the pension schemes that provide more than the statutory minimum requirements. In four cases the Commission found that the relevant schemes were discriminatory. However, although there still is direct discrimination against women and part-timers who are predominantly women, discrimination in the pension schemes has to a large extent disappeared thanks to the legal restrictions and the European jurisprudence.[34]

But there are still two major problems. The first one is that the employers are resisting the application of the EC Court of Justice's ruling of 1994 according to which women and part-timers ought to have had access to the pension schemes. The second problem concerns the retroactive aspect of the law. In this regard, it has to be taken into account that in December 1999 the Supreme Court of Netherlands ruled that the term of limitation was 30 years under the old Civil Code with the effect that reparation had to go back to April 1976. In addition, on November 6, 1998 the Supreme Court handed down a ruling that applied retroactively. It granted a retired stewardess a more favorable occupational pension scheme, which was open only to pursers and assistant pursers, positions for which women were not eligible at the time.[35]

The pension scheme was also the focus of contention in Ireland. The government introduced an Employment Equality Bill in 1996. According to Section 2(1) of the Bill, "remuneration" does not include pension rights.[36] Although the Bill passed through Parliament in March 1997,

---

Feb 3, 2005, has stayed its final decision on the matter until the Arbitration Council has rendered on the appeal lodged by Air Madagascar against the ruling of Nov 1997. See CEACR, *Direct Request, Madagascar*, 2007.

[34] CEACR, *Direct Request, Netherlands*, 2002.

[35] CEACR, *Direct Request, Netherlands*, 2002. Government stated that due to the European jurisprudence, the voluntary reparations of the pensions have become partially obligatory and that since the mid-1990s a large number of pension funds have begun correcting the pensions of women who were excluded in the past from pension arrangements. (See CEACR, Direct Request, Netherlands, 2003). With respect to the limited participation of women in supplementary pension schemes due to the exclusion of certain job categories (so-called white spots), the Government adopted the new Pensions Act to replace the Pension and Saving Funds Act. If this fails, the Government will introduce a formal obligation not to exclude employees from pension schemes See CEACR, *Direct Request, Netherlands*, 2006.

[36] CEACR, *Direct Request, Ireland*, 1997.

its constitutionality was challenged before the Supreme Court. In 1997 that Court held that certain provisions including the one on the concept of remuneration were unconstitutional.[37]

In addition to retirement age and pension, working hours could also affect how much women may earn. The discrepancy in salaries resulting from the difference of working hours was central in a Dutch case. The issue of the lower salary paid to a woman employed on a flexible basis (temporary contract and hourly wage) in relation to the pay received by the full-time employees on the permanent contract led to an important ruling by the Supreme Court of Netherlands.[38] The District Court upheld the plaintiff's claim for equal pay on the grounds that the employment relationship between the plaintiff and her employer was virtually the same as that between the full-time employees and the employer (in terms of the long duration and permanent character of her activities). The district court took into account the generally accepted principle that employees were entitled to fair pay, which means that equal work performed in the same conditions should receive equal pay, unless there were objective grounds that would justify otherwise. It held that under section 1638z of the Civil Code which requires acting as a good employer, the employer was obligated to remunerate the plaintiff in the same manner as her colleagues on the permanent contracts. The Supreme Court upheld this judgment.[39]

The differential treatment based on grounds of working hours in some legislation was held discriminatory in Germany. The Continued Payment of Wages Act prohibits workers whose employment has fewer than 10 hours of work per week or 45 hours per month from claiming wages during a period of incapacity.[40] The Federal Labor Court ruled in 1991 that it amounted to indirect discrimination as women were affected significantly more than men, and that this was not based on an objective factor.[41]

---

[37] Work has begun on revision of the text, in accordance with the terms of the judgment, with a view to submitting an amended Bill to Parliament. CEACR, *Direct Request, Ireland*, 1998.

[38] *Agfa judgment*, 8 April 1994, Case No. 15 292.

[39] CEACR, *Individual Observation, Netherlands*, 1997.

[40] Section 1(3), No. 2, of the Continued Payment of Wages Act.

[41] CEACR, *Direct Request, Germany*, 1995.

In Japan, the National Hospital Workers Union (JNHWU) issued a communication concerning the "wage-based" contract staff (chingin-shokuin), who were employed on a daily basis for a maximum of one year at a time in national hospitals, due to the shortage of permanent employees. According to JNHWU, there are substantial disparities between the treatment of the wage-based contract staff and the permanent staff employed in the national hospitals. A large portion (70 percent) of the contract staff are women. The government pointed out that the permanent staff was for the most part female as well. Since both the contract and permanent employment were equally female predominated, the government argued that there was no indirect discrimination. The CEACR agreed that the wage difference between the contract staff and the permanent staff in the national hospitals did not constitute pay discrimination based on gender.[42]

Seniority-related pay difference is also an issue in Japan. The Court found in the *Shiba Shinkin Bank* case that, in spite of their eligibility under an automatic seniority-based promotion system, the employer had failed to promote its female employees appropriately. Hence the court ordered the defendant to award those eligible women the promotion and corresponding back pay.[43]

Controversy has raged over whether the two-track system[44] that distinguishes the career path indirectly on the grounds of sex, may negatively affect women's ability to earn remuneration equal to that of men for work of equal value.[45] There is an interesting decision handed down by the Tokyo District Court in 2002. In this case a group of female employees filed suit against their employer. The Court held that the separate-track hiring and treatment of women and men applied by the employer were gender based and violated Article 14 of the Constitution (equality under the law) and section 6 of the Equal Employment Opportunity Act.[46]

---

[42] CEACR, *Individual Observation, Japan*, 2000.

[43] See "Women Win Sex Discrimination Suit", from http://www.jil.go.jp/jil/bulletin/year/1997/vol36-02/04.htm (accessed on Sep 30, 2007).

[44] One significant aspect of the career patterns in Japan is the two-track system. The system is split along gender line. Men and women are recruited immediately after high school for either the integrated track (who are trained to become managers and mostly males) or the clerical track (all females). See Y. Ogasawara (1998). *Office Ladies and Salaried Men: Power Gender and Work in Japanese Companies*. Los Angeles: University of California Press.

[45] CEACR, *Individual Observation, Japan*, 2003.

[46] Cases Nos.24,224 and 12,628.

Retirement age and other benefits, together with salary, are crucial to the welfare of working women. Therefore, an expansive definition, which includes elements such as retirement age and pension, should be adopted in order to close the gender wage gap and improve the conditions of female workers.

3. *Job Analysis*

How to compare jobs and determine the value of jobs is another difficult issue present before the domestic courts. As the following Swiss case indicates, it is complicated to determine whether the wage difference is the result of sex discrimination or other factors. In the case *M.B. v. the Canton of St. Gallen*, the Federal Tribunal found that, due to the lack of competition on the labor market, the lower pay was justified for the teachers of psychiatric nursing who were paid less than the teachers of technical professions in the vocational schools. It also held that the actual costs of their education could be taken into account for the wage determination. The Swiss Federation of Trade Unions commented that this ruling has had a rather adverse impact on the realization of equal pay for equal work and work of equal value.[47] The government stated that a reform of the teaching profession was discussed and it has seen the necessity to establish a federal legal framework for the health professions, which might ease the problem of differential treatments in allocating funds to the training of teachers in vocational schools and teachers in nursing.[48] Likewise, in Sweden, the objective factors of the market, age and collective agreement were the reasons for which the Labor Court held that the sex discrimination in pay had not been established, despite the fact that the jobs being compared were deemed to be of equal value.[49]

Some ratifying states have reached a limited interpretation of "equal work". For example, In Saudi Arabia, the Higher Commission for the Settlement of Disputes, decided that a worker could claim equal treatment as compared to his or her colleagues only when the circumstances and qualifications are equal.[50]

In contrast to the more limited approach, Iceland had a dramatic change in the judicial treatment of equal pay. The Supreme Court

[47] CEACR, *Direct Request, Switzerland*, 2002.
[48] CEACR, *Direct Request, Switzerland*, 2003.
[49] CEACR, *Direct Request, Sweden*, 2006.
[50] CEACR, *Individual Observation, Saudi Arabia*, 1993.

interpreted the main law[51] concerning equal pay and held that when comparing jobs, it is necessary to base the decision on a comprehensive evaluation.[52] It noted that jobs may be comparable in terms of equal value even though they differ in their individual aspects.[53] In 2005, the Supreme Court for the first time decided an equal pay case involving a comparison of jobs performed by women and men that were different in nature.[54] In this case, the female manager of the social affairs department of a municipality claimed her right to equal pay under the Equal Status and Equal Rights of Women and Men Act had been violated, by comparing her remuneration to that of an engineer employed by the same municipality. Relying on a job evaluation exercise that had assessed the two jobs with the same number of points, the Supreme Court considered that the plaintiff had advanced substantial arguments that the two jobs were so closely comparable that she had suffered discrimination, while the municipality did not succeed in demonstrating that the difference in pay resulted from the objective and relevant considerations.[55]

Similarly, in Norway, even though the Equal Status Law in force limits the application of the equal pay principle to work in the same enterprise, the Equal Status Appeals Board and the Labor Disputes have broadened the scope of comparison for the purpose of equal pay in some decisions. For example, the Appeals Board has determined that job comparisons do not have to be made between workers who are employed concurrently. A judgment of the Labor Disputes Court recognized that different occupations may be regarded as comparable if there are similarities regarding the training for the occupation and the job assignments involved and if the employees in such occupations work with some degree of collaboration at the same workplace. The Equal Status Ombud considers that comparison between workers with different types of specialized training should be further encouraged.[56]

---

[51] Act on Equal Status and Equal Rights of Women and Men on equal wages.

[52] In the Case No. 11/200 of May 31, 2000.

[53] CEACR, *Direct Request, Iceland*, 2001.

[54] Case No. 258/2004, decision of January 20, 2005.

[55] Directorate-General for Employment, Social Affairs and Equal Opportunities, European Union, *General Report on Developments in EU Gender Equality Law, 2005*. See http://ec.europa.eu/employment_social/gender_equality/docs/2005/groupexpertleg_general_report_04_05_en.pdf (accessed on Oct 30, 2007), at p. 6. Also see CEACR, *Direct Request, Iceland*, 2006

[56] CEACR, *Individual Observation, Norway*, 2001.

These decisions have widened the scope of job comparison. The judiciary in Norway, in this sense has become instrumental in promoting gender pay equity.

The Supreme Court of Chile, in contrast, has restricted the principle through its interpretation. According to Section 143 of the Labor Code of Chile, equal wages shall be paid for equal work performed in the same job, with the same working time and under the equal conditions of efficiency. The Supreme Court, through its judgment, interpreted Section 143 of the Labor code to the effect that in individual cases there is a strict requirement to fully demonstrate the equality of conditions of efficiency between the workers who receive different wages but work in the same enterprise and perform the same job with the same working time.[57]

There has not yet been an agreement as to what criteria should be used to determine "work of equal value". The Swedish Labor Court, in 2001, approved the use of a job evaluation method (using the four criteria for determining the value of a job-knowledge and competence, effort, responsibility and working conditions) in an equal pay case.[58] Even though it was decided that the wage difference between two midwives and a medical technician constituted no unlawful wage discrimination, the case is significant. The court stated in its opinion that the jobs of a midwife and a medical technician were of "equal value", which opens the possibility for further comparison between different jobs.[59]

Physical strength has been utilized as a primary criterion for some job classification in Germany. The Federal Labor Court of Germany has concluded in two decisions[60] that to define the term "light physical work", not only the previously accepted criterion of muscle demand should be taken into account, but also all factors that put pressure on workers and resulted in physical reactions (including standing or maintaining certain positions, repetitive work, nervous strain and noise, or the pulse rate at work). The Court also considered, having taken into consideration of the expert opinion on the average male and female physical capacity, that the difficulty inherent in the same job should be

---

[57] CEACR, *Direct Request, Colombia*, 1990.

[58] *Dom nr 13/01, mål nr A 190/97*. Also see CEACR, *Direct Request, Sweden*, 2000.

[59] See "*Labor Court Approves Job Evaluation in Wage Discrimination Case*", from http://www.eurofound.europa.eu/eiro/2001/03/feature/se0103187f.htm (accessed on Sep 30, 2007).

[60] 4AZR 707 and 4AZR 713/87 of 27 April 1988.

calculated according to the respective strength of the man or woman doing the job.[61] In a decision of July 29, 1992, the German Federal Labor Court held that a woman marking prices in the goods receipt department of a retail establishment ought to be classified in a higher wage category in the collective agreement, as her work generally required some heavy physical effort. In its decision confirming the reclassification, the Court stated that the characteristics of "heavy physical work" in the collective agreement in question did not refer exclusively to the muscular demand placed on the worker, but rather referred to all factors that placed a demand on the worker and led to the physical reactions (such as the posture necessary, time-controlled or repetitive work, nervous or sensory stress, noise and other environmental and social factors). However, as women are usually born physically weaker than men, the utilization of physical strength in general is likely to lead to discrimination. As a result, the Court also held that an increase in wages determined exclusively according to muscular demand, was lawful only if the overall wage system also included compensatory factors commonly associated with the female sex.[62]

Other countries have rejected the use of the criterion of "physical strength". For instance, in Austria the inclusion "physical capability" as an element for job analysis may lead to the invalidation of a collective agreement. Collective agreements enjoy great autonomy, neither the public authorities nor the legislative bodies could intervene in negotiations. Nevertheless, the legality of provisions in collective agreements could be challenged by the parties in individual litigation. In 1994, the Supreme Court of Austria, for the first time, discussed the issue of indirect discrimination against women. The case concerned a collective agreement containing a provision for two categories of temporary workers which employed the criterion of "physical capability" for classification in the higher category. The Court decided that this criterion for the job classification was obviously favorable to men. As there lacks criterion that takes into consideration of the typical female strength such as manual dexterity, the Court concluded that this lack of balance in the assessment criteria amounted to indirect discrimination against

[61] German Government's Eighth Report to the Federal Diet on the application of the principle of equal remuneration, under article 119 of the EEC Treaty, defines "wage groups for light work" as wage groups set out in collective agreements for physically light, unskilled (lower grade) work).CEACR, *Individual Observation, Germany*, 1993.

[62] CEACR, *Individual Observation, Germany*, 1995.

physically less strong women and therefore constituted a violation of section 2(2) of the 1979 Equality of Treatment Act as amended. Accordingly the relevant wage category provision contained in the agreement was ruled to be partially invalid.[63]

So what criteria should be employed to evaluate jobs and hence to decide whether gender discrimination exists? In Netherlands, the Court concluded that the exclusion of certain factors in job evaluation amounted to indirect discrimination. The Equal Treatment Commission in *Case 97–54* found that a salary-scale system applied by the Minister of Education, which was based only on the paid working experience and the last salary earned, while omitting the criteria such as education and unpaid experience relevant to the job, amounted to a form of indirect discrimination against women. This decision has been taken into consideration in the regular talks between the Minister of Education and the unions representing teachers on the criteria to be used in determining the salaries of women returning to work.[64]

The following case referred to the European Court of Justice provides a meaningful guideline as to what constitutes an objective job classification method.[65] In this case, Ms. Rummler, working for a printing firm in the Federal Republic of Germany, claimed that she should belong to a higher pay category. The pay scale in the printing industry was regulated by a framework Wage Rate Agreement for Industrial Employees of the Printing Industry, which provided for seven wage groups. This job classification was determined based on the four factors: a) degree of knowledge; b) concentration; c) muscular demand or effect; d) responsibility. Ms. Rummler argued that her work involved packing parcels weighing more than 20 kilograms and for her it constituted "heavy physical work". Therefore, her work should be classified as wage group Four instead of Three. Wage group Four requires weight to be more than 50 kilograms. The question centered on whether this job classification system heavily based on the criteria of muscle demand and the heaviness of work was in conformity with the principle of equal pay.

[63] 14.9. 1994, ObA 801/94. Also see Directorate-General for Employment, Social Affairs and Equal Opportunities, European Commission, *Report on Equal Pay*, from http://ec.europa.eu/employment_social/gender_equality/legislation/report_equal_pay.pdf (accessed on Oct 30, 2007), at p. 11.

[64] CEACR, *Direct Request, Netherlands*, 1999.

[65] See *Rummler v. Dato-Druck GmbH* (237/85).

The Court held that a job classification system "must be based on criteria which do not differ according to whether the work is carried out by a man or by a women and must be organized as a whole in such a manner that it has the practical effect of discriminating generally against workers of one sex".[66] It laid down three guiding principles:

> (a) "The criteria governing pay rate classification must ensure that work which is objectively the same attracts the same rate of pay whether it is performed by a man or a woman.
>
> (b) The use of values reflecting the average performance of workers of one sex as a basis for determining the extent to which work makes demands or requires effort or whether it is heavy constitutes a form of discrimination on grounds of sex contrary to the Directive.
>
> (c) In order for a job classification system not to be discriminatory as a whole it must, insofar as the nature of the tasks carried out in the undertaking permits, take into account criteria for which workers of each sex may show a particular aptitude.[67]

These guiding principles suggest that when a job classification system becomes a subject of dispute before the court, the court should decide whether this system is formal, analytical, factor-based and non-discriminatory.[68]

It was not until fairly recently that the argument that female-dominated lines of work have been historically undervalued was presented before the court. In the South Wales of Australia, a case was brought by the Liquor, Hospitality and Miscellaneous Workers' Union (LHMU) in 2004 claiming that the jobs of the childcare workers had been undervalued because of the highly feminized nature of this sector.[69] LHMU argued that childcare is a type of work that is based on skills of caring and nurturing children. This job is typically performed by women. As a result, the public tend to have a misconception that the skills associated with this job are innate to women. The uniqueness of this industry results in no male work comparator. Therefore, because of the absence of viable work comparators, it is difficult for these female

---

[66] *European Court Reports* 1987, pp. 37–38.

[67] *Ibid.*

[68] *Commission of the European Communities* 1993, p. 20.

[69] Michael Lyons & Meg Smith, "*Gender Pay Equity, Wage Fixation and Workchoices: Forward to the Past?*" from http://www.qwws.org.au/filestore/OWOL%20Papers/PDF/Lyons%20and%20Smith%20FINAL%20-%20DONE.pdf (accessed on Feb 01, 2008), pp. 116–119. Also see CEACR, *Direct Request, Australia*, 2007.

workers to seek legal redress based on the argument that there is a violation of the equal pay principle. Women working in the childcare industry have long suffered from low pay. The Industrial Relations Commission in the end granted considerable pay increase (from 20% to 50%) for the daycare workers.[70]

4. *Difficulties Facing Equal Pay Cases*

The concept of equal pay has made it difficult for a domestic judiciary to decide an equal pay case. Women workers also have trouble bringing and winning equal pay cases. In the United Kingdom, *Clark and others v. Bexley Health Auth*ority and the subsequent related case *Enderby v. Frenchay Health Authority* allowed the "material factor" defense presented by the employer. The employer argued that they had no choice in the matter of salary because they were obligated to pay their staff neither more nor less than the salaries authorized by the Secretary of State for Health.[71] The Court held that the employers had successfully established a material factor defense in conformity with the meaning of s. 1(3) of the Equal Pay Act 1970, by showing that the pay gap between NHS speech therapists and their comparators, pharmacists and clinical psychologists results from the historical differences in the bargaining structures. This case later was referred to the European Court of Justice (ECJ).[72] The ECJ decided that the burden of proof shall rest with the employer if there is a prima facie case of wage discrimination. However, its decision that market forces may constitute an objective justification for wage difference may become an enormous hurdle for women workers to succeed in their equal pay lawsuits.

The costly and time-consuming equal pay lawsuits such as the above prompted the UK government to adopt various measures to streamline the procedures for equal pay tribunal cases: the appointment of the specialist tribunal panels, the use of the case management discussions, and the provision of the special legal training along with the longer time limits for bringing cases under the Equal Pay Act. However, in the opinion of the Equal Opportunities Commission (EOC), the existing

---

[70] A similar case concerning child care workers took place in Queensland. *Ibid*, Lyons & Smith.

[71] See *Clark & Others v. Bexley Health Authority, Enderby v. Frenchay Health Authority*. CEACR, *Direct Request, UK*, 1990.

[72] See [1994] ICR 112, ECJ Case C-127/92. *European Court reports 1993 Page I-05535*. CEACR, *Direct Request, UK*, 1992.

legislation makes the lawsuits of equal pay costly for both employers and employees and therefore requires reform.[73] Nevertheless, according to the statistics of the Employment Tribunal (GB) there were a total of 3,943 equal pay cases filed in 2004–05, marking a significant jump from the previous reporting year (1,563). In spite of this remarkable increase in the caseload, there were in fact fewer successful cases at hearing (20) than in the previous reporting year (51).[74]

As the rampant gender wage gap still persists, it would be hasty to assume the lower number of cases implies less violation of equal pay principle. The low number of cases on equal pay can only reflect women workers' unsuccessful entry to judicial assistance. This is certainly the case in some ratifying states. For example, in Austria, between 1979 and 1990 the Equal Treatment Committee had only brought six cases against employers out of 18 complaints of wage discrimination and the rest of cases were settled.[75]

In Switzerland, women face significant difficulties in the majority of cases because they have to assume the burden of proof when lodging a complaint, according to the workers' representative of Norway.[76] The equality offices dealt with 120 cases between 1996 and 2000 of which a third concerned equal pay issues. But the Federal Tribunal of Switzerland has only had 18 cases relating to equal remuneration, of which 16 concerned communal or cantonal workers seeking the readjustment of their wages. According to the Government, the low number of equal pay cases in part could be explained by the fact that the equal pay procedure is typically very long and that an appeal to the Federal Tribunal does not necessarily guarantee that the compensation will be obtained.[77]

The low number of cases may also result from the lack of authority of the special agency dealing with equal pay. The Equal Status Council of Denmark had treated only five cases brought before it in 1996 and 1997. The government explained that no authority to try cases and to subpoena evidence might lead to the falling number of cases brought before the Council, since a similar decline has not been observed in the

[73] CEACR, *Direct Request, UK*, 2006.

[74] CEACR, *Direct Request, UK*, 2007.

[75] See CEACR, *Direct Request, Austria*, 1993.

[76] This is interesting. The Workers' member of Norway has paid attention to the welfare of their fellow workers in other countries. Gender pay gap is truly an issue for all workers in the whole world.

[77] CEACR, *Direct Request, Switzerland*, 2003.

courts or in the industrial relations system. As a result, the reform of the structure of the Equal Status Council has since been under discussion.[78]

In Japan, during the period 1996–2001 labor inspectors found 58 cases of violations of Section 4 of the Labor Standards Act, but no case was referred to the Prosecutor's Office. A referral to the Prosecutor's Office would be made only in the cases of the "grave or flagrant violation".[79] The CEACR is of the view that no court rulings or labor inspection reports concerning equal remuneration somehow indicates no violation of the principle set out in the Convention in practice. To some degree this is true. However, the absence of the court rulings and reports of violations could also be explained by the fact that in a country where the unemployment rate is high, workers prefer to remain silent and not to jeopardize their employment over denouncing the violation to the labor authorities.[80]

Other factors may also contribute to the low number of equal pay cases. For example, in Norway, the public has little information about the Equal Status Act and the mechanisms of appeal. Those with the necessary knowledge choose not to complain. The high rate of unemployment is arguably another explanation for this situation.[81]

Gender pay equity concerns not only employees but also employers. The national judiciaries have imposed more responsibilities on employers. In Israel, a case on the access to pay information was decided by the District Labor Court in the case *Simi Nidam v. Rali Electric and Electronics*. In this case the Court asked the employer to release the salary information.[82] In Austria, the court ruled that an employee

[78] CEACR, *Direct Request, Denmark*, 1999. The Equal Status Council is currently establishing a database containing decisions on equality issues from the courts, the industrial system and statements from the Council's own case work. According to the Government, the database will be structured in such a way that it will be possible to monitor developments in Danish lawsuits concerning equal remuneration and the effect of the reversed burden of proof provided for in the Equal Remuneration Act.

[79] CEACR, *Individual Observation, Japan*, 2003.

[80] CEACR, *Direct Request, Dominican Republic*, 1992.

[81] This is arguably also the case for Denmark in the 1980s. See Michael Rosholm & Nina Smith (1996). "The Danish Gender Wage Gap in the 1980s: A Panel Data Study", *Oxford Economic Papers* 48: 254–279, p. 274.

[82] *1576/99 Simi Nidam v. Rally Electric* (05.11.2003). In this case, the complainant was awarded the pay difference she received as opposed to the wages of her male counterparts in the same position. The complainant in the end was awarded a sum of 30,000 NIS. Also see CEACR, *Direct Request, Israel*, 2003.

may dispute his or her dismissal with regard to Section 105 of the Labor Constitutional Act, even if no grounds may warrant the appeal of the dismissal.[83]

Sweden is another example of increasing responsibilities for employers. Its Equal Opportunities Act requires employers to review annually the situation of the gender wage gap and to have an equality plan which includes the analysis of such gender wage gap.[84] The Equal Opportunities Ombudsman has asked the Church of Sweden, the Swedish Armed Forces, the biggest advertising companies, the banks and insurance companies and employment agencies, to present their equal opportunity plans. In this context, a complaint was filed against one employer before the Equal Opportunity Commission (EOC), concerning the access to pay information of employees.[85] There was also a test case brought by the Equal Opportunities Ombudsman before the Equal Opportunity Commission (EOC). In this case the Ombudsman requested that a subpoena be issued against an employer who had not conducted the wage survey as required by the Equal Opportunities Act. The dispute centered on the issue of whether the trade unions had access to the wage information of the employees who might not be their members. In December 1998, the EOC declined to issue the subpoena, holding that the employer was not obligated to supply such information. However, in the context of the adoption of Bill 1999/2000:143, trade unions would have greater access to salary information.[86] Recently, Sweden has introduced the opportunity for employees' associations to ask the Equal Opportunities Commission for a writ of subpoena against employers who are not fulfilling their legal obligations. It also shifted the burden of proof to employers.[87]

Generally speaking, even though there has been substantial advancement on the jurisprudence of gender pay equity developed by the national judiciaries, women workers still face considerable challenge as to lodging and winning equal pay cases. The challenge comes from not only substantive legal constraints but also procedural ones. Therefore, it requires a serious change on both substantive and procedural laws to facilitate women workers in utilizing judicial assistance.

[83] In a 1987 case handed down by the Vienna Labor and Social Welfare Tribunal, affirmed by the Higher Land Court of Vienna. CEACR, *Direct Request, Austria*, 1993.

[84] Sections 9(a) and 11 of the Equal Opportunities Act, 1991.

[85] CEACR, *Direct Request, Sweden*, 2000.

[86] CEACR, *Direct Request, Sweden*, 2001.

[87] Act No. 371 of 1974. CEACR, *Direct Request, Sweden*, 2004.

II. Typology of Judicial Compliance

In terms of implementing the international labor standard of equal pay, there are three basic types of national judiciaries: highly active judiciary, medium active judiciary, and inactive judiciary. The criteria for determining these types are mainly comprised of the following: Are the precedents of the regional courts cited? Are the judges informed of the international standards? Are the ratified ILO standards binding and used on courts? Are the courts dealing with a fair number of equal pay cases? Are the decisions of these cases favorable to the female employees? According to these criteria, while the judiciaries in some ratifying states such as Canada, Switzerland, Australia and the United Kingdom are somewhat active in this regard, others are inactive mostly because there has seldom been a court case on equal pay.

1. *Highly Active Judiciary*

Among those highly active judiciaries, the Australian courts have delivered a significant number of cases on equal pay. Two important decisions handed out by the Conciliation and Arbitration Commission (CAC) changed the landscape of the jurisprudence on gender pay equity in Australia. The case in 1969 granted the right to "equal pay for equal work"[88] and the case in 1972 expanded the right to equal pay for "similar work".[89] In 1985, the CAC agreed with certain therapists (occupational therapists, physiotherapists and speech pathologists) in the Australian Public Service that their qualifications, the application of scientific principles in their daily work, the factors of their work environment, the level of autonomy, responsibility, accountability and complexity of their work, were comparable to the ones of the scientists. Therefore these therapists should not be excluded from the science classification and they were awarded considerable salary increase.[90] This case essentially allowed the comparison between different jobs and broadened the scope of job comparison. It is noteworthy that the decision of the Australian Industrial Relations Commission (AIRC) on the *HPM Industries Equal Pay Test Case of 8 March 1998*

---

[88] See *Equal Pay Case 1969*, (1969) *Commonwealth Arbitration Reports*, vol. 127, p. 1142.

[89] See National Wage and Equal Pay Cases, 1972–1973 *Commonwealth Arbitration Reports*, vol. 147, pp. 172–181.

[90] *The APS Therapists Anomalies Case*, Print G1499, Sydney, December 23, 1985.

included extensive reference to the Convention and the 1986 General Survey on equal remuneration. The AIRC ruled that work value standards are preferable to competency standards[91] which, in absence of agreement, are not adequate tools to assess work of equal value.

2. *Medium Active Judiciary*

Most judiciaries in the world have not yet dealt with a large quantity of cases on equal pay. For example, over 25 years until the year of 2003 the Labor Dispute Court of Norway only decided eight cases regarding the equal pay/equal treatment legislation, among which merely 3 cases were determined according to the equal pay legislation. As to the other 5 cases even though the employee organizations brought out the legislation, the Court handled them on other legal grounds, such as the intent of the agreement. This practice is largely criticized, as the legal theory such as the collective parties have the control over their agreements does not favor the protection of employees and has as a matter of fact led to few cases brought to the Court.[92]

Nonetheless, gender pay equity has started to emerge on the agenda of some judiciaries that have rarely handled equal pay cases before. In Brazil, for instance, although there have not been many equal pay cases, one case brought by the Prosecutor's Office in the State of Piauí against Empresa Pintos, Ltda., headquartered in Teresina was significant, in the sense that it was the first equal pay case in the nation. The plaintiff alleged pay discrimination against female workers.[93] The Conciliation and Trial Board in Teresina found pay discrimination in its ruling issued in 1995. The judgment was then confirmed.[94]

The judiciary in the Republic of Korea has also made its first attempt at equal pay cases. The Supreme Court for the first time issued a ruling regarding the gender wage discrimination. It based its decision on the definition of equal pay for work of equal value provided in the Ministry of Labor's Regulation No. 422 on Handling Equal Employment Matters. According to the Regulation and the ruling, work of equal

---

[91] For a definition of "competency standards", see http://www.ambulancedriving.com/standard/whatcomstan.html (accessed on Oct 30, 2007).

[92] Directorate-General for Employment, Social Affairs and Equal Opportunities, European Commission. *Report on Equal Pay*, April 2006, see http://www.reteparioopportunita.it/Rete_Pari_Opportunita/UserFiles/news/equal_pay_report.pdf, (accessed on Oct 30, 2007), at p. 65.

[93] ACP No. 003/95.

[94] CEACR, *Direct Request, Brazil*, 2002.

value refers to jobs that are equal or almost equal.[95] Even though the ruling refers to the principle of equal pay for work of equal value, it in fact provides a more limited interpretation of the principle than the one enshrined in the Convention.

Likewise, the Latvian court in 2002 decided its first case with regard to the issue of gender-based salary discrimination. The case is currently on appeal to the Supreme Court of the Republic of Latvia.[96]

In general, equal pay is still new to these medium active judiciaries. They have not developed a comprehensive body of jurisprudence on gender pay equity. The number of equal pay cases they have dealt with is very limited. Moreover, the principle on equal pay endorsed in their decisions is narrower compared to the one contained in the Convention. It will take a while before these judiciaries become actively involved in the equal pay cases.

3. *In-Active Judiciary*

The judiciary in some ratifying states has not had any formal legal encounter with respect to equal pay, even though there may have been some complaints regarding equal pay. For example, in Lithuania, there are few cases concerning equal pay brought to the Court. The government has stated that most of the complaints alleging violations of the principle of equal remuneration lodged with the Office of Equal Opportunities Ombudsmen are groundless since most of the time women and men are paid differently because the work they are performing is different.[97] This statement by the government acutely reveals its misunderstanding of the Convention, which may be the main reason why its jurisprudence of equal pay is less developed.

The reason for the silence of these judiciaries on equal pay issues is complicated. It may be in part because of the lack of access to the international information. Judges and practitioners have little training in international law and the accurate digest of international law is hardly available. A bridge is needed to connect international law with these domestic courts.[98]

---

[95] Supreme Court Decision SCR2002 DO3883, 14 March 2003. CEACR, *Direct Request, Republic of Korea*, 2006.

[96] CEACR, *Direct Request, Latvia*, 2002.

[97] CEACR, *Direct Request, Lithuania*, 2005.

[98] Auturo Bronstein and Constance Thomas. *International and European Labor Standards in Labor Court Decisions, and Jurisprudence on Sex Discrimination*. Geneva: International Labor Office, 1995, p. 10.

Other factors influencing the actual use of the international labor standards in the national courts include the status of international law in their legal systems and the competence of the courts as well as judges' mindset towards the use of international law.[99] The National Labor Court of Israel provides an interesting example of how the international standards can play a significant role in its decisions. The Court has repeatedly cited the European Charter, the Universal Declaration of Human Rights and the ILO Conventions in its decisions. It tends to interpret its cases in favor of the international labor standards.[100] The court also frequently refers to the decisions made by other nations' courts, when there is no relevant domestic law on the issue at hand. This extensive reference to the international law and foreign law is mostly pragmatic as international law and foreign law are used to justify the court's decisions.[101] The frequent use of the international labor standards and foreign court decisions in the Israeli courts has been credited to the enormous access to the international law provided for the judges and practitioners, the open-minded attitude of the judges towards the use of international law. It is the obligation of the ratifying states to comply with international law, but as to the foreign law, states are not obligated to do so. However, the knowledge of foreign law can certainly facilitate policymakers in improving their own legal systems and can assist in solving legal problems present in their own legal systems and hence in improving these systems, as exhibited by the Israeli judiciary.[102]

For the purpose of promoting judicial compliance, the training of judges and practitioners on the international labor standards is of paramount importance. Some judges and practitioners in certain ratifying states may have no knowledge of the existing international labor standards. Without knowledge of the ILO Convention No. 100, how can we expect them to use it in court? These judges and practioners essentially bear the tremendous responsibility of connecting international law and domestic law.

There are several ways to enhance the knowledge of judges on the international labor standards. The first one is to incorporate

[99] *Ibid*, pp. 5–10.

[100] *Ibid*, p. 9. `

[101] *Ibid*, p. 10. Spanish Tribunal has also been found citing the opinions by the ILO CEACR, to support its decisions. *Ibid*, p. 9.

[102] Rene David & John Brierley (1978). *Major Legal Systems in the World Today* (2nd ed.). London: Stevens & Sons, pp. 5–8.

international labor law into the required curriculum for law schools (or training schools for judges) and into bar exams (or other legal professional entrance exams). By this way the future legal profession is required to get familiar with international labor law. Only if the legal profession has the proper training on how to research, interpret and apply international law, can international law have a chance to be complied with.

The second one is to develop an online international labor law library which is accessible to all judges and practitioners around the world. The ILO has built several very useful databases. Based on these databases, a more complete international labor law library could be constructed. The periodic training on how to use this library should be followed. In this regard, the ILO's technical support and training center in Turin can play a large role.

The third one is to encourage NGOs and other relevant organizations to organize seminars and conferences on international labor law, to spread the knowledge and to share the best practice. The importance of international labor law is still under estimated in many countries. The relevance of international labor law to workers has not been fully realized. Therefore it is crucial to raise the awareness of the existence of international labor law among those judges and practitioners who administer and implement the law.

Judges and practitioners need to learn the international obligations their governments are supposed to fulfill so that they can apply the law in a way that is consistent with these international obligations. In this sense, the training of judges and practitioners on international law is indispensable to the judicial compliance of international law.

The judicial compliance, like the legislative compliance, varies a great deal among the ratifying states. The interpretation of the courts on the principle of gender pay equity is constantly compromised to balance their obligation to the Convention and social reality of their own. So far, no single judiciary (not even the Canadian courts) has developed a very expansive concept of gender pay equity the Convention targets for. That is to say, the national judiciaries have a long way to go to fully comply with the Convention. After addressing the "internalization" and the "interpretation" of the "transnational legal process" of compliance, there is one element left- the "interaction", which will be examined in the following chapter.

CHAPTER V

THE PROCESS OF "INTERACTION"

The transnational legal process consists of three elements: the "internalization" of legal norms into the internal systems, the "interpretation" of the international legal norms to the situation, and the "interaction" between institutions.[1] Chapter III has examined those national legislation to disentangle the process of the "internalization" of the legal norm of gender pay equity into the domestic systems. Chapter IV has evaluated the court decisions and proceedings to explore how the international labor standards of gender pay equity are "interpreted" to the situation. In addition to the "internationalization" and "interpretation", the "interaction" between actors provides the opportunity to discuss, formulate and reinforce the international norms such as gender pay equity. As the process of the "interaction" is both horizontal and vertical, this chapter first analyzes horizontal "interaction" among the ILO, other international organizations, ratifying states and NGOs, during the process of compliance with the Convention. It then offers a comparative case study of the vertical "interaction" between the ILO and China and Japan, to delineate the process of compliance in more details. The data for this chapter come from the reports of the ILO, other UN agencies, the ratifying governments, the non-governmental organizations, as well as the secondary literatures.

I. Horizontal Interaction

The very nature of the ILO-the tripartite structure provides a valuable platform for the interaction among governments, employers and employees[2] who are the major actors in the area of gender pay equity. These three actors are equally important in implementing the principle of gender pay equity. Their tripartite cooperation enables the flow of information, the mutual understanding of their respective positions,

[1] Harold Hongju Koh (1997). "Why Do Nations Obey", *Yale Law Journal* 106: 2599, pp. 2600–02.

[2] The ILO also calls employers and employees organizations as "social partners".

and most importantly, the possible solution based on the agreement of all three actors.

The CEACR has repeatedly stressed the necessity of cooperation between organizations of employers and employees to ensure the successful implementation of the principle. As a matter of fact, the Convention specifically recognizes the need for this cooperation in Article 4.[3] At the international level, the ILO's treaty-making activities[4] and the annual International Labor Conference both exhibit to a large extent this type of tripartite cooperation.[5] Each member state is represented by two government officials, one workers' representative, and one employers' representative in the annual conference. All four representatives are equally involved in the process of adopting the labor conventions.

The tripartite structure is also evident at the national level, although the involvement of associations of employers and employees may differ. In Lithuania, a Tripartite Council was created. Recently it approved a methodology for the Assessment of Jobs and Positions in 2005 and recommended it for enterprises, institutions and organizations. The Methodology was presented during a number of tripartite meetings and workshops and it has been published as a brochure and on the website of the Council. The secretariat of the Tripartite Council agreed to set up workshops and to consult on the application of the Methodology for workers and employers' representatives.[6] Obviously this type of cooperation may increase the possibility of a successful implementation of the policy. In Sweden, the social partners were also heavily involved in the process of the equal pay policymaking. They worked with the legislators and other policymakers to develop and implement the gender pay equity plans that are tailored to the specific circumstances and needs of each company. In the process, the social partners received technical assistance and financial support from the relevant institutions.[7]

Interestingly, employees' associations in one state sometimes care not only for the welfare of their own members but also that of their

---

[3] Also see the Recommendation (Paras 1, 2, 3).

[4] Christopher C. Joyner (1997). *The United Nations and International Law* (2nd edition), Cambridge University Press, pp. 66–68.

[5] See the ILO Constitution, arts. 19 & 22.

[6] CEACR, *Individual Observation, Lithuania*, 2007.

[7] See Christina Jayne Colclough (2004). *Gender Equality Plans at the Workplace*. European Foundation for the Improvement of Living and Working Conditions.

counterparts in other states. The worker members of Norway even issued a communication to the CEACR about the difficulty the women workers in Switzerland face in filing lawsuits.[8] The horizontal interaction in this sense is "transnational".

The "interaction" occurs not only among tripartite constituencies, but also among the ILO and other UN organizations. After a close examination of the CEACR's reports, one can find the frequent references to other UN organizations' reports or the country reports to these organizations. The Human rights Committee,[9] the International Covenant on Economic, Social and Cultural Rights,[10] the Committee on the Elimination of all Forms of Discrimination against Women (CEDAW),[11] the UN Economic and Social Council,[12] the UN World Conference on Women[13] and the UNDP[14] are regularly mentioned in the Committee's reports. This cross-reference on the one hand, enables the Committee to verify the accuracy of information provided in the country reports, on the other hand, assists the Committee in placing the issue of gender pay equity in a broader context.[15]

From the CEACR's reports, one can also discern the "interaction" among the regional institutions concerning the gender wage gap. For example, in 2002 the Nordic Council of Ministers initiated a joint

---

8 ILCCR, *Individual Case, Switzerland*, 1988.

9 See, for example, CEACR, *Direct Request, Cambodia*, 2004. CEACR, *Direct Request, Switzerland*, 1999.

10 See, CEACR, *Direct Request, Russia*, 2004. CEACR, *Direct Request, Slovakia*, 2002. CEACR, *Direct Request, Uruguay*, 1999; CEACR, *Individual Observation, Nepal*, 1995; CEACR, *Direct Request, China*, 2007.

11 See CEACR, *Direct Request, Spain*, 2003; CEACR, *Direct Request, Thailand*, 2006; CEACR, *Direct Request, Turkey*, 2000; CEACR, *Direct Request, Uzbekistan*, 2006; CEACR, *Direct Request, Zimbabwe*, 2002; CEACR, *Individual Observation, Malaysia*, 2007; CEACR, *Direct Request, Angola*, 2006; CEACR, *Direct Request, Angola*, 2007; CEACR, *Direct Request, Bangladesh*, 2002; CEACR, *Direct Request, Belize*, 2004; CEACR, *Direct Request, Burkina Faso*, 2002, 2007; CEACR, *Direct Request, Equatorial Guinea*, 2005; CEACR, *Direct Request, Greece*, 2007; CEACR, *Direct Request, Israel*, 2006; CEACR, *Direct Request, Kyrgyzstan*, 2005; CEACR, *Direct Request, Nigeria*, 1999; CEACR, *Direct Request, Luxembourg*, 1999.

12 CEACR, *Direct Request, Uruguay*, 2002; CEACR, *Direct Request, Austria*, 2004.

13 CEACR, *Direct Request, Hungary*, 1997; CEACR, *Direct Request, Iceland*, 1997.

14 CEACR, *Direct Request, Mauritius*, 2006.

15 The source of CEACR's report has been very diverse.[15] It comes from both international organizations, and regional or national organizations such as European Industrial Relations Observatory (EIRO),[15] Council of Economic Analysis. See Constance Thomas (2003). "Information Sources and Measures of International Labor Standards on Employment Discrimination", *Comparative Labor Law and Policy* 24: 365. Also see CEACR, *Direct Request, Spain*, 2003; CEACR, *Direct Request, France*, 2001.

project (2003–06), seeking to improve the statistics on the gender wage gap. It developed useful tools and policies that are compatible with the changing economy and with the trend towards involving more local bargaining and individual wage settlements. As improved statistics are essential to a better implementation of the principle, this project is expected to facilitate the participating countries in developing a more efficient and tailored policy to narrow the gender pay gap. The collaboration also occurs in the Norwegian Centre for Gender Equality. The Center, with the collaboration with Austria, Denmark, Greece and the United Kingdom, took the project of the European Commission's Community Framework Strategy on Gender Equality (2001–05) entitled "Towards the closing of the gender pay gap (2001–05)". The project seeks to identify an efficient mix of tools to reduce the gender pay gap in those countries.[16]

Other similar projects aiming at the enhanced equal pay compliance include the project of "Guaranteeing Equal Pay Rights-Legislation and Mechanism for Ensuring Greater Protection", led by the Portuguese Commission for Equality in Labor and Employment, in cooperation with the Department of Equal Opportunities of Italy, the Department of Equality, Justice and Law Reform of Ireland, the Ministry of Children and Family Affairs of Norway and the Ministry of Gender Promotion of Luxembourg.[17] In Europe, there have been more than 20 similar projects on the equal pay issue.[18] All of them demand transnational cooperation. From this transnational cooperation one can see that the issue of the gender wage gap has become a "transnational" concern. As a result, governments have to interact and collaborate to solve the issue.

II. Vertical Interaction

The "interaction" occurs not only at the horizontal level, but also at the vertical level. The vertical "interaction" typically involves the interaction between the ILO and its member state governments. One significant aspect of the ILO/member-state interaction is through its reporting mechanism. It is fair to say that this reporting mechanism is by

---

[16] CEACR, *Direct Request, Norway*, 2003.

[17] See European Commission (2007). *Equal Pay: Exchange of Good Practices*. Luxembourg: European Commission, p. 34. This 2007 report also describes more than 20 similar projects on the equal pay issue.

[18] *Ibid.*

far working. The ratifying states' respect for the Convention could be ascertained in part by examining whether they take their reporting obligation seriously, as reporting to the governing body is one of the major responsibilities of the ratifying states. As the charts (see Table 8 and Figure 2) show, most of the ratifying states have fulfilled their reporting obligations. The average report rate (1990–2007) among the states that have ratified the ILO Convention No. 100 is about 78%. This frequent interaction between the ILO and the governments forces the member governments to constantly evaluate whether they have fulfilled their international obligations under the ILO Convention No. 100 and to adjust their policies accordingly. It constitutes an inherent part of compliance.

Table 8: The Ratifying States' Report Performance

Ratifying State	Ratification Year	Report Performance[19]
Afghanistan	1969	8/9
Albania	1957	3/4
Algeria	1962	8/11
Angola	1976	7/11
Argentina	1956	1
Australia	1974	1
Austria	1953	1
Azerbaijan	1992	6/7
Bahamas	2001	2/3
Bangladesh	1998	1
Barbados	1974	2/3
Belarus	1956	1
Belgium	1962	1
Belize	1999	1/2
Benin	1968	6/7
Bolivia	1973	3/4
Bosnia and Herzegovina	1993	1

[19] This rate equals the number of the reports on the implementation of the ILO Convention No. 100 actually submitted by the ratifying states during 1990–2007/the number of the reports on the implementation of the ILO Convention No. 100 supposed to be submitted by the ratifying states during 1990–2007. The source comes from the CEACR's reports on the ILO Convention No. 100 from 1990 to 2007.

Table 8: (*Cont.*)

Ratifying State	Ratification Year	Report Performance
Botswana	1997	1/2
Brazil	1959	1
Bulgaria	1955	9/10
Burkina Faso	1969	6/11
Burundi	1993	3/5
Byelorussian	1956	1
Cambodia	1999	2/3
Cameroon	1970	6/13
Canada	1972	1
Ced'Ivoire	1961	7/9
Central African Republic	1964	9/14
Chad	1966	10/13
Chile	1971	7/9
China	1990	1
Colombia	1963	1
Comoros	1978	1/3
Congo	1999	1/7
Costa Rica	1951	8/9
Croatia	1991	1
Cuba	1954	1
Cyprus	1987	7/10
Czech Republic	1993	4/7
Djibouti	1978	6/13
Dominica	1983	7/16
Dominican Republic	1953	1
Ecuador	1957	1
Egypt	1960	1
El Salvador	2000	1
Equatorial Guinea	1985	1
Eritrea	2000	3/4
Estonia	1996	1
Ethiopia	1999	1
Fiji	2002	1
Finland	1963	1
France	1953	1

Table 8: (*Cont.*)

Ratifying State	Ratification Year	Report Performance
Gabon	1961	2/3
Gambia	2000	1/2
Georgia	1993	3/4
Germany	1956	1
Ghana	1968	5/13
Greece	1975	1
Grenada	1994	1/2
Guatemala	1961	3/4
Guinea	1967	7/12
Guinea-Bissau	1977	5/13
Guyana	1975	7/10
Haiti	1958	3/7
Honduras	1956	8/9
Hungary	1959	7/8
Iceland	1958	8/9
India	1959	10/11
Indonesia	1958	9/10
Iran	1972	3/5
Iraq	1963	2/3
Ireland	1974	9/10
Israel	1965	2/3
Italy	1956	8/9
Jamaica	1975	5/12
Japan	1967	1
Jordan	1966	4/5
Kazakhstan	2001	1/2
Kenya	2001	1
Kyrgyzstan	1992	1/6
Latvia	1992	3/5
Lebanon	1977	2/3
Lesotho	1998	1/2
Libyan Arab Jamahiriya	1962	2/5
Lithuania	1994	1
Luxembourg	1967	6/7
Madagascar	1962	7/12
Malawi	1965	9/14

Table 8: (*Cont.*)

Ratifying State	Ratification Year	Report Performance
Malaysia	1997	1
Mali	1968	10/13
Malta	1988	4/5
Mauritania	2001	1
Mauritius	2002	1
Mexico	1952	1
Mongolia	1969	4/9
Morocco	1979	10/11
Mozambique	1977	10/13
Nepal	1976	9/11
Netherlands	1971	1
New Zealand	1983	1
Nicaragua	1967	1
Niger	1966	6/11
Nigeria	1974	3/5
Norway	1959	1
Pakistan	2001	1/3
Panama	1958	7/8
Papua New Guinea	2000	1/2
Paraguay	1964	7/11
Peru	1960	1
Philippines	1953	11/14
Poland	1954	1
Portugal	1967	1
Republic of Korea	1997	4/5
Republic of Moldova	2000	1
Romania	1957	1
Russian Federation	1956	6/7
Rwanda	1980	8/9
Saint Lucia	1983	3/16
Saint Vincent and the Grenadines	2001	1/2
San Marino	1985	7/10
Sao tome and Principle	1982	5/16
Saudi Arabia	1978	1

Table 8: (*Cont.*)

Ratifying State	Ratification Year	Report Performance
Senegal	1962	9/14
Servia and Montenegro	2000	1
Seychelles	1999	2/3
Sierra leone	1968	4/15
Singapore	2002	1
Slovakia	1993	6/7
Slovenia	1992	3/4
South Africa	2000	1
Spain	1967	1
Sri Lanka	1993	7/9
Sudan	1970	1
Swaziland	1981	9/13
Sweden	1962	8/9
Switzerland	1972	8/9
Syrian	1957	7/9
Tajikistan	1993	2/9
Tanzania	2002	1
Thailand	1999	2/3
Togo	1983	5/6
Trinidad and Tobago	1997	3/5
Tunisia	1968	10/13
Turkey	1967	9/10
UK	1971	1
Ukraine	1956	8/9
United Arab Emirates	1997	1
Uruguay	1989	1
Uzbekistan	1992	1/2
Venezuela	1982	9/10
Vietnam	1997	2/3
Yemen	1976	7/12
Zambia	1972	9/10
Zimbabwe	1989	1

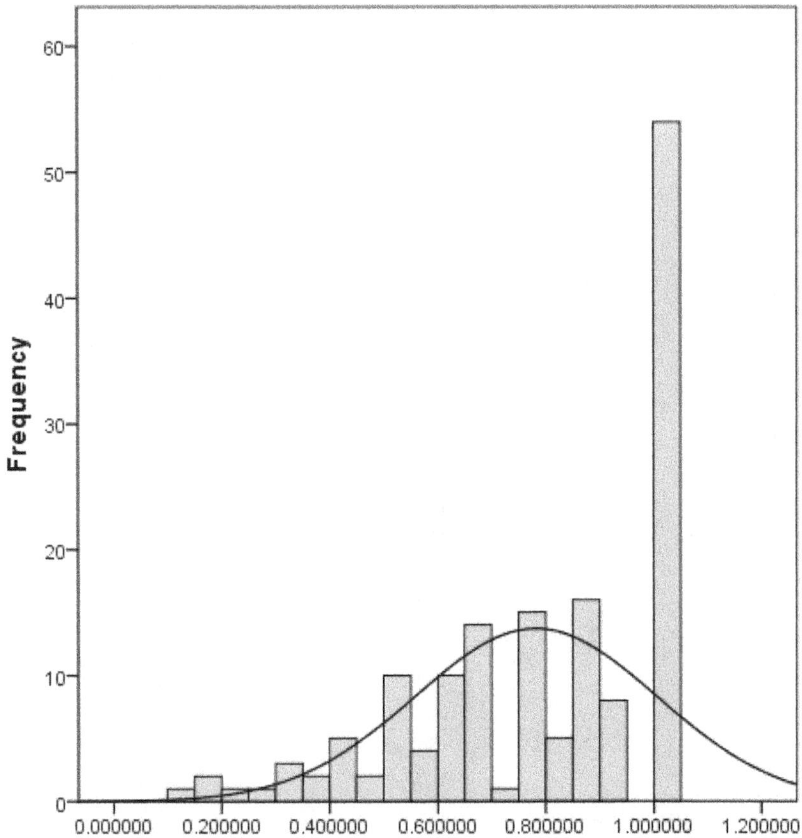

Figure 2: Frequency – Report Performance of the Ratifying States

The "vertical interaction" takes place in part through the ILO's technical program. This program has greatly helped various ratifying states by bringing together all sorts of resources and expertise. For example, the Labor Act of Cambodia was drafted with the assistance of the ILO and has contained several provisions that provide more protection for workers than before and has arguably successfully incorporated the principle of the Convention.[20] It is noteworthy that since the 1990s the ILO has been taking a new approach to its technical program and using it as a means to promote the implementation and compliance of the international labor standards in its member states,

[20] CEACR, *Direct Request, Cambodia*, 2004.

particularly those developing nations.[21] Therefore it is fair to say that the technical cooperation program is instrumental in bridging the ILO and its member states in ensuring the accurate understanding and hence the ultimate compliance with the international labor standards. The ILO's International Training Center in Turin has provided valuable training for judges, tribunal panel members and other dispute settlement bodies. The International Labor Office in Geneva also offers regular training seminars for judges and lawyers from all over the world. These seminars could enhance judges and lawyers' understanding of the relevant Conventions and thus facilitate the consistent implementation of these treaties.[22]

To better describe how the "vertical interaction" between the ILO and its member states, the following comparative case study focuses on a detailed process-tracing of how the ILO interacts with China and Japan.[23] The reasons to choose China and Japan for this comparative case study are as follows: first, these two countries have two different political systems. Japan is a democratic country, while China has an authoritarian regime. A comparative analysis between these two countries could shed light on whether the political system is a variable in terms of the level of "interacting" with the international governing body; second, the gender wage gap is a serious problem in both China and Japan.[24] China, as the biggest developing country, houses the

---

[21] See Hector Bartolomei De La Cruz et al (1996). *The International Labor Organization: the International Standards System and Basic Human Rights.* Oxford: Westview Press, p. 14.

[22] See Constance Thomas et al (2007). *The Use of International Labor Law in Domestic Courts: Theory, Recent Jurisprudence, and Practical Implications*, see http://training.itcilo.it/ils/ils_judges/training_materials/english/Article%20Beaudonnet,%20Oelz,%20Thomas.pdf (accessed on Oct 30, 2007). A cooperation agreement was signed between the ILO's International Training Center and the Institut superieur de la magistrature in Morocco in order to include international labor standards into the curriculum of the school on a permanent basis. As a result, each year, all future Moroccan judges are specifically trained on the use of international labor law. A similar initiative is being developed in Madagascar. Since 1984 the ILO has also provided technical support for the organization of Meetings of European Labor Court Judges and of Ibero-American Labor Judges which discuss both procedural and substantive issues, including human rights questions. See footnote No. 5.

[23] Another reason to choose China and Japan for this comparative case study is that these two countries seemingly share a similar cultural context in terms of the role of gender in industrial relations.

[24] Women earned 65.3% of what men earned in Japan, as in the year of 2001. See http://www.gender.go.jp/english_contents/women2003/news/n06.html; In China, as in the year of 2003, the gender wage gap is around 30 percent. See CEACR, *Direct Request, China*, 2007.

largest workforce in the world. The gender pay gap in Japan is the greatest among all highly industrialized nations. Therefore, promoting gender pay equity in these two countries is of significant importance. It will be insightful to learn whether and how the ILO plays a role in promoting the principle of gender pay equity in both countries.

As the subsequent text indicates, the overall relationships between the ILO and China and the ILO and Japan are quite different. But this overall relationship does not affect their "interaction" with the ILO on the issue of gender pay equity. Both Japan and China have trouble implementing the Convention. Over the years they both have interacted with the governing body to ensure that their obligation to implement the Convention is fulfilled.

1. *The Interaction between the ILO and Japan*

Generally speaking, the ILO and the Japanese government have maintained a close cooperative relationship. In 1974, the ILO and Japan established the ILO/Japan Multi-bilateral Program. This program has now extended its technical support to other countries in the Asia-pacific area and contributed to the discussion and cooperation concerning the issues of employment promotion, occupational health and safety and child labor. The ILO Tokyo Branch Office has played a significant role in promoting workers rights in the Asia-pacific area.[25] Japan also initiated the Program on Strategic Approaches toward Employment Promotion (PEP), which has provided valuable support for the Asian developing countries after the Asian economic crisis.[26]

The Japanese trade unions have also closely interacted with the ILO. They have been using the ILO as a forum to seek the benefit for their members. In 1998, The Japanese National Railway Workers' Union (Kokuro) and the Japanese National Railway Locomotive Engineers' Union (Zendoro) filed a complaint with the ILO, challenging the breakup and privatization of Japan's gigantic railway Company and alleging that discrimination in employment in the new companies violated the ILO Convention No. 87 and No. 98.[27] After examining the

---

[25] See, for example, *ILO Major Activities in Japan in 2000: In Partnership With ILO Constituents*, from http://www.ilo.org/public/english/region/asro/tokyo/newsletr/today2001.htm (accessed on April 20, 2005).

[26] http://www-ilo-mirror.cornell.edu/public/english/region/asro/bangkok/japanmb/index.htm (accessed on April 20. 2005).

[27] Takao Miura (1999). "Breakup and Privatization of Japan's Gigantic Railway Company and thoroughgoing Discrimination in Employment in the New Companies",

case, the Committee on Freedom of Association of the Governing Body issued recommendations in 2000: 1) urging all parties to accept the Four Political Party Agreement adopted in May 2000; 2) emphasizing the Convention No. 98 which includes the principle of the protection against acts of anti-union discrimination at all times.[28]

Another significant feature of the relationship between the ILO and Japan is that the ILO Conventions, reports and recommendations have been invoked before the Japanese courts, although there is no consensus concerning the legal status of the ILO reports and views. The ILO reports, ironically, were used to justify the limitations set by the Japanese government on the trade union rights.[29] For example, in the *Agriculture & forestry Trade Union* case of 1973, the Japanese Supreme Court selectively cited the ILO reports and held that it was constitutional and internationally acceptable to limit the trade union rights in public sectors.[30] The Japanese courts have also dismissed some arguments grounded on the ILO reports in a number of cases. In these cases, they generally decided that these reports are not legally binding.[31]

---

25 *Rodo-Soken Journal.* From http://www.yuiyuidori.net/soken/jour/j_25.html (accessed on April 20. 2005).

[28] http://www.ilo.org/public/english/region/asro/tokyo/newsletr/today2001.htm (accessed on April 20, 2005).

[29] Yuji Iwasawa (1998). *International Law, Human Rights, and Japanese Law.* Oxford: Clarendon Press. At p. 110.

[30] The Supreme Court referred to the Article 6 of ILO Convention No. 98 and some parts of Dreyer Report as well as several previous reports of the Committee on Freedom of Association: Case No. 60, Complaints Presented by the World Federation of Trade Unions...against the Government of Japan, *Report of the Committee on Freedom of Association (12th)*, Eighth Report of the ILO to the UN, App. II, at 202, 211 (1954). Case No. 179 Complaints Presented by the General Council of Trade Unions of Japan...against the Government of Japan, *Report of the Committee on Freedom of Association (54th)*, 44 I. L. O. Off. Bull. 274, 308 (1961). See Jedgt 25 Apr. 1973, Sup. Ct Grand Bench, 27 Keishu 547, Judgment Upon Case of Violation of the National Public Service Law Providing Crime of Inciting Public Officials to Acts of Dispute (Series of Prominent Judgments of the Supreme Court Upon Questions of Constitutionality, No. 14) (1976), in Lawrence W. Beer & Hiroshi Itoh, *The Constitutional Case Law of Japan*, 1970 Through 1990. Seattle: University of Washington Press, 1996. at p. 244. Likewise, the Tokyo High Court refered to the Report of the Committee on Freedom of Association in Case No. 792 to justify the government's position, but it claimed that "interpretation of ILO Conventions adopted in opinions and reports of the Committee of Experts on the Application of Conventions and Recommendations, and the Committee on Freedom of Association signifies no authoritative or juicial interpretation, ad are not of a nature to bind the interpretation of law by domestic courts". Judgt 26 may 1988, Tokyo High Ct, 519 Rodo Hanrei 73, 76.

[31] For example, in 1993, the Oita District Court claimed that: "Reports and recommendations of ILO organs do not bind the Parties, unless they amount to subsequent practice in the application of the treaty which establishes the agreement of the parties regarding its interpretation as provided for in the Vienna Convention on the Law of

However, even with this seemingly agreeable relationship, the ILO has frequently expressed its concern over various labor issues in Japan, such as the restricted rights of public employees in Japan,[32]

Treaties. It is obvious that the views of the ILO organs fall short of it." Judgt 19 Jan. 1993, Oita Dist. Ct, 1457 Hanrei Jiho 36, 49. In 1985, the Fukuoka District decided that "ungratified conventions, recommendations, reports and the like fall neighter within 'treaties concluded by Japan' nor within 'established laws of nations'", although it held that Articl 37 (1) of the Local Public Service Law which prohibited the local public employees from the right to strike is inconsistent with the views of ILO organs: "Views of various ILO organs... are nothing but calls to the governments to make arrangements in domestic laws in accordance with the object of the ILO Conventions. One cannot conclude that they have become sources of law as legally binding standars in interpreting and applying the Conventions, unlike a final decision of the International Court of Justice rendered in cases of doubts or disputes over the interpretation of a Convention (Article 3791) & (2) of the Constitution of the ILO). Judgt 26 Dec. 1985, Fukuoka Dist. Ct, 32 Shomu Geppo 2145, 2179–2180. In 1985, the Tokyo High Court also deineid that ILO reports are part of "international labor standard" and therefore "cannot have automatic binding force". Judgt 20 Nov. 1985, Tokyo High Ct, 466 Rodo Hanrei 65, 78, 79.

[32] See, for example, Kazuo Sugeno (1979). "Public Employee Strike Problems and Its Legal Regulation in Japan", In Witmore Gray (ed.), *Current Studies in Japanese Law*. Ann Arbor: University of Michigan Press. Also see "Does Japan's government continue to reject ILO recommendations", from http://www.japan-press.co.jp/2311/nov26.html (accessed on April 20, 2005). As a matter of fact, the right to strike is completely prohibited in Japan for public employees. Even though Japan ratified two of the most central ILO Conventions on trade union rights: the 1948 Convention on Freedom of Association and Protection of the Right to Organize (No. 87), and the 1949 Convention on the Right to Organize and Collective Bargaining (No. 98),[32] both of these two conventions did not specify whether the right to strike is applicable to public sectors. See Convention Concerning Freedom of Association and Protection of the Right to Organize, adopted on July 9, 1948, 68 U. N. T. S. 17 (ratified by Japan on June 14, 1966); Convention Concerning the Application of the Principle of the Right to Organize and Bargain Collectively, adopted on July 1, 1949 (ratified by Japan on Oct 20, 1954); But in 1983, the Committee of Experts suggested in a report that the prohibition of the right to strike of public employees may violate the 1948 Convention on Freedom of Association and Protection of the Right to Organize (No. 87). See *Freedom of Association and Collective Bargaining: General Survey by the Committee of Experts on the Application of Conventions and Recommendations, Report of the Committee of Experts*, International Labor Conference, 69th Sess. At 63 (1983). See also, e. g., *Report of the Committee on Freedom of Association* (222d), 66 I. L. O. Off. Bull., Ser., B, No. 1, 44–46 (1983). In 1964, the ILO Fact-Finding and Conciliation Commission on Freedom of Association launched an investigation on the issue of the lack of the right to strike of Japanese public employees. See *Report of the Fact-Finding and Conciliation Commission on Freedom of Association Concerning Persons Employed in the Public Sector in Japan*, 49 I. L. O. Off. Bull.. Spec. Supp. No. 1 (1966). This was the first case and one of the only five cases the Commission dealt with and the Commission. Also see James A. R. Nafziger (1969). "The International Labor Organization and Social Change: The Fact-Finding and Conciliation Commission on Freedom of Association", *New York University Journal of International Law and Policy* 1: 15. The ILO has stated in its recommendations that the ban on strikes by public sector is the violations of the ILO Conventions and urged Japanese government to revise its domestic law in conformity with its ILO obligation. See "Does Japan's government continue to reject ILO recommendations", from http://www.japan-press.co.jp/2311/nov26.html (accessed on April 20, 2005).

long working hours,[33] and sexual slavery.[34] The gender wage gap in Japan is another major concern for the ILO.

Japan ratified the ILO Convention No. 100 relatively early (in the year of 1967). This early ratification is generally attributed to the strong political will.[35] In 1986, Japan passed its Equal Opportunity Act, mainly to fulfill its international obligation after it ratified the UN Convention on the Elimination of All Forms of Discrimination against Women (CEDAW). This law was passed not due to the trade union pressures or a feminist movement. As a matter of fact, most feminist leaders opposed this law because they were concerned that those protective measures for women workers (i.e. prohibition of night work and menstruation leave, etc.) may be abolished. The employers' organizations were also against this law because they were concerned that it would be too costly to implement it. Despite the lack of support, the Japanese government in the end did manage to get this law passed, by emphasizing its international obligation under the CEDAW.[36]

However, even though there is such basic law on equal pay for equal work, the gender wage discrepancy persists in Japan. The ILO has long been concerned with the gender pay gap in Japan,[37] as this gap is greater in Japan than in other industrialized countries. The International Labor Conference Committee has discussed the gender wage gap in Japan as an "individual case" three times (in the years of 1993,

[33] In 1993, the ILO issued a report[33] showing that Japanese workers not only suffered from long hours of work, but also are the victims of *Karoshi* (death from overwork). See *ILO World Labor Report 1993*. Geneva: ILO, 1993. pp. 65–67. Also see http://www.ilocis.org/en/samplilo.html (accessed on April 20, 2005).

[34] In 1996, an ILO panel of experts said that Japan's use of Asian women as prostitutes to serve its soldier during the WWII (known as "comfort women") should be categorized as sexual slave and violates the ILO's 1930 Forced Labor Convention. The CEACR presented a report to the 91st Session of the International Labor Conference and expressed its concern about the failure of Japanese government in solving the problems of military "comfort women" and industrial forced labor during the WWII. In response to this concern, the National Confederation of Trade Unions of Japan (ZENROREN) urged the Japanese government to offer its formal apologies and to provide compensations of these acts. See http://www.arts.cuhk.edu.hk/NanjingMassacre/nmnwe96.html (accessed on April 20, 2005).

[35] Ryoko Akamatsu (2005). "Work and Gender-Symposium Commemorating the 50th Anniversary of Reopening of the ILO Office in Japan", from http://www.ilo.org/public/english/region/asro/tokyo/conf/2005tbo/ra.htm (accessed on Sep 30, 2007).

[36] Hiromasa Suzuki (1992). "Equal Pay and Equal Opportunity Issues in Japan", in Alan Gladstone et al. (eds.), *Labor Relations in a Changing Environment*. New York: Walter de Gruyter, pp. 441–442.

[37] The overall gender pay gap was 34.3% in the year of 2004. See ILCCR, *Individual Case*, Japan, 2007.

1994, 2007) since 1990.[38] The CEACR has also commented over years about the continual gender wage gap in Japan. But it appears that the Japanese government had been reluctant to take any proactive legal measure to address the issue of the gender wage gap. Japan has only a general provision on the principle of the right against discrimination in compensation.[39] This general provision is indeed vague. It does not state "equal pay for work of equal value" or even "equal pay for similar work".

The communication between the ILO and Japan has not always been futile. In response to the years' pleading from the ILO, in 2006, Japan revised its Equal Employment Opportunities Law (EEOL) to prohibit discrimination with respect to matters that have an effect on remuneration. The revision outlaws discrimination based on sex in respect of assignment of tasks and responsibilities, as well as any changes concerning a worker's occupation or employment contract (Article 60). However, the CEACR has explicitly expressed the view that Japan still has not fulfilled its obligation even with this new law.[40]

The most significant aspect of the "interaction" occurs among some NGOs in Japan and the ILO concerning the *Sumitomo* case. The Working Women's Network (WWN) submitted various reports on the conditions of the working women in Japan to the ILO and has been lobbying for international support for the plaintiffs in the *Sumitomo* case. The CEACR committee in several occasions referred to the reports of the WWN and urged the Japanese government to take initiatives in solving the gender wage gap in Japan.[41] The response from the ILO suggests that WWN's strategy to embarrass the government through exposing the discriminatory practices and highlighting the discrepancy between the ILO Convention No. 100 and the domestic policy in Japan has worked at least to a certain degree.

With the information gathered from the NGOs and by itself, the ILO has also been able to turn the government's attention to other relevant issues which significantly affect the gender wage gap, such as the wage system, the career track management and the indirect discrimination.[42]

---

[38] See ILCCR, *Individual Case, Japan*, 1993, 1994, 2007.

[39] See Article 4, Labor Standards Law of Japan, from http://www.campus.ne.jp/~labor/rootseiri/roukihou.html (accessed on Sep 30, 2007).

[40] CEACR, *Individual Observation, Japan*, 2007.

[41] See http://wwn-net.org/english/?cat=3 (access on Sep 30, 2009).

[42] See ILCCR, *Individual Case, Japan*, 2007.

2. *The Interaction between the ILO and China*

Compared to Japan that has a mostly smooth relationship with the ILO, China has endured a rocky road with the ILO. China was a founding member of the ILO in 1919. During the turbulent pre-1949 era, its relationship with the ILO was mainly about promoting better labor conditions in China and unifying the enforcement of the labor standards in the enterprises located in the foreign settlements. In 1923, the Chinese government set up an office in Bern, Switzerland, aimed at improving cooperation with the ILO. In 1934 China was elected as a member of the ILO governing body.[43]

The founding of the People's Republic of China in 1949 and its socialist system marked a temporary ending of its constructive relationship with the ILO. In particular, the two-China situation led to the loss of the membership of the mainland China's ILO membership. Taiwan's succession to the ILO stirred a fierce controversy. After China regained its status in the United Nations in 1971, the ILO offered China the membership again. But in the 1970s China was only a "non-active member"[44] and its relationship with the ILO was featured by the "specific exemption" and "specific entitlement". In other words, the China-ILO relationship is based on its claims to the special rights while seeking the special exemption from its organizational responsibilities.[45]

In 1978 China began the transition from an isolated to an open society. Its relationship with the international organizations and specialized UN agencies such as the ILO was also being transformed. In 1983 when China sent its delegation to the International Labor Conference, China resumed its role as an active member. Although China was not ready to accept the principle of freedom of association and the right to collective bargaining, its relationship with the ILO has fundamentally changed since. After 1983, China gained one of the ten non-elective Governing Body seats. From 1984, the ILO also had a Chinese Assistant Director-General. In 1985, the ILO Beijing Brand Office opened and in 1985 for the first time an ILO technical cooperation project

[43] See *China and ILO*, http://www.china-labour.org.hk/iso/article.adp?article_id=1166 (accessed on April 20, 2005). Also see Ann Kent(1999). *China, The United Nations, and Human Rights*. Philadelphia: University of Pennsylvania Press. At pp. 119–128.

[44] John Chen. *Formal cooperation masks rejection of key labour rights*. http://www.amrc.org.hk/4401.htm (accessed on April 20, 2005).

[45] For this characterization of Chinese international organizational behavior, see Samuel S. Kim (Summer, 1995). "China's Pacific Policy: Reconciling the Irreconcilable", *International Journal*, 464.

had a Chinese expert.[46] Before 1990, the All China Confederation of Trade Unions (ACFTU) also occupied a worker seat in the Governing Body.

Another crucial event influencing the relationship between China and the ILO was the Tiananmen Square Incident of 1989. It featured three stages. At the beginning, as a response to the violent repression of the Chinese workers, the ILO withdrew its technical assistance and the International Confederation of Free Trade Unions (ICFTU) filed a formal complaint against China to the ILO Committee on Freedom of Association (CFA),[47] which the Chinese government refuted as an "interference in its internal affairs". But later China gradually showed its willingness to cooperate with the ILO and supplied some information requested by the ILO. However, it still claimed that the ILO's action was interference into China's domestic affairs. During the last stage, China gave up its "interference" claim and further demonstrated its cooperative attitude towards the ILO, in part as an attempt at damage control in response to the 1989 Tiananmen Square Incident.[48]

Since the mid-1990s, the relationship between China and the ILO experienced a substantive improvement. China began to take its membership seriously and employ the ILO standards to protect workers in the foreign-owned enterprises and to ease the labor turbulence resulting from the rationalization of its state-owned enterprises.

Gender pay equity is an area where the ILO and China witness cooperation. China ratified the ILO Convention No. 100 in 1990 and has expressed its commitment to implementing the Convention. It has since cooperated with the ILO to ensure the implementation of the Convention. It even requested technical support from the ILO.[49]

---

[46] Victor-Yves Ghebali (1989). *The International Labour Organization: a case study on the evolution of U.N. specialised agencies*. Dordrecht; Boston; London: Martinus Nijhoff Publishers. At p. 125.

[47] International Labor Office, *268th Report of the Committee on Freedom of Association*, Case No 1500 (China), GB. 244/5/6, 244th Sess. (Geneva, November 1989), paras. 671, at 158–162; International Labor Office, 270th Report of the Committee on Freedom of Association, GB. 245/5/8, 245th Sess. (Geneva, February-March 1990), paras. 297–334, at 83–92; International Labor Office, *279th Report of the Committee on Freedom of Association*, GB. 251/8/11, 251st Sess. (Geneva, 11–15 November 1991), paras. 602–641, at 156–165; and International Labor Office, *281st Report of the Committee on Freedom of Association*, GB. 252/9/13, 252nd Sess. (Geneva, 2–6 March 1992), paras. 74–83, at 17–20.

[48] See http://www.china-labour.org.hk/iso/article.adp?article_id=1166 (accessed on April 20, 2005).

[49] CEACR, *Direct Request, China*, 2004.

In April 2006, the ILO held a workshop with the ACFTU on gender-sensitive statistics collection.[50] The CEACR has not shown particular discontent regarding the implementation of the Convention in China.

3. *A Comparative Study of the ILO/Japan and ILO/China Relationships*

In general, the evolution of China's relationship with the ILO exhibits an increasing procedural compliance and willingness to incorporate the ILO standards into its domestic law. The growing contact between China and other countries and its eagerness to participate in the world affairs are the leading factors resulting in such increasing cooperation between China and the ILO, As revealed by the following statement: "The All-China Federation of Trade Unions actively participates in ILO activities because it is a forum for extensive contacts with other countries and a platform for publicizing China's viewpoint and policies, an important channel for international exchange and cooperation on labor and social problems, as well as a window for understanding international labor movement news."[51] However, before a substantive reform occurs in the political regime, it is unlikely to see the Chinese government alter its attitude towards other labor issues such as freedom of association. But gender pay equity appears to have become an area where the positive interaction and cooperation has occurred.

Conversely, the ILO/Japan relationship has been consistently healthy and positive. The Japanese government is responsive to the ILO complaints and inquiry. The ILO has also become a partner to the Japanese government during the economic restructure and the economic recovery after the Asian economic crisis. More uniquely, the ILO reports and opinions have been frequently invoked before the Japanese courts,

---

[50] CEACR, *Direct Request, China*, 2007. The ILO held a tripartite seminar on women workers' rights in Beijing in 1996. See CEACR, *Direct Request*, China, 1997.

[51] As revealed by the following statement: "The All-China Federation of Trade Unions actively participates in ILO activities because it is a forum for extensive contacts with other countries and a platform for publicizing China's viewpoint and policies, an important channel for international exchange and cooperation on labor and social problems, as well as a window for understanding international labor movement news." See *Seventy Years of the All-China Federation of Trade Unions*. Beijing: China Worker's Press, July 1995.

which no doubt suggests the awareness of these documents among the Japanese workers and lawyers, and the influence of the ILO.

However, the disagreement between the ILO and Japan on the issue of the gender pay gap is acute. It seems that the ILO and Japan have not been able to reach a consensus over this issue. Despite the fact that the ILO has repeatedly insisted that a more proactive and comprehensive measure is needed to resolve the issue of the gender wage differential in Japan, the Japanese government has not yet dealt with the issue in the way the ILO desires.

The difference between the ILO/China and ILO-Japan relationships mostly stem from the different political systems in these two countries. China's turbulent twentieth century has witnessed so many dramatic changes. The change of the political regime in 1949, the reform era starting from the late 1970s and early 1980s, and the retreat from the political reform after 1989 all affected the ILO/China relationship. In contrast with China, Japan's political history after WWII was relatively quiet. There was no overhaul of a political regime. This political stability contributed to a consistent policy towards the ILO-Japan relationship and therefore their constructive cooperation. Obviously, it is easier for the ILO to work with a government with a stable policy. But if a government such as China realizes that the benefit of cooperating with the ILO outweighs its cost, the ILO could have an opportunity to enforce its international labor standards in that country, even though the political culture and climate of that state is not particularly favorable to certain ILO policies.

After assessing the nature of China and Japan's interaction with the ILO, it is fair to conclude that as a widely praised specialized agency, the ILO has played a crucial role in establishing and promoting the international labor standards including gender pay equity in its member states. Its relationship with China and Japan epitomizes both success and failure. Japan's experience with the ILO is mainly a success story. The impact of the ILO can be seen from the frequent quotes of the ILO reports and recommendations in the Japanese courts. However, ironically, the ILO has to battle with Japan concerning the issue of gender pay equity.

The ILO-China story is more complicated. At the beginning of the 1980s, the ILO encountered a battle with China regarding the issue of freedom of association. But it is this battle that in the end brought China closer to the ILO. It is through this constant engagement that China incorporated many international labor standards, including gender pay equity into its own domestic labor law. Through its interaction with the ILO, China earned a reputation for respecting the Convention. China certainly could benefit from this cooperative image in the era of globalization. For the long-term purpose, the continuous pressure yet cooperation appears to have produced more positive results than the mere isolation. In this sense, the ILO handles the "hard case" (China)[52] very well.

The interaction between the governing body and its member states is essentially a process in which the governing body seeks compliance from its members and its member states frequently make a compromise between their international obligations and their domestic practice. It is through this constant engagement and interaction that international law achieves its maximum relevance and international organization works to its greatest capacity.

The interaction not only occurs between the governing body and its member states, as the above text suggests, but also among other actors. Trade unions, employer's organizations, courts, lawyers, and NGOs all interact with the governing body (the ILO) and the governments. This network consists of various actors at various levels. The interaction among these actors within this network is both horizontal and vertical, which may not always produce harmony and agreement. Nonetheless, this transnational interaction certainly makes international law relevant and thus elevates the status of international law and promotes the ultimate compliance.

Hence, here goes the complete process of the transnational legal process of compliance: internalization, interpretation and interaction. This process of compliance is full of the essential contradiction between fulfilling a ratifying state's international obligations and prioritizing its own domestic policies. From time to time a member state's international obligation is compromised. As a global issue, gender pay equity should be implemented without any compromise, which ought to be the ultimate goal for both the ILO and the ratifying states.

[52] See Alastair Lain Johnston (2007). *Social States: China in International Institutions, 1980–2000*. Pinceton: Princeton University Press, p. 37.

CHAPTER VI

CANADA V. JAPAN: THE BEST V. THE WORST

Canada is generally considered as the most successful country in achieving the greatest degree of compliance with the principle of gender pay equity laid out in the ILO Convention No. 100 on Equal Pay. Japan, in contrast, has the worst record among the highly industrialized nations in terms of compliance of gender pay equity. This chapter provides a comparative study on Canada and Japan, two highly industrialized countries with the opposite compliance records, with the attempt to unravel the key factors for compliance/non-compliance.

I. Canada

1. *Legislative Compliance*

a. *Concept of "Equal Pay for Equal Work and Work of Equal Value"*

After ratifying the Convention No. 100 in 1972, Canada has adopted a comprehensive legislative approach to gender pay equity, through its human rights acts, relevant anti-discrimination laws and specific legislation on equal pay at both the federal jurisdiction and a number of provinces.[1] In 1978, the Canadian Human Rights Act in its section 11 made it unlawful to pay women less than men for doing work of equal value. Through the Equal Wages Guidelines the Act now applies to the federal public service and federally-regulated undertakings. The Guidelines specify the basis for the comparison of work of equal value in the same establishment and prescribes that gender is not a reasonable factor justifying the pay differential. The act has had a significant impact on the lives of women workers in public sectors through various court cases.[2]

---

[1] Most jurisdictions in Canada include equal pay provisions in their human rights legislation, except, equal pay provisions are included in human rights legislation, with the exception of Manitoba, New Brunswick, Nova Scotia, Saskatchewan and the Yukon Territory (private sector) where such provisions are included in employment standards legislation. See http://www.rhdcc-hrsdc.gc.ca/eng/labour/labour_law/esl/equal_pay_tb.shtml#_ednref22 (accessed on Sep 10, 2007).

[2] One landmark case is *Public Service Alliance v. Treasury Board of Canada (1998), T.D. 7/98 (Canadian Human Rights Tribunal).*

Like its federal counterpart, the provincial approach to gender pay equity is also remarkable. Quebec passed a proactive Pay Equity Act[3] in 1996 covering both public and private sectors, in addition to its Charter on Human Rights and Freedoms that prohibits discrimination based on gender. The Act requires employers to redress differences in compensation due to the systemic gender discrimination suffered by people who occupy positions in the predominately female job classes. It identifies wage discrimination through a comparison between female-dominated and male-dominated jobs for the same employer or the same establishment, an evaluation of these jobs using a non-discriminatory method of analytical job evaluation, and an estimate of the pay gap between these jobs. It then assigns responsibility for employers to ensure gender pay equity which increases with the size of an enterprise.[4] The Act obligates employers with more than ten but fewer than 50 employees to adjust compensation in order to afford the same remuneration for work of equal value to employees occupying positions in the female-dominated jobs.[5] Employers with more than 50 employees are obligated to set up a pay equity plan.[6] Those enterprises employing 100 or more employees have to establish a pay equity committee.[7] Bipartite sector-based committees may be set up to facilitate the establishment of pay equity plans in a particular sector.[8] Pay equity plans must be developed in four steps: 1) the identification of predominantly female and predominantly male job classes; 2) the description of the job evaluation method and instrument; 3) the job evaluation exercise and the determination of the necessary adjustments in compensation; and 4) the determination of the terms and conditions of payment.[9]

[3] See the Quebec Pay Equity Act of 1996. Proactive laws "encourage or require employers to implement a pay equity plan even when no discrimination complaint has previously been lodged against them. See M.T. Chicha (2006). *A Comparative Analysis of Promoting Pay Equity: Models and Impacts*. Geneva: ILO. From http://www.ilo.org/dyn/declaris/DECLARATIONWEB.DOWNLOAD_BLOB?Var_DocumentID=6596 (accessed on Oct 10, 2007), p. 9.

[4] See *Pay Equity Act*, from http://www.canlii.org/qc/laws/sta/e-12.001/20051019/whole.html (accessed on Sep 10, 2007).

[5] Section 34 of the Pay Equity Act of 1996.

[6] *Ibid*, section 31.

[7] *Ibid*, section 16.

[8] *Ibid*, Chapter III.

[9] See Quebec, Pay Equity Act 1996 from http://www.ces.gouv.qc.ca/documents/publications/anglais.pdf (accessed on Oct 30, 2007). Also see http://www.equalpaycoalition.org/other_prov.php (accessed on Oct 30, 2007).

This mandatory pay equity policy has enjoyed considerable success. The women workers in the public sector, particularly those who have union representation, have attained a substantial compensation adjustment. The employers, imposed major obligations on to ensure gender pay equity, admitted that the mandatory pay equity laws as a matter of fact were beneficial.[10] The positive effects of the Quebec Pay Equity Act 1996 have led to the plea for a similar approach to be adopted by the federal system.[11]

In addition to Quebec, Ontario's equal pay law of 1951 is similarly effective. It has been proven to have narrowed the gender wage gap from the 1950s to the 1970s.[12] Ontario is also "unique" in the sense that it was the first province in Canada to have extensive equal pay legislation.[13] In 1987 it passed the Pay Equity Act, the sole purpose of which is to "redress systemic gender discrimination in compensation for work performed by employees in female jobs".[14] The Act not only applies to the public sector but also to the private sector. It is not complaint-based. Instead it requires employers to take initiatives to discern a gender wage gap and to tackle the issue accordingly through actions such as providing compensation adjustment to the employees concerned. In essence Ontario has adopted a legislative approach to gender pay equity as proactive as the one in Quebec.

It is noteworthy that Manitoba passed the first Canadian legislation that requires affirmative action with regard to gender pay equity. It guarantees a statutory right to equal pay for work of comparable worth for about 60,000 workers in Manitoba's public sector. As a result, a job re-evaluation was conducted among all public sectors and some 4, 900 employees in the female-predominated jobs were granted pay equity increases.[15]

---

[10] Positive results include improved working climate and relations, increased productivity, a more positive perception of fairness within companies, a better understanding of jobs involved and updated or newly introduced wage policies. See Andree Cote & Julie Lassonde (2007). *Status Report on Pay Equity in Canada*, from www .http://www. nawl.ca (accessed on Oct 30, 2007).

[11] *Ibid.*

[12] See R Malarkey. et. al (1989). "The Socio-legal Impact of Equal Pay Legislation in Ontario, 1946–1979". *Osgoode Hall Law Journal* 27: 295–336.

[13] See Kenneth A. Kovach (1996). "Comparable Worth: the Canadian Legislation", *Business Horizon* 41–46, p. 43.

[14] Section 4 (1).

[15] Brian P Smeenk (1993). "Canada's Pay Equity Experiments: A Difficult Principle to Oppose, Pay Equity has become an Attractive, yet Controversial, Political Policy", *HR Magazine* 38: 58–61, p. 59.

b. *Job Evaluation*

At the federal level, the Equal Wages Guidelines of 1986 (Guidelines) under the Canadian Human Rights Act specify the factors to be considered in assessing the skill, effort and responsibility required in work and the conditions under which work is performed. For example, intellectual and physical qualifications acquired by experience, training, and education or natural ability are the factors for assessing the skills required for the performance of work.[16]

In addition to this basic model, Canada has made a notable effort to establish an objective job evaluation system. It has undertaken a thorough reform of the job classification and evaluation system in the federal public sectors. In 1992 it introduced a new job evaluation utilizing the Universal Classification Standard (UCS) 2.0. This standard was developed to assist public servants in more efficiently managing the wide variety of jobs performed for the interests of the public, and also to streamline a job evaluation system which had more than 30 years of history.[17] It is comprised of four factors for measuring the various requirements of a job: responsibility (measures responsibility in the work for people, ideas and things); skill (measures what employees need to know about, or to be able to do in order to perform the work assigned); effort (measures the mental and physical exertion required by the work); and working conditions (measures the physical and psychological conditions under which the work is performed and their potential effects on the health of employees). Each of the four factors is subdivided into elements to allow an evaluation of the whole range of jobs carried out in the public service. For example, working conditions include: (i) the level of danger (underground, working in tunnels, high altitude, high speed, under water, maritime work and exposure to flammable and explosive materials); (ii) the level of hazard (exposure to high temperature, radiative heat, low temperatures, dust, noise and other toxic and hazardous materials); and (iii) the degree of physical

---

[16] http://www.rhdcc-hrsdc.gc.ca/eng/labour/labour_law/esl/equal_pay.shtml#_ednref1 (accessed on Sep 10, 2007).

[17] It has three fundamental goals: universality (the Standard is capable of evaluating the full range of work characteristics within the public service of Canada); gender neutrality (the Standard can identify and positively value the characteristics of work done by women and men, including work that has been historically "invisible" or undervalued); and simplicity (the design and administration of the Standard can support a straightforward and efficient method of valuing and describing work). To meet these goals the Standard must be capable, for example, of comparing the work of care giving with the work of policy analysis, administration or ship repair.

and mental impairment caused by the natural environment and by different shifts (work on a plateau, an open field, maritime and flight operations, long night and rotating shifts).[18]

The Standard is considered as in conformity with the Canadian Human Rights Act, which stipulates that "in assessing the value of work performed by employees employed in the same establishment, the criterion to be applied is the composite of the skill, effort and responsibility required in the performance of the work and the conditions under which the work is performed". The government states that this system of appraisal (which covers around 30 million workers) will help avoid undervaluing the amount of labor contributed in those sectors where the posts are dominated by women workers, thus assist in ensuring the implementation of the principle. The Government further indicated that this post and skill wage system is playing the role of an objective appraisal of jobs based on the work performed, as required by the Convention, and that it is no longer necessary to compare the different posts of men and women, as suggested by the CEACR.

However, the Canadian federal government concluded that a single unified system is too inflexible for more than 150,000 positions in the federal public service and ceased the use of this single classification standard in 2002.[19] The government is now working on a new classification and evaluation system which is intended to be "less rigid" and "more tailored" to occupational needs.[20] While acknowledging that the system, as described, does not involve consideration of the sex of the worker, the CEACR emphasizes that even though this is a gender-neutral approach, it does not address the goal of the Convention that is to ultimately eliminate the wage discrimination for women workers through ensuring equal remuneration for work of equal value. Nevertheless, despite the fact that there are several aspects that may demand improvement, the CEACR is of the view that this Standard is a quantitative method of analysis enabling the relative value of jobs to be determined, and it serves as a good example for other States.[21]

---

[18] CEACR, *Individual Observation, Canada*, 2002.

[19] See *A Profile of the Public Service of Canada: Current Good Practices and New Developments in Public Service Management*. Commonwealth Secretariat, 2004. P. 14.

[20] See CEACR, *Individual Observation, Canada*, 2004. Also see http://www.tbs-sct.gc.cal/classification/ (accessed on Sep 10, 2007).

[21] CEACR, *Direct Request, China*, 1997.

The reform and effort to create an objective job appraisal method is also carried out at the provincial level. The 1993 amendments to the Pay Equity Act of Ontario establish two new methods of achieving pay equity: proportional value comparisons[22] and proxy comparisons.[23] Both new methods require a gender neutral comparison of skill, effort, responsibility and working conditions between male and female job classes. In such cases employers must determine the relationship between the value of the work performed and the pay received by male job classes and apply the same principles and practices to female job classes.[24]

In sum, with some exceptions such as British Columbia, Manitoba, Prince Edward Island and the Yukon Territory, most provinces in Canada often include skill, effort and responsibility required in the performance of work, and conditions under which work is performed, as the factors of assessing what constitutes "substantially the same work". In Prince Edward Island, the Human Rights Act prescribes that education and experience must be taken into consideration for assessing "substantially the same work".[25]

c. *Special Agencies*

In Canada, gender pay equity as an issue has been elevated to such a point that it demands a special agency. Ontario created the Pay Equity Commission[26] to battle the issue of the gender wage gap and to promote gender pay equity. The Commission is composed of two separate and distinct bodies. The Pay Equity Office is responsible for implementing and enforcing the *Pay Equity Act*. It "investigates,

[22] Proportional value comparisons are to be used by both public and private employers in situations where there is an insufficient number of equal or comparably valued male job classes to make direct comparisons. In such cases employers must determine the relationship between the value of the work performed and the pay received by male job classes and apply the same principles and practices to paying female job classes. See http://www.payequity.gov.on.ca/peo/english/pubs/tools_regress_pv.html (accessed on Oct 30, 2007).

[23] Proxy comparisons are to be used only in the public sector where there are insufficient male classes to use the other methods. The proxy method requires employers to make comparisons to jobs outside the employers' establishment. See http://www.payequity.gov.on.ca/peo/english/pubs/proxycomp.html (accessed on Oct 30, 2007).

[24] CEACR, *Individual Observation, Canada*, 1994.

[25] http://www.rhdcc-hrsdc.gc.ca/eng/labour/labour_law/esl/equal_pay.shtml#_ednref1) (accessed on Sep 10, 2007).

[26] See http://www. labour.gov.on.ca/pec/index_pec.html (accessed on Sep 10, 2007).

mediates and resolves complaints and provides programs, tools and services to help public and private sector employers, employees and bargaining agents understand and comply with the Act". It also provides educational seminars, an e-learning program, and outreach to employers' organizations, trade unions and other stakeholders.[27] The Pay Equity Hearings Tribunal is responsible for "adjudicating disputes that arise under the *Pay Equity Act*".[28]

Quebec has also established a "Commission on Pay Equity" which has a monitoring, advisory, research, promotional and regulatory role.[29] It has the authority to receive complaints and to carry out non-advisory investigations.[30] The Commission on Pay Equity is also authorized to resolve any questions concerning pay equity between a predominantly female job class and a predominantly male job class in enterprises with fewer than ten.[31] It has been active in awareness-raising and training activities and in developing tools.[32]

In general, Canada has achieved a legislative success on "equal pay for similar work" in most of its jurisdictions. However, the legislative development of gender pay equity within Canada exhibits discrepancy. Unlike Ontario, Quebec, Manitoba, Prince Edward Island, New Brunswick and Nova Scotia, Saskatchewan, Newfoundland, British Columbia, and Alberta still have not enacted any specific pay equity

---

[27] http://www.ilo.org/wcmsp5/groups/public/—ed_norm/—relconf/documents/meetingdocument/wcms_103484.pdf (accessed on Sep 30, 2009), p. 365.

[28] See http://www.payequity.gov.on.ca/index_pec.html (accessed on Sep 10, 2007). Also see the example of Norway: upon the joint suggestion from the Gender Equality Ombudsperson and the Director of the Center for Gender Equality, as well as the leader of the Confederation of Higher Education Unions, the Equal Pay Commission was created to focus on providing information on pay differences between men and women as well as considering the causes and measures to help eradicate these differences. The social partners will also have a role in the functioning of the Commission through their participation in an appointed task force. The Equality and Anti-discrimination Ombud and Tribunal were established on 1 January 2006, integrating the tasks of the former Gender Equality Ombud and Gender Equality Board of Appeals. The new agency assumes responsibility for enforcing the Gender Equality Act, including the equal pay provision under section 5. See Directorate-General for Employment, Social Affairs and Equal Opportunities, European Union (2005). *General Report on Developments in EU Gender Equality Law*. See http://ec.europa.eu/employment_social/gender_equality/docs/2005/groupexpertleg_general_report_04_05_en.pdf (accessed on Oct 30, 2007), at p. 6. Also see CEACR, *Direct Request, Norway*, 2007.

[29] Chapter V, Division I, of the Pay Equity Act of 1996.

[30] Chapter VI, Division I, *Ibid.*

[31] CEACR, *Individual Observation, Canada,* 1999.

[32] http://www.ilo.org/wcmsp5/groups/public/—ed_norm/—relconf/documents/meetingdocument/wcms_103484.pdf (accessed on Sep 30, 2009), p. 365.

legislation.[33] Saskatchewan and British Columbia did undertake an Equal Pay for Work of Equal Value and Pay Equity Policy Framework,[34] which nevertheless bears no legal sanctity. Furthermore, it has yet to fully incorporate "equal pay for work of equal value" into its legislation. Even for those jurisdictions that have adopted "equal pay for work of equal value", the comparison of "equal value" is limited to the same establishment other than different establishments that the CEACR has consistently urged the government to do.

2. *Judicial Compliance*

In addition to the proactive legislations on gender pay equity, the Canadian courts have developed an advanced jurisprudence regarding gender pay equity. Both federal courts and state courts have intervened in various gender pay equity cases.[35] At the federal level, even though in 1978, the Canadian Human Rights Act made it discriminatory to pay women less than men for performing work of equal value (section 11), it was the Court's 1998 decision in *Public Service Alliance v. Treasury* that clearly made this legislation relevant to women workers. The decision thoroughly examined the meaning, scope and proper application of the gender pay equity provisions of the Act. It contains some important findings on the key issues related to gender pay equity, such as the appropriate methodology to determine wage adjustments, how far back retroactive wage adjustments should go, whether there should be interest payments on the wage adjustments, and whether damages should be awarded to employees. The Public Service Alliance of Canada (PSAC) brought the case to the Human Rights Tribunal, claiming that government employees in the female-dominated job categories, such as the secretaries, clerks, hospital workers and librarians, were not receiving equal pay for work of equal value. The Tribunal ordered that the payments to the employees be calculated based on a job comparison formula put forward by the CHRC and that the Treasury Board and the PSAC would have one year to agree on the distribution of payments.[36]

---

[33] http://www.equalpaycoalition.org/other_prov.php (accessed on Sep 30, 2009).

[34] http://www.ilo.org/wcmsp5/groups/public/—ed_norm/—relconf/documents/meetingdocument/wcms_103484.pdf (accessed on Sep 30, 2009), p. 365.

[35] According to Lexisnexis, Canadian courts have decided over 200 cases on equal pay since 1983. See http://www.lexisnexis.com.steenproxy.sfasu.edu:2048/hottopics/lnacademic/? (accessed on Jan 10, 2007).

[36] See *PSAC v. Treasury Board* (1998), T.D. 7/98 (Canadian Human Rights Tribunal). Also see CEACR, *Direct Request, Canada,* 1999.

This 1998 decision was of historic significance. It strongly supports the principle of gender pay equity and argues that gender pay equity is fundamentally an issue of "social justice".[37] More notably, the expert testimony made by Mr. Durber on the Convention played a significant part. He testified that the Convention, together with the Royal Commission of the Status of Women's Report directly led to the enactment of the Canadian Human Rights Act of 1978.[38] This historical connection between the Convention and the Act suggested that the court ought to interpret the Act in light of the Convention.

The federal complaint-based equal pay law in Canada has usually led to costly and lengthy legal battles. But the results are also financially remarkable. Women workers have received major settlements. Bell Canada's 4765 telephone operators received a $104 million gender pay equity settlements in 2006 which included the gender pay equity settlement money, the payment for pain and suffering and the adjustment to pensionable earnings.[39] The Canadian federal government also paid out approximately $3 billion pay equity adjustments to the women in the predominantly female jobs within the government.[40]

At the provincial level, according to the decision of the Ontario Court (General Division), the amendments to the Pay Equity Act contained in the Savings and Restructuring Act of 1996 (Bill 26) which discontinued the proxy method[41] for achieving pay equity, were unconstitutional. This decision results in the proxy method being reinstated under the Pay Equity Act. As a consequence, the Government states that it has committed funds to cover retroactive proxy pay equity, and funds for pay equity programs.[42] These court cases may carry a considerable financial impact. Most notably, 100,000 of the lowest paid public

---

[37] For a detailed case analysis, see George T. Sulzner (2000). "A Pay Equity Saga: The Public Service Alliance of Canada vs. The Treasury Board of Canada Secretariat", *Journal of Collective Negotiations* 29(2), pp. 89–122.

[38] *Decision of the Tribunal- Phase II, PSAC v. Treasury Board*, from http://www.chrt-tcdp.gc.ca/search/view_html.asp?doid=166&isruling=1&lg=_e#SUBMISSIONS%20OF%20THE (accessed on Sep 30, 2007).

[39] See more cases: *Bell Canada v. CEPU* (No. 5) (1998), 32 C.H.R.R. D/183 (F.C.T.D.). *Bell Canada v. CEP and CTEA*, [1998] A-222–98 (F.C.A.). *Bell Canada v. CEPU* (No. 6) (1998), 32 C.H.R.R. D/213 (F.C.T.D.). *PSAC v. Government of the Northwest Territories,* [1998] No. T470/1097 (F.C.T.D.). *CUPE v. Canadian Airlines International and Air Canada* (1998), T.D. 9/98 (Canadian Human Rights Tribunal).).

[40] Chicha, *supra* note 1.

[41] For the definition of proxy method, see http://www.payequity.gov.on.ca/peo/english/pubs/proxycomp.html (accessed on Sep 30, 2007).

[42] CEACR, *Direct Request, Canada*, 1999.

sector women working in the predominantly female workplaces such as the child care centers and nursing homes have received hundreds of millions of dollars in the pay equity adjustments as a result of a landmark agreement between five unions and four women and the Ontario government.[43]

In Quebec, the Superior Court judgment declared Chapter IX of the Pay Equity Act and the subsequent amendments to the Act unconstitutional in 2004. According to the Superior Court, Chapter IX was maintaining a system of systemic pay discrimination, contrary to the objective of the Act. As a result of this decision, 60 large employers were obligated to undertake equal pay programs pursuant to the Act. Quebec has also tackled those hidden sex discrimination in pay. By adopting a regulation in 2005, it allows enterprises that do not have a male-dominated class to undertake a pay equity exercise, out of the concern that since discrimination is embedded in the social and economic context, the absence of a male-dominated class in an enterprise does not necessarily indicate an absence of pay discrimination based on sex.[44]

The financial implication of some equal pay cases in Quebec is extraordinary as well. Ten years after Quebec passed its Pay Equity Act, the Quebec Government in 2006 settled an equal pay lawsuit, which entitled some 327, 000 women in the public sector to the sizable pay equity adjustments and 1.5 billion in back pay with the total settlement valued at an estimated $ 4 billion. This case was brought by a public sector union but the result also covered non-unionized women working in other public sector workplaces.[45]

In addition to the legislative and judicial actions, various initiatives have been undertaken by the governments to combat the gender wage gap. The New Brunswick government in its Five Year Wage Gap Action Plan lays out "clear and measurable benchmarks and targets for achieving pay equity, through changing societal attitudes, increased sharing of family responsibilities, reducing the job clustering of women and increasing the use of pay equity practices to better value work".[46] The Saskatchewan government introduced the Equal Pay for Work of

---

[43] See "Pay Equity Victory for Women and Unions", from http://www.childcareontario.org/res/fsheets/pdf/payequitysummary03.pdf (accessed on Oct 30, 2007).

[44] CEACR, *Direct Request, Canada*, 2007.

[45] Chicha, *supra* note 1.

[46] http://www.ilo.org/wcmsp5/groups/public/—ed_norm/—relconf/documents/meetingdocument/wcms_103484.pdf (accessed on Sep 30, 2009), p. 365.

Equal Value and Pay Equity Policy Framework that has proven to be effective in narrowing the gender wage gap in every participating department and agency.[47]

The Canadian model has for the most part achieved equal pay for equal work in practice. However, from the perspective of the ultimate realization of equal pay for work of equal value, there is still a long way to go. Many scholars have criticized the existing federal system on gender pay equity as not being proactive enough. In 2004, the Pay Equity Task Force of Canada reached a conclusion that the present scheme was not effective and recommended an adoption of a more proactive act.[48] Even in Quebec and Ontario where there has been substantial success, non-compliance is not uncommon in the private sector and non-unionized sector.[49] Nonetheless, public and scholarly attention to and involvement in this issue in Canada is undeniably remarkable. It is through this process of the constant self-examination and reexamination that gender pay equity in Canada progresses.

II. Japan

Among the highly industrialized countries, Japan has a persistently large gender wage gap. In Japan female workers only earn about two-thirds of what men earn. The gap is twice the OECD average.[50] The factors contributing to this gap are complex, including "two-thirds of the non-regular employees being female, a lack of women in supervisory roles (under 10% compared to around a third in the UK, Austria, Canada and Ireland), and women being underrepresented in management track career positions ('sogoshoku'), where females make up a meager 3.5%."[51] In addition to these factors embedded in the economic

[47] http://www.ilo.org/wcmsp5/groups/public/—ed_norm/—relconf/documents/meetingdocument/wcms_103484.pdf (accessed on Sep 30, 2009), p. 365.

[48] See Pay Equity Task Force (2004). Pay *Equity: A New Approach to a Fundamental Right*. From http://www.justice.gc.ca/en/payeqsal/6000.html (accessed on Sep 10, 2007).

[49] See Speech of Emmunuela Heyninck, Ontario pay Equity commissioner, Ontario Federation of labor, *Pay equity Maintenance: Union Obligations and Liabilities* (Nov. 14, 2006), from http://www.google.com/search?hl=en&q=Heyninck%2C+Ontario+pay+Equity+commissioner%2C+Ontario+Federation+of+labor%2C+Pay+equity+Maintenance&btnG=Search (accessed on Sep 10, 2007).

[50] See http://www.oecd.org/dataoecd/20/20/39696303.pdf (accessed on Sep 10, 2007).

[51] *Ibid.*

system, the Japanese government's hesitance to tackle the issue in the same proactive way as the Canadian government is certainly one of the reasons too.

1. *Legislative Compliance*

In a sense Japan was in a good position to fully conform to the Convention when it signed the treaty. Before Japan ratified the ILO Convention No. 100 on equal pay in 1967, there had been legal enactment about equal pay in place: Article 4 of the Labor Standards law which was passed in 1947. It provides "equal pay for equal work".[52] Article 4 stipulates that an employer may not discriminate in pay "by reason of the worker being a woman".[53] The concept of "pay" prescribed in the Labor Standards Law embraces all kinds of elements of remuneration, as required in the Convention. It not only covers the basic wage, but also includes bonuses, lump-sum allowances, welfare benefits, retirement pay or gratuities, and other allowances.[54] The Labor Standards Law also imposes certain legal obligations on employers. For example, employers are responsible to draw up documents concerning wages, including the amounts of basic wages and allowances, the names of employees, their gender, the basic period for calculation of wages, the number of working days, working hours, amount of overtime work and night work, and so on.[55] They have an obligation to keep such documents for at least three years.[56] Additionally, they must supply information promptly when the labor inspector requests it with regard to the implementation of the Labor Standards Law.[57]

It was the demand of labor for the economy and the invitation from the ILO to participate in the International Year for Human Rights that paved the way for the Japanese government to ratify the Convention.[58] However after the ratification of the Convention in 1967, the labor shortage eased[59] and the Japanese government since has been

[52] See Article 4 of the Labor Standards Law of 1947.

[53] Kazuo Sugeno, *Japanese Employment and Labor Law* 161 (Leo Kanowitz trans., Carolina Academic Press 2002) (1992).

[54] See Article 11 of the Labor Standards Law.

[55] See Article 108 of the Labor Standards Law.

[56] See Article 109 of the Labor Standards Law.

[57] See Article 110 of the Labor Standards Law.

[58] Tadashi Hanami (1981). "The Influence of ILO Standards on Law and Practice in Japan". *International Labor Review* 765, at pp. 767–769.

[59] *Ibid.*

disproportionately slow in taking actions to fulfill its international obligation under the Convention. There is no subsequent legal enactment in Japan that explicitly prescribes "equal pay for similar work and work of equal value". In 1985, Japan enacted the Equal Employment Opportunity Laws (EEOL). The EEOL was partly a response of the Japanese government to the international pressure particularly from the United Nations to deal with the issue of employment discrimination against women during the "Decade of Women".[60] The EEOL requires that employers "shall endeavor" not to discriminate against women in hiring and recruiting.[61] That hints the EEOL is largely voluntary in nature and provides no sanctions on those employers who discriminate.[62] Moreover, it does not specifically refer to the issue of wage discrimination.

Japan revised its Equal Employment Opportunities Law in 2006 to prohibit discrimination with respect to matters in employment that may have an effect on remuneration. The amendment prohibits discrimination based on sex in respect of assignment of tasks and responsibilities, as well as any changes concerning a worker's occupation or employment contract (Article 60). Nonetheless, this amendment does not cover pay discrimination itself. Therefore, as the CEACR stated, it does not fully reflect the principle of the Convention.[63]

Compared to the high compliance states such as Canada, there are not many legal and mandatory measures imposed on the employers in Japan. Nevertheless, the Japanese government is keen in the voluntary code of practice. The government issues guidelines concerning measures of improving wage and employment management, in order to eliminate the wage disparity between men and women. The government also assists employers and workers in monitoring the situation by preparing the wage disparity reports.[64]

Even though the EEOL assigned the Ministry of Labor to handle those gender-based discrimination complaints,[65] in Japan there is no

---

[60] Loraine Parkinson (1989). "Note, Japan's Equal Employment Opportunity Law: An Alternative Approach to Social Change", *89 Columbia Law Review 604,* at p. 614.

[61] Michael S. Bennett (1992). "Gender-Based Employment Discrimination in Japan and the United States", 15 *Loyola L.A. International & Comparative Law Journal* 149, at p. 155.

[62] Allen D. Madison (1997). "The Context of Employment Discrimination in Japan". 74 *University of Detroit Mercy law Review* 187.

[63] CEACR, *Individual Observation, Japan*, 2007.

[64] CEACR, *Individual Observation, Japan*, 2007.

[65] Parkinson, *supra* note 60, at p. 606.

special agency designated to solely deal with the issue of gender pay equity. Instead, the existing administrative agency such as the Prefectural Labor Standards Inspection Office is responsible for the enforcement of the Labor Standards Law including Article 4 on equal pay. The lack of a special agency partly reflects the fact that the issue of gender pay equity has not been placed at the center of the country's agenda. In this sense an establishment of a special agency whose main purpose is to address gender pay equity may largely help raise the awareness of the issue.

Another absence from the Japanese system on equal pay is an objective job appraisal method, which is an important part of the Convention No. 100. The conversation about objective job appraisal methods only started recently. The Japanese Trade Union Confederation (JTUC-RENGO) proposed in 2007 that an objective job evaluation method should be used as a means to implement the equal pay principle provided in the Convention.[66] However, it is unrealistic to assume that we will see the occurrence of an objective job evaluation system in Japan in the near future.

The gender wage gap in Japan is a product of the systemic discrimination against women in the workplace. Women face discrimination right from recruiting until retirement. For instance, in response to the 1986 EEOL, many major Japanese employers adopted a dual career-track system for employees: one is for career track employees ("*sogo-shoku*") that allows for intra-company transfers and promotion to officer positions (managerial track); and the other is for general employees ("*ippanshoku*") (general track). Even though this dual career-track system is seemingly gender-neutral, it has a detrimental effect on many female employees' career and salaries, as they tend to fall within *ippanshoku* and count only a small percentage (2.5%) of *sogoshoku*.[67] The adoption of the dual career-track system is not only an example of the ineffectiveness of the EEOL, but also a reflection of the resistance from the Japanese employers to realize the genuine gender equality. This sort of ingrained discrimination towards female employees certainly cast doubt on the efficacy of the voluntary code of

[66] CEACR, *Individual Observation, Japan*, 2008.

[67] Kazutoshi Kakuyama (1997). "Litigating Sexual Discrimination Employment Cases in Japan: Legal Developments", from http://www.tuj.ac.jp/newsite/main/law/lawresources/TUJonline/SexualDiscrimination/kakuyamasexualdiscrimination.html (access on Sep 30, 2007).

practice the Japanese government has been promoting. To eradicate the gender wage gap and fully comply with the principle of gender pay equity embodied in the Convention, Japan should adopt an aggressive legislative approach instead of just a voluntary code of practice.

2. *Judicial Compliance*

In general, the legal enactment of equal pay in Japan is not only inadequate, but also ineffective. Women workers rarely file a lawsuit based on Article 4 of the Labor Standards Law. Because Article 4 does not define "equal work" and is generally vague, it is extremely difficult to determine what constitutes 'equal work", considering the complicated employment and wage structure in most Japanese employers.[68] In practice, female workers hardly ever won the case based on Article 4.[69]

The Japanese courts have had relatively more gender wage discrimination cases than age discrimination or race discrimination cases. In this sense, the Japanese judiciary has been comparatively vigorous in dealing with wage discrimination prevalent in Japan. As a matter of fact, the employment law is an area that arguably has witnessed judicial activism from the Japanese courts[70], even though Japan is a so-called civil law system where judges presumably play a very limited role in law-making as compared to their common law counterparts because of non-existence of "stare decisis"[71].

The landmark 1975 *Akita Sogo Bank Case* is one of the few cases in which the Japanese court upheld the principle of "equal pay for equal work" based on Article 4 of the Labor Standards Law. In this case, the company applied the different wage tables for the female employees and male employees. The court held that the company cannot provide a reasonable justification for the wage difference and therefore violated Article 4.

The court's interpretation of "pay" has incorporated family allowance as in *Iwate Bank case* (1985), bonus as in *Nihon Tekko Renmei*

[68] F. Eyraud et al (1992). *Equal Pay Protection in Industrialized Market Economies: In Search of Greater Effectiveness*. Geneva: International Labor Office, p. 105.

[69] http://www.ilo.org/public/libdoc/ilo/P/09661/09661(2008-97-1A).pdf, pp. 380–382.

[70] Daniel H. Foote (1996). "Judicial Creation of Norms in Japanese Labor Law: Activism in the Service of —Stability". 43 *UCLA Law Review* 635.

[71] *Ibid.*

Case (1986), and increased wage that results from promotion as in *Shakai Hoken Shinryo Hoshu Shiharai Kikin* Case (1990). The components of the concept of "pay" through the court's interpretation have been expanded beyond the mere salary.

For a long while, the Japanese courts left the promotion decisions to the employers. But in 1996, the Tokyo District Court in *Shiba Shinyo Kinko* Case for the first time declared that the promotion practice that results in the male-female wage difference may be discriminatory. The company's wage system requires its employees to be promoted to a certain job grade in order to receive a pay raise. The promotion of the female employees was delayed considerably compared to that of the male employees. The court decided that this promotion practice violated the company's own rule of no gender discrimination. The female employees were found to be qualified for promotion and awarded the wage difference. However, the court held that promotion to a higher position should be the decision of the company.[72]

Not only may promotion result in the wage difference, but lateral hiring also may affect it. In *Ishizaki Hontern Case*, the company determined the wages based on age for those male lateral hires. But for the female lateral hires, the company used the starting wage for a high school graduate. The company was unable to justify this differential treatment and found unlawful under Article 709 of the Civil Code that provides that "a person who intentionally or negligently has infringed upon the rights of another person is liable for the resulting damages". In this case, the Court had the opportunity to explicitly uphold the right of "equal pay for equal work" but refused to declare so. Instead the Court maintained that wage determination should be employers' decision.

Overall, the Japanese courts have been hesitant to explicitly endorse the principle of "equal pay for equal work" provided by Article 4 of the Labor Standards law, even though from time to time they may award the female plaintiffs the wage difference based on other laws. In most cases, the monetary compensation provided to plaintiffs is very limited considering the extent of the discriminatory practice. The *Sharp Electronics* case 2000 by far awarded the largest wage discrimination judgment (58 million yen).[73]

---

[72] Kakuyama, *supra* note 67.
[73] Toyko Metropolitan Government, 2000.

As the Labor Standards Law is generally vague, the courts over the years have developed a "public order doctrine"[74] based on Article 90 of the Civil Code.[75] In 2005, the Osaka District Court ordered Sumitomo Metal Industries to pay 63 million yen to four employees who suffered the sexual discrimination in wages and promotions, stating that the employer's practices went against "public order".[76]

However, the courts in Japan have been relatively reluctant in developing the "public order doctrine" to invalidate the discriminatory practices in the area of initial hiring that has a significant impact on an employee's salary.[77] Without a more express and active approach from the legislative branch on wage discrimination, the courts are likely to continue to apply the "public order doctrine" sparely and inconsistently.[78]

Even though the Japanese judiciary, as compared to the Canadian courts, has not been active in creating the norms of "equal pay for equal and similar work", it does regularly address its concern for gender inequality in terms of wage. For example, in the 2003 *Sumitomo Electric* Case, the Chief Justice Toshio Igaki of the Osaka Appeals Court, refers to the International Convention on the Elimination of All Forms of Discrimination against Women (1985) and appeals to the Japanese society to "keeping with the international trends" of making progress in gender equality.[79]

III. Conclusion

When compared to Canada, a country with an impressive record of tackling the issue of the gender wage gap, Japan is overshadowed by the

[74] Kazuo Sugeno, *Japanese Employment and Labor Law* 161 (Leo Kanowitz trans., Carolina Academic Press 2002) (1992), at p. 163.

[75] Minpo, art.90, translated in Milhaupt et al., The Japanese Legal System: Cases, Codes and Commentary 749 (2006). Civil Code Article 90: "A juristic act which has for its object such matters as are contrary to public policy or good morals is null and void."

[76] See Sumitomo Kinzoku Kogyo, (Osaka D. Ct., Mar. 28, 2005), available at http://www.courts.go.jp/search/jhsp0030?action_id=dspDet ail&hanreiSrchKbn= 01&hanreiNo=6578&hanreiKbn =03, discussed in Sumitomo Metal Guilty of Gender Bias, Japan Times, Mar. 29, 2005, available at http://search.japantimes.co.jp/print/nn20050329a3.html.

[77] Foote, supra note 70, at p. 672.

[78] Megan L. Starich (2007). "The 2006 Revisions to Japan's Equal Opportunity Employment Law: A Narrow Approach to a Pervasive Problem". 16 *Pacific Rim law and Policy* 551, at p. 568.

[79] http://wwn-net.org/english/?p=22 (accessed on Sep 30, 2010).

lack of initiatives from both the legislative and judiciary branches. Obviously the "gradualism"[80] the Japanese government has followed all these years is simply not working in terms of narrowing down its notorious gender wage differential. Japan can always claim that its ingrained cultural uniqueness makes it difficult to change. But if both branches take no action, how can anyone expect any change?

[80] Kiyoko Kamio Knapp (1999). "Don't Awaken the Sleeping Child: Japan's Gender Equality Law and the Rhetoric of Gradualism". 8 *Columbia Journal of Gender and law* 143.

CHAPTER VII

CONCLUSION

The current international law on gender pay equity has achieved a general acceptance and compliance. However, the ILO conventions on equal pay are ahead of reality and far from being reflected in actual practice. The general international labor standards on gender pay equity are still vague and incomprehensible to the public.

Compliance (not without compromise) with the international treaty does occur in the area of gender pay equity, as this book demonstrates, which justifies the further promotion of the international labor treaties, and the international instruments in general. This general compliance with the international labor treaty also elevates the role of the International Labor Organization that was largely responsible for the emergence of the international labor standards including gender pay equity.

The "internalization" of the principle of gender pay equity into the domestic legislation has gone a long way from "equal pay for equal work", to "equal pay for similar work", and to "equal pay for work of comparable worth". Although there is a trend in the developed countries to encompass a broad principle of equal pay, as defined in the Convention, the majority of the developing countries still struggle to do so. A comprehensive legislative approach is suggested to further undertake the issue of the gender wage gap.

Various factors contribute to the low legislative compliance: the lack of knowledge and information of the real situation; the inadequate data and research; the limited comprehension of the concept of equal value set out in the Convention; the insufficient knowledge of the principles of job appraisal; and the shortage of the financial resources necessary to collect and analyze data, and to institute systems of job evaluation. Certain culture practices may hinder the ratifying governments from recognizing the gender wage gap as an issue. The systemic gender discrimination is even more difficult to deal with. The historical and structural discrimination against women is the fundamental barrier to realize gender equality. Many female predominated job classes are customarily undervalued, which is the main factor causing the gender wage gap. I suggest that an overhaul of the existing job evaluation system may help in this regard.

The "interpretation" of the domestic courts on the principle of gender pay equity has often been compromised to balance their obligation to the Convention and the social reality of their own. Most judiciaries agree to the concept of "equal pay for equal work" or "equal pay for similar work", but not yet "equal pay for work of equal value". In fact, no judiciary has embraced the concept of "equal pay for work of equal value". More and more elements are included in the concept of "remuneration". In general, the jurisprudence of gender pay equity developed by the judiciaries of the ratifying states is far from being the one enshrined in the Convention.

The reasons for the inactive judiciaries on the equal pay issue are complex. They may include the following reasons: the lack of access to and training on international law, the status of international law in their legal systems, the competence of the courts, and the judges' mindset towards the use of international law. I offer several suggestions as to how to enhance the knowledge of the judges on the international labor standards, such as to incorporate international labor law into the curriculum of law schools and bar exams, to develop an online international labor law library which is accessible to all judges and practitioners throughout the whole world, to encourage NGOs and other relevant organizations to organize seminars and conferences on international labor law, and to spread the knowledge and share best practice.

As part of the "transnational legal process", the "interaction" not only occurs between the governing body and its member states, but also among other actors. This network of "interaction" consists of various actors at various levels. The interaction among these actors within this network is both horizontal and vertical. As the comparative case study of the vertical "interaction" between the ILO-Japan and the ILO-China indicates, the interaction between the governing body and its member states may not always generate harmony and agreement. The difference between the ILO/China and ILO-Japan relationships mostly stems from the different political systems in these two countries. The international pressure is proven to play a significant role. Through the transnational/international interaction, international law is made relevant and compliance is ensured.

The comparative case study between Canada and Japan suggests that if the ratifying states take initiatives like the Canadian government has been doing, there is a better chance of narrowing the genderwage gap. That is, governments' no action in part is to blame for the persistent wage discrimination women workers' have long faced.

This study is an attempt to broaden the scope of the subject in the field of international labor law. As domestic industrial relations and labor conditions have been seriously challenged by globalization, various international labor standards have been proposed to safeguard and promote labor rights. However, an important question remains: are these rules and standards enforceable and well enforced? This book seeks to contribute to the existing literature with its study of an issue that has not been addressed before—the international labor standards. It is certainly just a baby step to expand the scope of the subject. Further empirical investigation is needed for other subareas such as child labor.

I strongly advocate the inclusion of labor rights into the human rights scholarship. Core international labor standards including gender pay equity ought to be considered as fundamental human rights. In general, the human rights literature on labor rights is more problem-solving, policy-oriented while theoretically fragmented. This book incorporates labor rights into the emerging literature on the compliance of international human rights law, with the hope that other human rights such as the right against forced labor could be systemically and empirically explored by the human rights scholars in the near future.

The "transnational legal process" theory, which vividly outlines the process of compliance as comprised of the "internalization", the "interpretation" and the "interaction", stays mainly as a theory that requires an empirical application. This study applies the theory to a specific area (the international labor law of equal pay) and intends to supply it with substance. The transnational legal process theory provides an alternative approach to explaining the relationship between international institutions and domestic politics, and international law and national law. This is also the area in which political scientists and international law scholars might entertain more collaboration. Even though the theory of the "transnational legal process" was first proposed by an international law scholar,[1] it undoubtedly could be insightful for political scientists and could present a new perspective for future research on international relations.

The literature on "compliance" has long suffered from being inconsistent and imprecise. A test on how to examine whether compliance exists may reunify the literature. Out of this concern, this study seeks to provide such tests. To discern whether a state has achieved "high

[1] See Harold Hongju Koh (1997). "Why Do Nations Obey International Law", *Yale Law Journal* 106: 2599.

legislative compliance" on the international law on gender pay equity, the following test could be useful: a) if a state has an explicit legal enactment on the principle of "equal pay for work of equal value" other than just "equal pay for equal work", and comprehensive guidelines on how to implement the principle; b) if a state has a judicial or semi-judicial institution which is specifically entrusted with handling the issue of equal pay; c) if female workers have been awarded substantial monetary compensation because of certain legislation. As to whether there exists a highly active judiciary, the following criteria should be considered: a) if the courts have dealt with a fair number of equal pay cases; b) if these decisions are favorable to the female employees; c) if the ILO standards or other regional law are cited and binding on courts. Even though these are the tests for the compliance of the international law on gender pay equity, they may be insightful for the compliance of other areas of international law as well.

Practically speaking, these two tests could be used for the policy-makers for the purpose of self reflection on whether their state has fulfilled its international obligations. They could also be helpful for the agenda setting of the relevant NGOs. The ILO could also utilize them as the guideline to examine whether high compliance occurs. The tests could be useful for the compliance of other areas of international law than gender pay equity.

The national judiciaries are proven to be mostly supportive of international labor standards, particularly in Canada and various European countries. As there lacks an international tribunal to adjudicate the issue related to the violation of the international labor standards and core international labor treaties still do not have a strong enforcement mechanism, national judiciaries are therefore particularly instrumental in achieving gender pay equity since they provide irreplaceable alternative platforms to the equal pay disputes. It should not be presumed as a "hollow hope"[2] to rely on the courts to resolve disputes and advance social change, as the conventional public law literature suggests. The policy reform may have an impact in a grand scale, but individuals certainly can make a change through lawsuits on their own. However, the conditions leading a court to support the implementation of gender pay equity in the developing countries certainly demands further research.

[2] See Gerald N. Rosenberg (1991). *The Hollow Hope*. Chicago: University of Chicago Press, Chapter 12.

For the advocates who are concerned with the persistent gender wage gap, I offered a comprehensive approach that involves all levels of laws and institutions. This approach at a minimum should include ratifying the relevant international treaty (the ILO Convention No. 100 in particular); an explicit legal enactment of the principle of "equal pay for equal work and work of equal value", a broad definition of "remuneration", and an objective appraisal of jobs based on the work to be performed; working with employers, NGOS and other relevant organizations during various stages of policy-making; incorporating code of conduct and affirmative action into the policy; and developing adequate programs on awareness raising and capacity building.

BIBLIOGRAPHY

Abrahamsson, Bengt et al. (1980). *The Rights of Labor*. (Translated from the Swedish by David McCune). Beverly Hills, California: Sage Publications.

Aceves, William J (2001). "Critical Jurisprudence and International Legal Scholarship: A Study of Equitable Distribution", *Columbia Journal of Transnational Law* 39: 299.

Acharya, Sarthy et al. (1995). *The Equal Remuneration Acts and Labor Markets: A Study of Maharashtra*. Bombay, India: Tata Institute of Social Sciences.

Act affording protection to working women, strengthening their rights to employment opportunities in both private and public sectors and strengthening the prohibition on discrimination against women with respect to their employment. Senate No. 1114. 9th Congress of the Philippines.

Act No. 83–635, to amend the Labor Code and the Penal Code as to equality in employment between women and men. Dated 13 July 1983. Legislative Series 1983-Fr.2. France.

Act providing for equal employment opportunity and for other purposes. Senate Bill No. 871.Congress of the Philippines.

Act respecting contracts of employment. 30 April 1970. Finland.

Act respecting equality between women and men. 8 August 1986. Finland.

Act respecting the Equality Ombudsman and the Equality Board. 8 August 1986. Finland.

Act strengthening the prohibition on discrimination against women with respect to terms and conditions of employment, amending for the purpose article 135 of the Labor Code, as amended. Senate Bill No. 65. 1987. Philippines.

Act strengthening the prohibition on discrimination against women with respect to terms and conditions of employment, amending for the purpose article 135 of the Labour Code, as amended. Approved 12 May 1989. Republic Act No. 6725. Philippines. Labor Law Documents 1989-PHL 3, ILO.

Act to establish equality for men and women (Second Equality Act - 2. GleiBG). Germany, Bundesgesetzblatt, 30 June 1994, No. 39. Labor Law Documents, 1994-DEU 2. ILO.

Act to promote and ensure equal employment opportunities in the Philippines, establish an Equal Employment Opportunities Authority, provide penalties for violations thereof, and for other purposes. House Bill No. 6338. Republic of the Philippines.

Adams, Kirstine & Byrnes, Andrew (1999). *Gender Equality and the Judiciary: Using International Human Rights Standards to Promote the Human Rights of Women and the Girl-child at the National Level: Papers and Statements from the Caribbean Regional Judicial Colloquium, Georgetown, Guyana, 14–17 April 1997*. London: Commonwealth Secretariat.

Adams, Lorna; Carter, Katie; Schafer, Staefan (2006). *Equal Pay Reviews Survey 2005*. Manchester, UK: Equal Opportunities Commission.

Affirmative Action (Equal Employment Opportunity for Women) Act 1986. No. 91 of 1986. Australia.

Affirmative Action (Equal Employment Opportunity for Women) Amendment Act 1992. Australia.

Agócs, Carol (Ed.) (2002). *Workplace Equality: International Perspectives on Legislation, Policy and Practice*. The Hague & New York : Kluwer Law International.

Agrawal, Anuja (2006). *Migrant Women and Work*. New Delhi & Thousand Oaks, California: Sage Publications.

Agarwal, N (1990). "Pay Equity in Canada: Current Developments," *Labor Law Journal*, 518 at 520–1.

Aharonian, Taline (1995). "Equal Value in the European Union: Fiction or Reality", *the Buffalo Journal of International Law* 2: 91.

Akamatsu, Ryoko (2005). "Work and Gender-Symposium Commemorating the 50th Anniversary of Reopening of the ILO Office in Japan", from http://www.ilo.org/public/english/region/asro/tokyo/conf/2005tbo/ra.htm (accessed on Sep 30, 2007).

Armstrong, Pat, Cornish, Mary & Millar, Elizabeth (2003). "Pay equity: Complexity and contradiction in Legal Rights and Social Processes", in *Changing Canada: Political Economy as Transformation*, ch. 7 (Wallace Clement & Leah F. Vosko, Eds.). Canada: McGill-Queen's University Press.

Albrecht, James & Vroman, Susan (1993). "Evaluating Policies to Reduce the Gender Gap: An Economic Approach", *Georgetown Law Journal* 82: 69.

Alston, Philip (2004). "Core Labor Standards and Transformation of International Labor Rights Regime", *European Journal of International Law* 15(3): 457.

—, (Ed.) (2005). *Labor Rights as Human Rights*. Oxford: Oxford University Press.

—, (1999). "Transplanting Foreign Norms: Human Rights and Other International Legal Norms in Japan", *European Journal of International Law* 10(3): 625.

Alter, Karen J (2000). "Do International Courts Enhance Compliance with International Law?" *Review of Asian and Pacific Studies* 25: 51–78.

—, (1996). "The European Court's Political Power", *West European Politics* 19: 458.

Alvarez, Jose E (1998). "Why Nations Behave", *Michigan Journal of International Law* 19: 303.

American Society of International Law (2002). "How Are Nations Behaving?" *American Society of International Law Proceedings* 96: 205.

Ames, Linda J (1995). "Fixing Women's Wages: the Effectiveness of Comparable Worth Policies", *Industrial and Labor Relations Review* 48:4.

Ancheta-Sabilano, Aura (1991). "GO-NGO Collaboration to Improve the Working Conditions of Homeworkers". *Philippine Labor Review* 15(1).

Anker, Richard (1997). "Theories of Occupational Segregation by Sex: An Overview." *International Labor Review* 136: 315–339.

Anti-Discrimination Act. Act No. 48, 1977. The Statutes of New South Wales, Australia.

Anti-Discrimination Act 1991. Act No. 85 of 1991. Queensland, Australia.

Amorim, Anita, Badrinath, Sandhya & Murray, Una (2005). *Gender Equality and Child Labor: A Participatory Tool for Facilitators*. Geneva: International Labor Office.

Arend, Anthony Clark (1998). "Do Legal Rules Matter? International Law and International Politics", *Virginia Journal of International Law* 38:107.

Arnull, A (1986). "Article 119 and Equal Pay for Work of Equal Value", *European Law Review* 19(11): 200–208.

Arrowsmith, David (1986). *Pay Equity: Legislative Framework and Cases*, Industrial Relations Centre, Queen's University at Kingston, Research and Current Issues Series No. 43. Kingston: Ontario.

Avery, P (2004). "The Diluted Equal Pay Act: How was it Broken? How can it Be Fixed?" *Rutgers Law Review* 56 (3): 849–75.

Baer, Judith A (1978). *The Chains of Protection: the Judicial Response to Women's Labor Legislation*. Westport, Conn.: Greenwood Press.

Bamber, Greg et al. (Eds.) (2004). *International and Comparative Employment Relation: Globalization and the Developed Market Economies*. London; Thousand Oaks, California: SAGE.

Banda, F (2006). "Blazing a Trail: the African Protocol on Women's Rights Comes into Force", *Journal of African Law* 50: 72–84.

Banks, Kevin (2004). "Globalization and Labor Standards- A Second Look at the Evidence", *Queen's Law Journal* 29: 533.

Banks, Robert F & Steiber, Jack (Eds.) (1977). *Multinationals, Unions, and Labor Relations in Industrialized Countries*. Ithaca : New York State School of Industrial & Labor Relations, Cornell University.

Barnett, E (1986). "Comparable Worth", *Trial* 22: 22–26.

Barrett, Nancy S (1979). "Women in the Job Market: Occupations, Earnings, and Career Opportunities, in Ralph E. Smith (Ed.), *the Subtle Revolution: Women at Work*, Washington, D.C.: The Urban Institute.

Barrington, Linda; Troske, Kenneth R (2001). *Workforce Diversity and Productivity: An Analysis of Employer-Employee Matched Data*. New York, The Conference Board.

Bartlett, Robert V. et al. (Eds.) (1995). *International Organizations and Environmental Policy*. Westport, Conn.: Greenwood Press.

Barth, Erling & Mastekaasa, Arne (1996). "Decomposing the Male/Female Wage Gap: Within and between Establishment Differences", *Labor* 10(2): 339–56.

Bartholet E. (1985). "Pay Equity: The Concept of Equal Pay for Work of Comparable Worth", *Proceedings of the Annual National Conference on Labor* (New York): 38: 1–11.

Bartolomei de la Cruz, Hector et al. (1996). *The International Labor Organization: the International Standards System and Basic Human Rights*. New York: Westview Press.

Basu, Kaushik (2003). *International Labor Standards: History, Theory, and Policy Options*. Malden, MA: Blackwell Publishing.

Bederman, David J (2000). "What's wrong with International Law Scholarship? I Hate International Law Scholarship (Sort of)", *Chicago Journal of International Law* 1: 75.

Beer, Lawrence W. & Itoh, Hiroshi (1996). *The Constitutional Case Law of Japan, 1970 through 1990*. Seattle: University of Washington Press.

Beijing Declaration and Platform for Action, (Beijing, September 4–15 1995), UN Doc. A/Conf. 177/20 (1995) and UN Doc A/Conf. 177/20/Add.1 (1995): 138.

Bennett, Laura (1988). "Equal Pay and Comparable Worth and the Australian Conciliation and Arbitration Commission", *Journal of Industrial Relations* 30(4): 533–545.

Bennett, Michael S. (1992). "Gender-Based Employment Discrimination in Japan and the United States", 15 *Loyola L.A. International & Comparative Law Journal* 149.

Benson, M (1985). "Equal Pay for Work of Equal Value", *Israel Yearbook on Human Rights* 174(15): 66–87.

Berik, Gunseli, Rodgers, Yana van der Meulen & Zveglich, Joseph E Jr (2003). *International Trade and Wage Discrimination: Evidence from East Asia*. The World Bank, Policy Research Working Paper Series: 3111.

Betten, Lammy (1993). *International Labor Law: Selected Issues*. Deventer, the Netherlands: Kluwer law and Taxation Publishers.

Billington, James (1987). "Realism and Vision in American Foreign Policy", 66 *Foreign Affairs* 630.

Bisschop, Siebrand (2004). "Equal Pay for Work of Equal Value: the Role of Job Evaluation Schemes", in Janet Cormak, Ed., *Towards the Uniform and Dynamic Implementation of EU Anti-discrimination Legislation: the Role of Specialized Bodies*. Dutch Equal Treatment Commission.

Black, Sandra E. & Brainerd, Elizabeth (2004). "Importing Equality? The Impact of Globalization on Gender Discrimination", *Industrial & Labor Relations Review* 57 (4): 540–559.

Blackburn, R. J (1995/1996). "Comparable worth and the Fair Pay Act of 1994", *Kentucky Law Journal* 84: 1277–1302.

Blankenship, Kim M (1993). "Bringing Gender and Race in: U. S. Employment Discrimination Policy", *Gender and Society* 7(2): 204–226.

Blanpain, R. (Ed.) (2001). *Labor law, Human Rights and Social Justice*. Hague: Kluwer Law International.

Blanpain, R. (Ed.) (2001). *The ILO and the Social Challenges of the 21st Century: the Geneva Lectures*. The Hague; Boston: Kluwer Law International.
Blau, Francine D (1977). *Equal Pay in the Office*. Lexington, Mass.: Lexington Books.
—–, (1996). *Where Are We in the Economics of Gender? The Gender Pay Gap*. National Bureau of Economic Research Work Paper Series.
Blau, Francine D & Kahn, Lawrence M (2000). *Gender Differences in Pay*. United States: Russell Sage Found.
—–, (1992). "The Gender Earnings Gap: Learning from International Comparisons", The American Economic Review 82(2): 533–538.
—–, (1999). "Analyzing the Gender Pay Gap", *Quarterly Review of Economics and Finance* 39: 625–646.
—–, (2007). "The Gender Pay Gap", *Economists' Voice* 1–6.
Block, Richard N et al. (Eds.) (2006). *Justice on the Job: Perspectives on the Erosion of Collective Bargaining in the United States*. Kalamazoo, Mich.: W.E. Upjohn Institute for Employment Research.
Blum, Linda M (1991). *Between Feminism and Labor: the Significance of the Comparable Worth Movement*. Berkeley: University of California Press.
—–, (1987). *Re-evaluting Women's Work: The Significance of the Comparable Worth Movement (California)*. PhD Dissertation. University of California, Berkeley 0028.
Böhning, W. R (2005). *Labor Rights in Crisis: Measuring the Achievement of Human Rights in the World of Work*. Basingstoke,England: New York : Palgrave Macmillan.
Bolyard, Wendy Lynn (2006). *Identifying Factors that Influence Gender Disparities in Physician Income: Implications for Public Policy*. Ph. D. Dissertation. University of Central Florida 0705.
Bonjour, Dorothe & Gerfin, Michael (2001). "The Unequal Distribution of Unequal Pay- An Empirical Analysis of the Gender Wage Gap in Switzerland", *Empirical Economics* 26: 407–427.
Borland, Jeff (1999). "The Equal Pay Case- Thirty Years on", *The Australian Economic Review* 32(3): 265–272.
Borzaga, Matteo (2006). "Company and Labor Law: Accommodating Differences: Discrimination and Equality at Work in International Labor Law", *Vermont Law Review* 30: 49.
Bouis, Howarth E (1998). *Gender Equality and Investment in Adolescents in the Rural Philippines*. Washington, D. C.: International Food Policy Research Institute.
Bowden, Ellen M. (1994). "Closing the Pay Gap: Redefining the Equal Pay Act's Fourth Affirmative Defense", *Columbia Journal of Law and Social Problems* 27: 225–67.
Boyle, Francis (1985). *World Politics and International Law*. Duke University Press.
Bradford, William (2005). "International Legal Compliance: Surveying Field", *Georgetown Journal of International Law* 36: 495.
Brasted, H. V. (2000). "Piecing Together the Jigsaw: Indian Women in the Urban Wage Labour Force", *Asian Studies Review* 24(2): 195–211.
Broadhurst A (1973). "Equal Pay: The Discriminating Act", Industrial and Commercial Training 5(1): 35–38.
Bronstein, Autoro & Thomas, Constance (1995). *International and European Labor Standards in Labor Court Decisions, and Jurisprudence on Sex Discrimination*. Geneva: International Labor Office.
Brookes, Mick, Hinks, Timothy & Watson, Duncan (2001). "Comparisons in Gender Wage Differentials and Discrimination between Germany and the United Kingdom", *Labor* 15(3).
Brophy, Julia & Smart, Carol (1981). "From Disregard to Disrepute: The Position of Women in Family Law", *Feminist Review* 9: 3–16.
Brown, Chris (2002). *Sovereignty, Rights and Justice: International Political Theory Today*. Cambridge: Polity Press.

——, (1999). "Universal Human Rights: A Critique", in Tim Dunne & Nicholas J. Wheeler, (Eds.). *Human Rights in Global Politics*. New York: Cambridge University Press.

Browne, K. R (1989). "Comparable Worth: An Impermissible Form of Affirmative Action?" *Loyola of Los Angeles Law Review* 22: 717–60.

Browne, M. N et al. (1987). "The Socially Responsible Firm and Comparable Worth", *American Business Law Journal* 25: 467–86.

——, (1999). "Individualism and the Market Determination of Women's Wages in the United States, Canada, and Hong Kong", *Loyola of Los Angeles International and Comparative Law Journal* 21(3): 355–98.

Brunnee, Jutta & Toope, Stephen J (2002). "Persuasion and Enforcement: Explaining Compliance with International Law", *Finnish Yearbook of International Law* 13: 1.

Brynin, Malcolm (2006). "Gender, Technology and Jobs", *The British Journal of Sociology* 57(3): 437–453.

Buckley. JE (1974). "Equal Pay: Progress and Problems (America)", *International Journal of Social Economics* 1(1): 84–95.

Bull, Hedley (1977). *The Anarchic Society: A Study of Order in World Politics*. New York: Columbia University Press.

Burton, C. (1987). *Women's Worth: Pay Equity and Job Evaluation in Australia*. Australian Government Publishing Service, Canberra.

——, (1990). *Pay Equity-Obligations, Costs and Benefits*. IRR conference on Preventing Discrimination in the Workplace, Sydney, September, 1990.

Butler, W. E (1991). Control over Compliance with International Law. Dordrecht, Boston: Martinus Nijhoff.

Cameron, James, Werksman, Jacob & Roderick, Peter (1996). *Improving Compliance with International Environmental Law*. London: Earthscan.

Cameron, Louisa May (1996). *Women and Gender in the Japanese Workplace and Society*. PhD Dissertation. Columbia University 0054.

Canadian Human Rights Act 1976–1977, Office Consolidation, Jan.1989, chapter H-6.

Candland, Christopher (2001). *The Politics of Labor in a Global Age: Continuity and Change in Late-industralizing and Post-socialist Economies*. Oxford & New York: Oxford University Press.

Cao, Le Thi & Phillip G Buchanan, Phillip G. "The Gender Gap in Accounting: Salary Disparity among Management Accountants", 18 *Akron Business and Economic Review* 34–43.

Carey, Sabine C. et al. (Eds.) (2004). *Understanding Human Rights Violations: New Systematic Studies*. Aldershot, Hants, England; Burlington, Virginia: Ashgate.

Carlson, Barbara Mackey & McEnrue, Mary Pat (1985). "Eliminating the Gender-Based Earning Gap: Two Alternatives", *Business Horizons* 76–81.

Carr, E. H (1949). *The Twenty Years' Crisis 1919–1939*. London: Macillman.

Cassel, Douglass (2001). "Does International Human Rights Law Make a Difference?" *Chicago Journal of International Law* 121.

Chamallas, M (1986). "Women and Part-time Work: The Case for Pay Equity and Equal Access", *North Carolina Law Review* 64: 709–775.

Charlesworth, Hilary (1998). "The Unbearable Lightness of Customary International Law", *American Society of International Law Proceedings* 92:44.

Chayes, Abram & Chayes, Antonia Handler (1995). *The New Sovereignty: Compliance with International Regulatory Agreements*. Cambridge: Harvard University Press.

Chaykowski RP (1988). *Pay Equity Legislation: Linking Economic Issues and Policy Concerns*. Kingston: Pay Equity and Comparable Worth: A Dialogue On Issues and Implementation.

Chen, Derek H. C (2004). *Gender Equality and Economic Development: The Role of Information and Communication Technologies*. Washington, D. C: World Bank.

Chen, John. *Formal Cooperation Masks Rejection of Key Labor Rights*. http://www.amrc.org.hk/4401.htm (accessed on April 20, 2005).
Cherry, Robert (1988). Discrimination by Gender: Economic Theories and Policy Implications, in Vroman, Georgine M etc (Eds.) *Women at Work: Socialization toward Inequality*. New York: Gordian Press.
Cheung, A (1995). "Pay Equity for Hong Kong: A Preliminary Exploration", *Hong Kong Law Journal* 33(25): 383–400.
Chicha, M.T. (2006). *A Comparative Analysis of Promoting Pay Equity: Models and Impacts*. Geneva: ILO. From http://www.ilo.org/dyn/declaris/DECLARATIONWEB.DOWNLOAD_BLOB?Var_DocumentID=6596 (accessed on Oct 10, 2007).
China and ILO http://www.china-labour.org.hk/iso/article.adp?article_id=1166 (accessed on April 20, 2005).
Cihon, P. J et al. (1988). "Comparable Worth: the U.S./Canadian Experience", *Loyola of Los Angeles International and Comparative Law Journal* 10: 57–107.
Cingranelli, David L. (1999). "Respect for Human Rights after the End of the Cold War". *Journal of Peace Research*, Vol. 36, No. 5. Pp. 511–534.
Civil Rights Act – The Public Health and Welfare, Subchapter VI. – Equal Employment Opportunities, 2000e, Title 42. Vol. 9, 1964 edition, United States Code.
Clauss, Carin Ann (1986). "Comparable Worth-The Theory, Its Legal Foundation and the Feasibility of Implementation", *University of Michigan Journal of Law Reform* 20:7.
Cobbah, J. A. M (1987). "African Values and the Human Rights Debate: An African Perspective", *Human Rights Quarterly* 9: 309.
Cockburn, Cynthia (1984). "Introduction: Trade Unions and the Radicalizing of Socialist Feminism", *Feminist Review* 16: 43–46.
Coicaud, Jean-Marc (2002). *Globalization of Human Rights*. New York: United Nations Publications.
Colclough, Christina Jayne (2004). *Gender Equality Plans at the Workplace*. European Foundation for the Improvement of Living and Working Conditions.
Commission Staff Working Paper (2003). *Gender Pay Gaps in European Labor Markets*. Brussels: EU.
Commission's Network of Legal Experts (2007). *Legal Aspects of the Gender Pay Gap*. From http://ec.europa.eu/employment_social/gender_equality/legislation/report_equal_pay.pdf (accessed on Dec 30, 2007).
Compa, Lance A (2003). "Assessing Assessments: A Survey of Efforts to Measure Countries Compliance with Freedom of Association Standards", *Comparative Labor Law and Policy Journal* 24 (2): 283–320.
——, (1996). *Human Rights, Labor Rights, and International Trade*. Philadelphia: University of Pennsylvania Press.
Compa, Lance & Lyle, Fay (2003). *Justice for All: A Guide to Worker Rights in the Global Economy*. Washington, D. C: American Center for International Labor Solidarity/AFL-CIL.
"Comparable Worth: A Symposium", *University of Michigan Journal of Law Reform* v. 20 (Fall 1986): 1–215.
"Comparable Worth: The Next Step toward Pay Equity under Title VII", *Denver University Law Review* v. 62 (1985): 417–45.
"Comparable Worth: Will It Close the Earnings Gap or Widen the Gender Gap?" *The Florida Bar Journal* v. 59 (April 1985): 27–32.
"Comparable Worth and the Courts: How Fear of the Market Place is Changing the Face of Title VII", *Houston Law Review* v. 23 (October 1986): 1185–1214.
"Comparable Worth and the Market Defense: A National Debate", *Golden Gate University Law Review* v. 16 (Fall 1986): 475–513.
"Comparable Worth and the Presumption of Equality: What does 'Justice' Require?. *West Virginia Law Review* v. 87 (Summer 1985): 837–57.

"Comparable Worth and Title VII: The Case against Disparate Impact Analysis", *Pacific Law Journal* v. 16 (April 1985): 833–851.
Constitution of the International Labor Organization, (1948) 15 U.N.T.S. 194.
Constitution Act of Finland. 17 July 1919.
Constitution of the Fourth Republic of Ghana (Promulgation) Law, 1992.
Constitution of the German Democratic Republic. Gesetzblatt der Deutschen Demokratischen Republic, 8 Oct. 1949, No. 1. Legislative Series 1949-Ger.D.R.1. ILO.
Constitution of the Philippines. 1987.
Constitution of Zambia Act, No. 1 of 1991. Supplement to the Republic of Zambia Government, Gazette dated the 30th August, 1991.
Confessor, Nieves R (1991). "Equality for Women Workers: Some Considerations", *Philippine Labor Review* 15(1).
Conforti, Benedetto (1993). *International Law and the Role of Domestic Legal Systems*. Martinus Nijhoff Publishers.
Conforti, Benedetto and Francioni, Francioni (Eds.) (1997). *Enforcing International Human Rights in Domestic Courts*. Martinus Nijhoff Publishers.
Confusion at ILO? From http://www.hartford-hwp.com/archives/55/293.html (accessed on April 20, 2005).
Constance, Thomas et al. (2007). *The Use of International Labor Law in Domestic Courts: Theory, Recent Jurisprudence, and Practical Implications*. See http://training.itcilo.it/ils/ils_judges/training_materials/english/Article%20Beaudonnet,%20Oelz,%20Thomas.pdf (accessed on Oct 30, 2007).
Convention on the Elimination of All Forms of Discrimination against Women, GA Res. 34/180, UN GAOR, 34th Sess. (Supp. No. 46), U.N. Doc. A/34/46, (1982) Can. T.S. 1982 No. 31.
Cook, AH (1975). "Equal Pay: Where is It?" *Industrial Relations* 14(2): 158–177.
Corley, Mary C. & Mauksch, Hans O (1987). "Registered Nurses, Gender and Commitment", in Anne Statham and et al. (Eds.), *The Worth of Women's Work*, Albany: State University of New York Press.
Cornish, Mary (2006). "Closing Global Gender Pay Gap: Securing Justice for Women's Work", *Comparative Labor Law & Policy* 28(2).
——, (1966). "Employment & Pay Equity in Canada: Success Brings Both Attacks and New Initiatives," *Canada-United States Law Journal* 22:255.
Cornish, Mary et al. (2006). "Securing Gender Justice: Challenges Facing International Labor Law", in John D. R. Craig & S. Michael Lynk, *Globalization and the Future of Labor Law* 377.
Cortis, Natasha (2000). "Gender, Pay Equity and Human Service Work: A New South Wales Case Study", *Australian Journal of Political Science* 35(1): 49–62.
Costello, Cathryn & Davies, Gareth (2006). "The Case Law of the Court of Justice in the Field of Sex Equality since 2000", *Common Market Law Review* 43 (6): 1567–1616.
Côte, Pierre-André (2000). *The Interpretation of Legislation in Canada*, Third Edition Toronto: Carswell.
Côte, Pierre-André & Lassonde, Julie (2007). "Status Report on Pay Equity in Canada", from http://www. nawl.ca (accessed on Oct 30, 2007).
Côte, Roland (2002). "Pay Equity at Last in Quebe?" *Labor Education* 128: 57–60.
Cotter, Anne-Marie (1998). *Gender Justice: Equality in Employment with Regards to Laws and the Courts Including the North American Free Trade Agreement and the European Economic Community Treaty*. Ph. D. Dissertation. Concordia University (Canada) 0228.
Council of Economic Advisers (1998). *Explaining Trends in the Gender Wage Gap*. Washington, D.C: White House.
Council of Europe (1986). *Case Law on the European Social Charter: Supplement no. 1*. Strasbourg: Council of Europe.

——(1987), *Case Law on the European Social Charter: Supplement no. 2.* Strasbourg: Council of Europe.

——(1983), Case *Law on the European Social Charter: Supplement no. 3.* Strasbourg: Council of Europe.

Council of the European Communities, *Council Directive of 10 February 1975* on the approximation of the laws of the Member States relating to the application of the principle of equal pay for men and women (75/117/EEC).

——, *Council Directive of 9 February 1976* on the implementation of the principle of equal treatment for men and women as regards access to employment, vocational training and promotion, and working conditions (76/207/EEC).

Covington, R. N (1988). "Equal Pay Acts: A Survey of Experience under the British and American Statues", *Vanderbilt Journal of Transnational Law* 1(21): 649–730.

Cox, Enid Elaine (1992). *Pay Equity: An Assessment of Equity, Job Satisfaction, and Performance Perceptions (Performance Assessment, Merit Ratings).* ED. D. Dissertation. Gonzaga University 0736.

Crampton, Suzanne M, Hodge, John W & Mishra, John W (1997). "The Equal Pay Act: The First 30 Years", *Public Personnel Management* 26(3): 335–344.

Craver, C. B (2004). "If Women Don't Ask: Implications for Bargaining Encounters, The Equal Pay Act, and Title VII", *Michigan Law Review* 102(6): 1104–1129.

Crosby, Faye J, Williams, Joan C & Biernat, Monica (2004). "The Maternal Wall", *Journal of Social Issues* 60(4): 675–682.

Crossen, Teall (2004). "Multilateral Environment Agreements and the Compliance Continuum", *Georgetown International Environmental Law Review* 16: 473.

Cruz, Hector Bartolomei De La et al. (1996). *The International Labor Organization: the International Standards System and Basic Human Rights.* Oxford: Westview Press.

Cuneo, Carl J (1990). *Pay Equity: the Labor-Feminist Challenge.* Toronto: Oxford University Press.

Cunnison, Sheila (1991). "Equal Value Legislation and the Unions: A Case Study from the UK", *Journal of Gender Studies* 1(1): 12–28.

Curran, Michael R (1996/1997). "On Common Ground: Using Cultural Bias Factors to Deconstruct Asia-Pacific Labor Law", *George Washington Journal of International Law and Economics* 30: 349.

Currie, Janet (1993). *Gender Gaps in Benefits Coverage.* National Bureau of Economic Research Working Paper Series.

Curtin, D (1987). "Labor Law–Equal Pay–Equality's Riddle", *Dublin University Law Journal* 9:132–6.

D'Amato, Anthony (1982). "The Concept of Human Rights in International Law", *Columbia Law Review* 82:1110.

D'Silva, Alan L.W. (1991). "Giving Effect to Human Rights Legislation - A Purposive Approach," *The Windsor Review of Legal And Social Issues* 3:45.

Daly, John L (2001). "Gender Equality Rights versus Traditional Practices: Struggles for Control and Change in Swaziland", *Development Southern Africa* 18(1): 45–56.

David, Rene & Brierley, John (1978). *Major Legal Systems in the World Today* (2nd ed.). London: Stevens & Sons.

De Lange, S. E (2007). Toward Gender Equality: Affirmative Action, Comparable Worth, and the Women's Movement. *New York University Review of Law and Social Change* 31(2):315–60.

Deléchat, Corinne et al. (1996). *Trade, Employment, and Labor Standards: a Study of Core Workers' Rights and International Trade.* Paris: Organization for Economic Co-operation and Development; Washington, DC: OECD Washington.

Department for International Development (2007). *Gender Equality at the Heart of Development-Why the Role of Women is Crucial to Ending Poverty.* See http://www.dfid.gov.uk/pubs/files/gender-equality.pdf (accessed on Dec 30, 2007).

Devine, Philip E (1987). "Comparable Worth", *International Journal of Applied Philosophy* 3: 11–19.

Dickens, Linda (1999). "Beyond the Business Case: a Three-pronged Approach to Equality Action". *Human Resource Management Journal* 9:1.

——, (1993). *Collective Bargaining and the Promotion of Equality: The Case of the United Kingdom. Equality for Women in Employment: An Interdepartmental Project.* Geneva: International Labor Office.

——, (1995). "UK Part-Time Employees and the Law - Recent and Potential Developments", *Gender, Work and Organization* 2(4): 207–215.

Dijkstra, A. Geske & Plantenga, Janneke (Eds.) (1997). *Gender and Economics: A European Perspective.* London and New York: Routledge.

Directorate-General for Employment, Social Affairs and Equal Opportunities, European Union (2005). *General Report on Developments in EU Gender Equality Law*, from http://ec.europa.eu/employment_social/gender_equality/docs/2005/groupexpertleg_general_report_04_05_en.pdf (accessed on Oct 30, 2007).

——, (2006). *Report on Equal Pay*, from http://www.retepariopportunita.it/Rete_Pari_Opportunita/UserFiles/news/equal_pay_report.pdf, (accessed on Oct 30, 2007).

Discrimination Act 1991. Australian Capital Territory, Australia.

Does Japan's Government Continue to Reject ILO Recommendations, from http://www.japan-press.co.jp/2311/nov26.html (accessed on April 20, 2005).

Donnelly, Jack (1986). "International Human Rights: A Regime Analysis", *International Organization* 40: 599.

Doumbia, Saliha & Meurs, Dominique (2003). "Gender Equality at Work in Sub-Saharan Africa: a Case Study of Mali's Modern Sector", *International Labor Review* 142 (3): 295–316.

Downs, George W, David M. Rocke, & Barsoom, Peter N (1996). "Is the Good News About Compliance Good News About Cooperation?" *International Organization* 50: 379.

Downs, George W, Danish, Kyle W & Barsoom, Peter N (2000). "The Transformational Model of International Regime Design: Triumph of Hope or Experience", *Columbia Journal of Transnational Law* 38: 465.

Doyle, W. E (2005). "Implications of Smith v. City of Jackson on Equal Pay Act Claims and Sex-Based Pay Discrimination Claims under Title VII", *the Labor Lawyer* 21(2):183–98.

Dresang, D. L., et al. (1985). "Comparable Worth: Defensive Strategies vs. Corrective Actions", *Wisconsin Bar Bulletin* 58: 8–9.

Du, Plessis Novitz R & Jaber, N (1990). "Pay Equity, the 'Free' Market and State Intervention", *New Zealand Journal of Industrial Relations* 15(3): 251–262.

Drzemczewski, Andrew (1988). *The European Human Rights Convention in Domestic Law: A Comparative Study.* New York: Clarendon Press.

Dwasi, Jane (1999). "Kenya: A Study in International Labor Standards and Their Effect on Working Women in Developing Countries: The Case for Integration of Enforcement Issues in the World Bank's Policies", *Wisconsin International Law Journal* 17: 347.

Edwards, Paul & Elger, Tony (Eds.) (2000). *International and Comparative Industrial Relations: The Global Economy, National States, and the Regulation of Labor.* New York: Continuum.

Edwing, K. D et al. (Eds.) (1994). *Human Rights and Labor Law: Essays for Paul O'Higgins.* New York, N.Y.: Mansell.

Ehrenberg, Daniel S (1996). "From Intention to Action: An ILO- GATT /WTO Enforcement Regime for International Labor Rights", in Lance A. Compa & Stephen F. Diamond. (Ed.). *Human Rights, Labor Rights, and International Trade: law and Policy Perspectives.* Philadelphia: University of Pennsylvania Press.

Elliott, Kimberly Ann (2000). "The ILO and Enforcement of Core Labor Standards", *International Economics Policy Briefs* 00–6: 1–7.

Elliott, Kimberly Ann et al. (2003). *Can Labor Standards Improve under Globalization?* Washington, DC: Institute for International Economics.

Elliott, Kimberly Ann and Freeman, Richard B (2003). *Can Labor Standards Improve Under Globalization?* Washington, DC: Institute for International Economics.

Ellis, Evelyn (1998). *EC Sex Equality Law*. Oxford: Clarendon Press.

Employment Act 1989 (Chapter 38). Her Majesty's Stationery Office, London.

Employment (Amendment)(No. 2) Regulations, 1990. Statutory Instrument No. 61 of 1990.Government of Zambia.

Employment Equity Act 1990. No. 61. New Zealand.

Employment (Miscellaneous Provisions) (Northern Ireland) Order 1990. No. 246 (N.I. 2).

Employment Standards Act 1987. Ch. E110. Re-enacted Statutes of Manitoba. Vol. II, Manitoba, Canada 1987.

England, Paula (1992). *Comparable Worth: Theories and Evidence*. Hawthorne, New York.: Aldine de Gruyter.

England, Paula (1999). "The Case for Comparable Worth", *Quarterly Review of Economics and Finance* 39: 743–755.

Ephron, SH (1986). "Equal Pay Guarantee in the EEC", *Comparative Labor Law Journal* 7(2): 197–209.

Epstein, Richard A (1993). "Some Reflections on the Gender Gap in Employment", *Georgetown Law Journal*, 82:75.

Equal Opportunities Commission of UK, Code of Practice on Equal Pay, from http://www.equalityhumanrights.com/Documents/Welsh%20language%20publications/Comisiwn%20Cyfle%20Cyfartal/Gender%20Code%20of%20practice%20on%20equal%20pay.pdf (accessed on Oct 30, 2007).

——, (1989). *Equal Pay: Making it Work; Review of the Equal Pay Legislation: Consultative Document*. London: H. M. S. O.

——, (2003). *Equal Pay Review in Practice*. Manchester: EOC.

——, (2005). *Equal Pay Reviews Survey 2005*. Manchester: EOC.

Equal Opportunity Act 1984. No. 95 of 1984. South Australia, Australia.

Equal Pay Act 1970 (Chapter 41). Her Majesty's Stationery Office, London.

Equal Pay Act 1972. No. 118. New Zealand.

Equal Pay Act 1972. No. 118. R.S. Vol. 18. Reprinted Act with Amendments Incorporated.Reprinted as on 1 March 1986. New Zealand.

Equal Pay Act (Northern Ireland) 1970. C. 32 (N.I).

Equal Pay Act of 1963 amends the Fair Labor Standards Act (FLSA), by adding section 206*(d)* to the FLSA. Title 29 – Labor. United States.

Equal Pay Act – Part 1620. Chapter XIV – Equal Employment Opportunity Commission. Labor -code of federal regulations. Containing a Codification of Documents of General Applicability and Future Effect. Revised as of July 1, 1992. Published by the Office of the Federal Register National Archives and Records Administration. Washington 1992.

Equal Pay Amendment Act 1991. No. 25. New Zealand.

Equal Pay (Amendment) Regulations 1983. (S.I. No. 1794 of 1983). Her Majesty's Stationery Office, London.

Equal Pay (Amendment) Regulations (Northern Ireland) 1984.

Equal Remuneration Act, 1976. No. 25 of 1976. A Manual of Labor Laws by Jagdish Lal. Law Publishers (India) Private Ltd. 12th Edition, Vol. I, 1990 India.

Equal Remuneration (Amendment) Act, 1987. No. 49 of 1987. The Gazette of India, Extraordinary, Part II, Section I, India.

European Commission (1996). *A Code of Practice on the Implementation of Equal Pay for Work of Equal Value for Men and Women*. Brussels: Office for Office Publications of the European Communities.

——, (2006). *Equality for Women and Men: European Community Acts*. Luxembourg: Office for Official Publications of the European Communities.

——, (2000). *Gender Equality in the European Union: Examples of Good Practices (1996–2000)*. Luxembourg: Office for Official Publications of the European Communities.

——, (2007). *Equal Pay: Exchange of Good Practices*. Luxembourg: Office for Official Publications of the European Communities.
European Economic Community (1957), *the Treaty of Rome*.
Evans, Patricia M. & Wekerle, Gerda R (Eds.) (1997). *Women & the Canadian Welfare State: Challenges & Change*. Toronto: University of Toronto Press.
Eyraud, F (1993). "Equal Pay and the Value of Work in Industrialized Countries", *International Labor Review* 132(1): 33–48.
Eyraud, F et al. (1993). *Equal Pay Protection in Industrialized Economies: In Search of Greater Effectiveness*. Geneva: International Labor Office.
Falk, Richard (2000). *Human Rights Horizons*. New York: Routledge.
——, (1964). "On Identifying and Solving the Problem of Compliance with International Law", *American Society of International Law Proceedings* 58:1.
Farrell, Warren (2005). *Why Men Earn More: the Startling Truth Behind the Pay Gap– and What Women Can Do About It*. New York: American Management Association.
Fieldes, Diane (2002). *'Some are more Equal Than Others': Australian Trade Union Campaigns for Equal Pay, 1968–1975*. Ph. D. Dissertation. University of New South Wales (Australia) 0423.
Fields, Robin (2006). *Increasing Inequities at Work: As China Enters New Prosperity, Past Efforts to Equalize Women and Men Have Been Overshadowed by a Growing Income Gap*. From HTTP://WWW.LATIMES.COM/BUSINESS/LA-FI -CHIWOMEN25NOV25,1,6453650.STORY?PAGE=1&CTRACK=1&CSET=TRUE (accessed on Oct 29, 2006).
Figart, Deborah M (2001). "Wage-Setting under Fordism: The Rise of Job Evaluation and the Idealogy of Equal Pay", *Review of Political Economy* 13(4): 405–25.
——, (2001). "Equal Pay for Equal Work: The Role of Job Evaluation in an Evolving Social Norm", *Journal of Economic Issues* 34(1): 1–19.
——, (1997). "Gender as More Than a Dummy Variable: Feminist Approaches to Discrimination", *Review of Social Economy* 55(1): 1–32.
Fillmore, Catherine J (1990). "Gender Differences in Earnings: A Re-Analysis and Prognosis for Canadian Women", *Canadian Journal of Sociology* 15(3): 275–299.
Filmer, Deon, Walle, Dominique Vande & Grosh, Margaret (1999). *Pay and Grade Differentials at the World Bank*. The World Bank, Policy Research Working Paper Series: 1912.
Finnemore, Martha (1996). *National Interests in International Society*. Ithaca: Cornell University Press.
Fischel, D. R., et al. (1986). "Comparable Worth and Discrimination in Labor Markets", *The University of Chicago Law Review* 53: 891–918.
Fisher, Roger (1981). *Improving Compliance with International Law*. Charlottesville: University Press of Virginia.
Fitzpatrick, R. B (1987). "European Women Entitled to Equal Pay for Work of Equal Value", *Federal Bar News & Journal* 34: 384–388.
Flax, Jane (1981). "A Materialist Theory of Women's Status", *Psychology of Women Quarterly* 6(1): 123–136.
Florini, Ann (1996). "The Evolution of International Norms", *International Studies Quarterly* 40: 363.
Fogel, W (1984). Equal Pay Act: Implications for Comparable Worth. New York: Praeger.
Fogel, W (1986). "Intentional Sex-based Pay Discrimination: Can it Be Proven?" *Labor Law Journal* 37: 291–299.
Foley, Conor (2000). *Global Trade, Labor and Human Rights*. London: Amnesty International United Kingdom.
Fonda, N., Glucklich, P., Goodman, J. & Morgan, J. (1979). "Job Evaluation without Sex Discrimination", *Personnel Management* (February): 34–37.
Fong, M. S (1976). "The Early Rhetoric of Women's Liberation: Implications for Zero Population Growth", *Journal of Marriage and the Family* 38(1): 127–140.

Foote, Daniel H. (1996). "Judicial Creation of Norms in Japanese Labor Law: Activism in the Service of —Stability", *UCLA Law Review* 43: 635.

Forsythe, David (1993). *Human Rights and Peace: International and National Dimensions*. Lincoln: University of Nebraska Press.

Fox, Hazel & Meyer, Michael (Eds.) (1993). *Armed Conflict and the New Law-Effecting Compliance*. London: British Institute of International and Comparative Law.

Francis, Becky (2005). *Gender Equality in Work Experience Placements for Young People*. Manchester: EOC.

Franck, Thomas M (1995). *Fairness in International Law and Institutions*. Oxford: Clarendon Press.

Franklin, R. J (2001). "America's Ambiguity towards Equal Pay for Women". Southern California Review of Law and Women's Studies 11(1): 233–81.

Freedom of Association and Collective Bargaining: General Survey by the Committee of Experts on the Application of Conventions and Recommendations, Report of the Committee of Experts, International Labor Conference, 69th Sess. (1983).

Friesen, Jane (1993). "Alternative Economic Perspective on the Use of Labor Market Policies to Redress the Gender Gap in Compensation", *Georgetown Law Journal* 82: 31.

Frischmann, Brett (2003). "A Dynamic Institutional Theory of International Law", *Buffalo Law Review* 51: 679.

Frundt, Henry J (1998). *Trade Conditions and Labor Rights: U.S. Initiatives, Dominican and Central American Responses*. Gainesville: University Press of Florida.

Fudge, Judy & MdDermott, Patricia (Eds.) (1991). *Just Wages: A Feminist Assessment of Pay Equity*. Toronto: University of Toronto Press.

Gaal, J., et al. (2002). "Gender-based Pay Disparities in Intercollegiate Coaching: The Legal Issues", *The Journal of College and University Law* 28(3): 519–68.

Galenson, Walter (1981). *The International Labor Organization: An American View*. Wisconsin: University of Wisconsin Press.

"Gender-based Wage Discrimination and the Bennett Amendment: County of Washington v. Gunther {101 S. Ct. 2242}", *Brigham Young University Law Review* v. 1982 (1982): 401–15.

George, Alexander L, & McKeown, Timothy J (1985). "Case Studies and Theories of Organizational Decision-making", *Advances in Information Processing in Organizations* 2: 21.

Gerards, J (2004). "Intensity of Judicial Review in Equal Treatment Cases", *Netherlands International Law Review* 16(51): 135–183.

Gerry, C. J., Kim, B. Y et Li, C. A (2004). "The Gender Wage Gap and Wage Arrears in Russia: Evidence from the RLMS. *Journal of Population Economics* 17(2): 267.

Ghebali, Victor-Yves (1989). *The International Labor Organization: a Case Study on the Evolution of U.N. Specialized Agencies*. Dordrecht, Boston & London: Martinus Nijhoff Publishers.

Giampetro-Meyer, A. M (2000). "Recognizing and Remedying Individual and Institutional Gender-based Wage Discrimination in Sport". *American Business Law Journal* 37(2): 343–86.

Giampetro-Meyer, A. M (1994). "Resurrecting Comparable Worth as a Remedy for Gender-based Wage Discrimination", *Southwestern University Law Review* 23: 225–251.

Giapponi, Catherine C. & McEvoy, Sharlene A. (2005). "The Legal, Ethical, And Strategic Implications Of Gender Discrimination In Compensation: Can The Fair Pay Act Succeed Where The Equal Pay Act Has Failed?" *Journal of Individual Employment Rights* 12(2): 137–150.

Giles, Wenona (1992). "Gender Inequality and Resistance: The Case of Portuguese Women in London", *Anthropological Quarterly* 65(2): 67–79.

Ginsburg, Tom & Adams, Richard (2004). "Adjudicating in Anarchy: An Expressive Theory of International Dispute Resolution", *William and Mary Law Review* 45:1229.

Godbey, K. L (1988/1989). "Comparable Worth and its Relevance to Nursing", *University of Florida Journal of Law and Public Policy* 2: 107–124.

Goldhar, Revital (2004). *Restructuring Pay Equity in the Era of the New Economy.* L.L.M Thesis. University of Toronto (Canada) 0779.

Goldin, Claudia (1985). "Understanding the Gender Gap", *New Perspectives* 17: 9–13.

Goldman, Frances Lee (1996). *Comparable Worth: Agenda Setting and Policy Adoption. Winners and Losers.* Ph. D. Dissertation. State University of New York at Binghamton 0792.

Goldsmith, Jack (2000). "Sovereignty, International Relations Theory, and International Law", *Stanford Law Review* 52: 959.

Goldsmith, Jack & Posner, Eric A (2003). "International Agreements: A Rational Choice Approach", *Virginia Journal of International Law* 44: 113.

——, (2005). *The Limits of International Law.* New York: Oxford University Press.

——, (1999). "A Theory of Customary International Law", *University of Chicago Law Review* 66: 1113.

Goldstein, D. H (1995). "Sex-based Wage Discrimination: Recovery under the Equal Pay Act, Title VII, or both", *The Alabama Lawyer* 56: 294–301.

Goodman, Ryan & Jinks, Derek (2004). "How to Influence States: Socialization and International Human Rights Law", *Duke Law Journal* 54:1.

——, (2002). "Measuring the Effects of Human Rights Treaties", *European Journal of International Law* 13: 171.

Gottfried, Heidi, & Reese, Laura (2004). *Equity in the Workplace: Gendering Workplace Policy Analysis.* New York: Lexington Books.

Gradin, Carlos et al. (2006). *Poverty and Women's Labor Market Activity: the Role of Gender Wage Discrimination in the EU.* Society for the Study of Economic Inequality Working Paper Series, from http://www.ecineq.org/milano/WP/ECINEQ2006-40 .pdf (accessed on Oct 30, 2007).

Gray, Witmore. (Ed.) (1979). *Current Studies in Japanese Law.* Ann Arbor: University of Michigan Press.

Green, Carole & Ferber, Marianne A (2005). "Do Detailed Work Histories Help to Explain Gender and Race/Ethnic Wage Differentials?" *Review of Social Economy* LXIII (1): 55.

Greenlaw, Paul S & Kohl, John P (1995). "The Equal Pay Act: Responsibilities and Rights", *Employee Responsibilities and Rights Journal* 8(4): 295–307.

Greenlaw, Paul S & Lee, Robert D (1993). "Three Decades of Experience with the Equal Pay Act", *Review of Public Personnel Administration* 13: 43–58.

Gregory, Charles Oscar (1979). *Labor and the Law.* New York: Norton.

Gregory, Jeanne (1992). "Equal Pay for Work of Equal Value: The Strengths and Weaknesses of Legislation", *Work, Employment & Society* 6: 461.

Gregory, Jeanne (1996). "Dynamite or Damp Squib? – An Assessment of *Equal* Value Law", *International Journal of Discrimination and the Law* 1 (4): 313–333.

Gregory, Jeanne etc (Eds.) (1999). *Women, Work, and Inequality: The Challenge of Equal Pay in a Deregulated Labor Market.* New York: St. Martin's Press.

Gregory, R. G & Ho, V (1985). *Equal Pay and Comparable Worth: What can the U.S. Learn from the Australian Experience?* Canberra: Australian National University Press.

Greven, Thomas (2003). *Clash of Globalizations? : the Politics of International Labor Rights in the United States.* Frankfurt am Main; New York: Peter Lang.

——, (1982). "Equal Pay and Sex Discrimination: Why Women Are Giving up the Fight", *Feminist Review* 10: 75–89.

Grimshaw, Damian & Miozzo, Marcela (2003). *Minimum Wages and Pay Equity in Latin America.* Geneva: International Labor Office.

Grint, Keith (1988). "Women and Equality: The Acquisition of Equal Pay in the Post Office 1870–1961", *Sociology* 22(1): 87–108.

Gross, James (Ed.) (2003). *Workers' Rights as Human Rights*. Ithaca: Cornell University Press.

Gunderson, Morley (1994). *Comparable Worth and Gender Discrimination: an International Perspective*. Geneva: International Labor Office.

—, (1994). "Pay and Employment Equity in the United States and Canada", *International Journal of Manpower* 15(7): 26–43.

—, (1991). "Equal Pay for Work of Equal Value: Canada's Experience", *Advances in Industrial and Labor Relations* 5: 151–168.

Gupta, Nabanita Datta & Rothstein, Donna (2005). "The Impact of Worker and Establishment-level Characteristics on Male-Female Wage Differentials: Evidence from Danish Matched Employee-Employer Data", *Labor* 19(1): 1–34.

Guzman, Andrew T (2001). *International Law: A Compliance Based Theory*. Boalt Working Papers in Public Law. Paper 84. See http://repositories.cdlib.org/boaltwp/84 (accessed on Dec 30, 2007).

Haas, Linda (2003). "Parental Leave and Gender Equality: Lessons from the European Union", *Review of Policy Research* 20(1): 89–114.

Hadfield, Gillian K (1993). "Households at Work: Beyond Labor Market Policies to Remedy the Gender Gap", *Georgetown Law Journal* 82: 89.

Hakim, Catherine (2003). "The Search for Equality", *Work and Occupations* 30(4): 401–411.

Hallock, Margaret (2000). "Pay Equity: What is the Best Union Strategy?" *Labor Studies Journal* 25(1): 27–44.

—, (1999). "Pay Equity: The Promise and Practice in North America", *Labor & Industry* 10: 53.

Hanami, Tadashi (1981). "The Influence of ILO Standards on Law and Practice in Japan". *International Labor Review* 765.

Handman, Suzanne and Karen Jensen (1999). "Pay Equity in Canada: An Overview," *Canadian Labor & Employment Law Journal* 7: 65.

Hansson, Göte (1983). *Social Clauses and International Trade: an Economic Analysis of Labor Standards in Trade Policy*. London: Croom Helm; New York: St. Martin's Press.

Hardy, S (2002). *Small Step or Giant Leap? Towards Gender Equality at Work*. London: The Work Foundation.

Harrod, Jeffrey et al. (Eds.) (2002). *Global Unions?: Theory and Strategies of Organized Labor in the Global Political Economy*. London & New York: Routledge.

Hart, HLA (1994). "International Law", in *the Concept of Law*. Oxford: Clarendon Press.

Hart, Susan M (2002). "The Pay Equity Bargaining Process in Newfoundland: Understanding Cooperation and Conflict by Incorporating Gender and Class", *Gender, Work and Organization* 9(4): 355–371.

Hartmann, H. & Treimann, D. (1983). "Notes on the NAS Study of Equal Pay for Jobs of Equal Value", *Public Personnel Management* (Winter): 404–417.

Hathaway, Oona A (2002). "Do Human Rights Treaties Make a Difference?" *Yale Law Journal* 111: 1935.

Hathaway, Oona A (2005). "Between Power and Principle: An Integrated Theory of International Law", *University of Chicago Law Review* 71(2): 469–536.

Hatt, Sue (1996). *Gender, Work and Labor Markets*. New York: Palgrave Macmillan.

Heather, Joshi & Marie-Louise, Newell (2000). *Pay Differences between Men and Women: Longitudinal Evidence from the 1946 Birth Cohort*. CEPR Discussion Papers: 156 1987.

Heaton, Norma et al. (1997). "'The Differences between Women are More Marginal'... Catholic and Protestant Women in the Northern Ireland Labor Market", *Work, Employment and Society* 11 (2): 237–261.

Heery, Edmund (2006). "Equality Bargaining: Where, Who, Why?" *Gender, Work and Organization* 13(6): 522–542.

Heide, Ingeborg (2004). "Sex Equality and Social Security: Selected Rulings of the European Court of Justice", *International Labor Review* 143(4): 299–339.

—, (1999). "Supranational Action against Sex Discrimination: Equal Pay and Equal Treatment in the European Union", *International Labor Review* 138(4): 381–410.

Henderson, James P (1992). "Equal Pay vs. Equal Job Opportunity for Women: The Debate in Great Britain from 1891 to 1923", *International Journal of Social Economics* 19: 298–316.

Henkin, Louis (1967). *How Nations Behave*. New York: Columbia University Press.

Hepple, B. A (1984). *Equal Pay and the Industrial Tribunals*. London: Sweet and Maxwell.

—, (Ed.) (2002). *Social and Labor Rights in a Global Context: International and Comparative Perspectives*. Cambridge & New York: Cambridge University Press.

Heyns, C. H (2002). *The Impact of the United Nations Human Rights Treaties on the Domestic Level*. The Hague; New York: Kluwer Law International.

Hertwig, Kim (1999). "Pay Equity Legislation in Canada: A Study of the Public Service of Canada Case", *Canadian Woman Studies* 19(1–2): 186–193.

Hervey, Tamara K (2003). *Economic and Social Rights under the EU Charter of Fundamental Rights: a Legal Perspective*. Oxford & Portland, Oregon: Hart.

Heyns, C. H (2002). *The Impact of the United Nations Human Rights Treaties on the Domestic Level*. Hague & New York: Kluwer Law International.

Higgin, Rosalyn (1994). *Problems and Process-International Law and How We Use it*. Oxford: Clarendon Press.

Hill, Judith M (1987). "Pay Equity", *International Journal of Applied Philosophy* 3: 1–9.

Hlongwane, Nomagugu (2004). *Commentary on South Africa's Position Regarding Equal Pay for Work of Equal Value: a Comparative Perspective*. L.L.M Thesis. University of The Western Cape.

Ho, Daniel E (2002). "Compliance and International Soft Law: Why Do Countries Implement the Basle Accord?" *Journal of International Economic Law* 5: 647.

Ho, Virginia Harper (2003). *Labor Dispute Resolution in China: Implications for Labor Rights and Legal Reform*. Berkeley, Calif.: Institute of East Asian Studies, University of California - Berkeley.

Hodges-Aeberhard, Jane (1999). "Affirmative Action in Employment: Recent Court Approaches to a Difficult Concept", *International Labor Review* 138(3): 247–272.

Hoffman, Stanley (1984). "The Problem of Intervention", in H. Bull (Ed.), *Intervention in World Politics*. New York: Oxford University Press.

Holzhauer, J. D 1986). "The Economic Possibilities of Comparable Worth", *The University of Chicago Law Review* 53: 919–33.

Honoree, Andre L. & Terpstra, David E (2005). "Employees' Responses to Merit Pay Inequity", *Compensation and Benefits Review* 37(1): 51–58.

Horrigan, J., et al.(1988). "Comparable Worth: Public Sector Unions and Employers Provide a Model for Implementing Pay Equity", *Labor Law Journal* 39: 704–11.

Hoskyns, Catherine (1996). *Integrating Gender: Women, Law and Politics in the European Union*. London: Verso.

Huang, Peter H (2002). "International Law and Emotional Rational Choice", *Journal of Legal Studies* 31: 237.

Hughes, Helen (1998). "Equal Pay for Work of Equal Value: Moving toward, or Away from, Wage Justice for Women?" *Policy* 14(3): 29–34.

Hum, D (1987). "Fair Wages in the Republic: An Essay on Equal Pay Legislation for the Private Sector", *Manitoba Law Journal* 16: 203–19.

Human Rights Act 1984. Ch. 22. Statutes of the Province of British Colombia. Victoria, Canada1985.

Human Rights Act 1993. No. 82. New Zealand.

Human Rights Commission Act 1977. No. 49. New Zealand.

Human Rights Watch (2001). *Trading Away rights: the Unfulfilled Promise of NAFTA's Labor Side Agreement*. New York: Human Rights Watch.

Humphreys, Brad R (2000). "Equal Pay on the Hardwood: The Earnings Gap between Male and Female NCAA Division I Basketball Coaches", *Journal of Sports Economics* 1(3): 299–307.

Hunt, M (1997). *Using Human Rights Law in English Courts*. Oxford: Hart Publishing.

Hunt, Audrey (1988). *Women and Paid Work: Issues of Equality*. London: Macmillan.

Hungtington, Samuel (1989). "American Ideas versus American Institutions", in G. John Ikenberry (Ed.), *American Foreign Policy: Theoretical Essays*. Glenview: Scott Foresman & Co.

Hunter, Laurie & Rimmer, Sheila (1995). "An Economic Exploration of the UK and Australian Experiences", *Gender, Work and Organization* 2(3): 140–156.

Hunter, Rosemary (1993). "A Feminist Response to the Gender Gap in Compensation Symposium", *Georgetown Law Journal* 82:147.

Hurd, Ian (1999). "Legitimacy and Authority in International Politics", *International Organization* 53: 379.

Hutchinson, T. N (1996). "The Fair Pay Act of 1994", *Indiana Law Review* 29: 621–46.

Hutner, Frances (Ed.) (1986). *Equal Pay for Comparable Worth: the Working Woman's Issue of the Eighties*. New York: Praeger.

Hyman P. (1993). "Equal Pay for Women after the Employment Contracts Act: Legislation and Practice- the Emperor with No Clothes?" *New Zealand Journal of Industrial Relations* 18(1): 44–57.

——, (1988). "Equal Pay for Work of Equal Value: Job Evaluation Issues", New *Zealand Journal of Industrial Relations* 13(3): 237–255.

Hutchison, Harry G (2000). "The Semiotics of Labor Law, Trade Unions and Work in East Asia: International 'Labor Standard' in the Mirror of Culture", *Emory International Law Review* 14:1451.

ILO (2004). *A Fair Globalization: Creating Opportunities for All*. Geneva: International Labor Office.

——, (2005). *Decent Work in Asia: Reporting on Results 2001–2004*. From www.ilo.org/public/english/region/asro/bangkok/14tharm/index_arm.htm (accessed on Dec 30, 2007).

——, (2007). *Equality at Work: Tackling the Challenges: Global Report under the Follow-up to the ILO Declaration on Fundamental Principles and Rights at Work (Part B)*. Geneva: International Labor Office.

——, (2004). *Gender Equality and Decent Work: Good Practices at the Workplace*. Geneva: International Labor Office.

——, (2006). *Gender Equality and Decent Work: Selected ILO Conventions and Recommendations Promoting Gender Equality*. Geneva: International Labor Office.

——, (2006). *Gender Equality in the World of Work: The Experience of Conducting Gender Training for Journalists*. Moscow: International Labor Office.

——, (2004). *Gender Equality through Collective Bargaining*. Jakarta: International Labor Office.

——, (2005). *ILO Major Activities in Japan in 2000: In Partnership With ILO Constituents*, from http://www.ilo.org/public/english/region/asro/tokyo/newsletr/today2001.htm (accessed on April 20, 2005).

——, (2007). *Protecting Labor Rights as Human Rights: Present and Future of International Supervision*, from http://www.ilo.org/public/english/standards/norm/download/resources/colloquium80ceacr.pdf. (accessed on Sep 10, 2007).

——, (2003). *Time For Equality at Work: Global Report Under the Follow-up to the ILO Declaration on Fundamental Principles and Rights at Work* (International Labor Conference, 91st Sess., Report I(b)).

——, (2003). *World Labor Report*. Geneva: International Labor Office.

——, (1989). *268th Report of the Committee on Freedom of Association*, Case No 1500 (China), GB. 244/5/6,244th Sess. (Geneva, November 1989).

——, (1990). 270th Report of the Committee on Freedom of Association, GB. 245/5/8, 245th Sess. (Geneva, February-March 1990).

——, (1991). *279th Report of the Committee on Freedom of Association*, GB. 251/8/11, 251st Sess. (Geneva, 11-15 November 1991).
——, (1992). *281st Report of the Committee on Freedom of Association*, GB. 252/9/13, 252nd Sess. (Geneva, 2-6 March 1992).
——, (1993). *286th Report of the Committee on Freedom of Association*, GB. 255/5/11, 255th Session (Geneva, 1-4 march 1993).
——, (1994). *292nd Report of the Committee on Freedom of Association*, GB. 259th sess. (Geneva, March 1994).
——, (1995). *297th Report of the Committee on Freedom of Association*, GB. 262/7/1, 262nd sess. (Geneva, march-April 1995).
——, (1950–1951). *Equal Remuneration for Men and Women Workers for Work of Equal Value. Seventh Item on the Agenda*. Geneva: International Labor Office.
——, (1975). *Equal Remuneration: Summary of Reports on Unratified Conventions and on Recommendations, (article 19 of the Constitution): Third Item on the Agenda, Information and Reports on the Application of Conventions and Recommendations*. Geneva: International Labor Office.
——, (2003). *Fundamental Rights at Work and International Labor Standards*. Geneva: International Labor Office.
"Increasing Protection for Women in the Area of Gender-based Wage Discrimination: County of Washington v. Gunther {101 S. Ct. 2242}", *New England Law Review* v. 17 (1981/1982): 549–578.
Individual's Rights Protection Act. Ch. I-2. Revised Statutes of Alberta. Vol. 3, Edmonton,Canada 1980.
Industrial and Labor Relations Act, No. 27 of 1993. Dated 30 April 1993. Zambia. Labour Law Documents, 1993-ZAM 1.
Industrial Relations Act, 1990. Dated 23 January, 1991. Zambia. Labour Law Documents,1990-ZAM 1.
Industrial Relations Reform Act 1993. No. 98 of 1993. Australia.
Industrial Relations Reform Act 1994. Act No.12 of 1994. Queensland, Australia.
Institute for Labor Studies-Department of Labor and Employment (2000). "Gender Equality at Work: Progress after Beijing and Continuing Challenges", *Philippine Labor Review* 24(1): 15–81.
International Covenant on Civil and Political Rights, GA Res/ 2200A (XXI), 21 UN GAOR, (Supp. No. 16) 52, UN Doc A/6316 (1966), 999 U.N.T.S. 171, Can. T.S. 1976 No. 47.
International Covenant on Economic, Social and Cultural Rights, GA Res. 2200A (XXI), 21 UN GAOR (Supp. No. 16), U.N. Doc. A/6316 (1966), 993 U.N.T.S. 3, Can. T.S. 1976 No. 46.
International Labor Organization, *Convention (No. 111) Concerning Discrimination in Respect of Employment and Occupation*, June 25, 1958, 362 U.N.T.S. 31: 128.
International Labor Organization, *Convention (No. 100) Concerning Equal Remuneration for Men and Women Workers for Work of Equal Value*, (1953) 165 U.N.T.S. 303.
International Labor Organization CEACR and ILCCR's reports (General Surveys, Individual Cases, General Observations, Individual Observations, Direct Requests) on individual ratifying states (164 states in total, as the year of 2007) on the implementation of the ILO Convention No. 100 on Equal Remuneration, 1990–2007.
Isbell, B. T (1996). "Gender Inequality and Wage Differentials between the Sexes: Is It Inevitable or Is There an Answer?" *Washington University Journal of Urban and Contemporary Law* 50: 369–400.
Iwasawa, Yuji (1993). "Implementation of International Trade Agreements in Japan", in *National Constitutions and International Economic Law*, edited by Mehinhard Hilf and Ernst Ulrich Petersmann. Boston, MA: Kluwer Law and Taxation Publishers.
——, (1998). *International Law, Human Rights, and Japanese Law: The Impact of International Law on Japanese law*. Oxford: Clarendon Press.

Iyer, Nitya (2002). *Working Through the Wage Gap: Report of the Task Force on Pay equity* (Commissioned by the British Columbia Government), from http://www.ag.gov.bc.ca/public/working_through_the_wage_gap.pdf (accessed on Sep 10, 2007).

Jackson, Brooks (2000). *Gender Wage Gap Decided by More than Discrimination*. From http://archives.cnn.com/2000/US/05/10/gender.bender/ (accessed on Nov. 6, 2006).

Jackson, Robert (2000). *The Global Covenant*. Oxford: Oxford University Press.

Jacob, Herbert et al. (1996). *Courts, Law, and Politics in Comparative Perspective*. New Haven: Yale University Press.

Jacobson, Harold K (1998). "Conceptual, Methodological and Substantive Issues Entwined in Studying Compliance", *Michigan Journal of International Law* 19: 569.

Jankelson, M (1990). "Remuneration Trends and Issues: Looking Forward, Looking Back", *Asia Pacific HRM* 28(2): 27–43.

Jarman, Jennifer (1994). "Which Way Forward? Assessing the Current Proposals to Amend the British Equal Pay Act", *Work, Employment & Society* 8(2): 243–254.

Jefferson, M (1985). "Equal Pay for Work of Equal Value: A Comment on Hayward versus Cammel Laird", *Industrial Relations Journal* 16(2): 76–80.

Jennings, K., et al. (1986). "A Neglected Consideration in Sex Based Wage Discrimination Cases", *Labor Law Journal* 37: 412–22.

Jewell, N (2002). "Equal Pay Act", *Georgetown Journal of Gender and the Law* 4(1): 625–38.

Jill, Andrews (1994). "National and International Sources of Women's Right to Equal Employment Opportunities: Equality in Law versus Equality in Fact", *Northwestern Journal of International Law and Business* 14: 413.

Johnson, B. S (1998). "Ensuring Equality: Pursuing Implementation of the Equal Pay Principle via the Institutions of the European Union, the North American Agreement on Labor Cooperation, and Corporate Codes of Conduct", *Virginia Journal of International Law* 15(38): 849–876.

Johnston, Alastair Lain (2007). *Social States: China in International Institutions, 1980–2000*. Pinceton: Princeton University Press.

Jones, David R & Makepeace, Gerald H (1996). "Equal Worth, Equal Opportunities: Pay and Promotion in an Internal Labor Market", *Economic Journal* 106(435): 401–09.

Jones, F. L (1983). "Sources of Gender Inequality in Income: What the Australian Census Says", *Social Forces* 62(1): 134–152.

Joy, Lois (2003). "Salaries of Recent Male and Female College Graduates: Educational and Labor Market Effects", *Industrial & Labor Relations Review* 56(4): 606–621.

Joyce, James A (1980). *World Labor Rights and Their Protection*. New York: St. Martin's Press.

Joyner, Christopher C (1998). "Recommended Measures under the Antarctic Treaty: Hardening Compliance with Soft International Law", *Michigan Journal of International Law* 19: 401.

——, (1997). The United Nations and International Law (2nd edition). Cambridge University Press.

Jurajda, Stephan (2003). "Gender Wage Gap and Segregation in Enterprises and the Public Sector in Late Transition Countries". *Journal of Comparative Economics* 31: 199–122.

Juriansz, Russel G (1987). "Anti-Discrimination Law, Part II," *Ottawa Law Review* 19: 667.

Kabeer, Naila (2005). "Gender Equality and Women's Empowerment: A Critical Analysis of the third Millennium Development Goal", *Gender and Development* 13(1): 13–24.

Kahler, Miles (2000). "Conclusion: The Causes and Consequences of Legalization", *International Organization* 54: 661.

Kahne, Hilda & Giele, Janet Z (Eds.) (1992). *Women's Work and Women's Lives: the Continuing Struggle Worldwide*. Boulder: Westview Press.
Kahn, Peggy & Figart, Deborah M (1998). "Reviving Pay Equity: New Strategies for Attacking the Wage Gap", *WorkingUSA* 2(2): 8–17.
Kakuyama, Kazutoshi (1997). "Litigating Sexual Discrimination Employment Cases in Japan: Legal Developments", from http://www.tuj.ac.jp/newsite/main/law/lawresources/TUJonline/SexualDiscrimination/kakuyamasexualdiscrimination.html (accessed on Sep 30, 2007).
Kalet, Joseph E (1994). *Primer on FLSA & Other Wage & Hour Laws*. Washington, D.C.: Bureau of National Affairs.
Kaplan, Gail C (1987–1988). "Pay Equity or Pay Up", *Los Angeles Law Review* 21:305.
Karamessini, Maria & Ioakimoglou, Elias (2007). "Wage Determination and the Gender Pay Gap: A Feminist Political Economy Analysis and Decomposition", *Feminist Economics* 13(1): 31–66.
Kates, Carol A. (1994). "Pay Equity and Wage Justice", *Review of Radical Political Economics* 26: 1–23.
——, (1994). "Pay Equity in Local Government: A Case Study", *Labor Studies Journal* 48–66.
Katz, Katarina (2001). *Gender, Work and Wages in the Soviet Union: A Legacy of Discrimination*. New York: Palgrave.
Kaufman, Bruce E (2004). *The Global Evolution of Industrial Relations: Events, Ideas and the IIRA*. Geneva: International Labor Office.
Kearney, Richard C (2001). *Labor Relations in the Public Sector*. New York: Marcel Dekker.
Keck, Margaret & Sikkink, Kathryn (1998). *Activists beyond Border*. Ithaca: Cornell University Press.
Kelly, Alison et al. (1982). "Gender Roles at Home and School", *British Journal of Sociology of Education* 3(3): 281–295.
Kelly, Claire R (2005). "Enmeshment as a Theory of Compliance", *NYU Journal of International Law and Politics* 37: 303.
——, (2001). "The Value Vacuum: Self-Enforcing Regimes and the Dilution of the Normative Feedback Loop", *Michigan Journal of International Law* 22: 637.
——, (2004). "Realist Theory and Real Constraints", *Virginia Journal of International Law* 44: 545.
Kelly, Rita Mae & Bayes, Jane (1986). "Symposium: Implementing Comparable Worth in the Public Sector: Theory and Practice at the State and Local Level", *Policy Studies Review* 5: 769–870.
Kemp, Alice Abel (1981). *Male-female Earnings Differences in Task Homogeneous Occupations*. Ph. D. Dissertation. University of Georgia 0077.
Kennan, George (1985–1986). "Morality and Foreign Policy", *Foreign Affairs* 64:205.
Kent, Ann (1999). *China, the United Nations, and Human Rights*. Philadelphia: University of Pennsylvania Press.
Keohane, Robert (1992). "Compliance with International Commitments: Politics Within a Framework of Law", *American Society of International Law Proceedings* 86: 176.
——, (1997). "International Relations and International Law: Two Optics", *Harvard Journal of International Law* 38: 487.
Kim, Samul S (1995). "China's Pacific Policy: Reconciling the Irreconcilable", *International Journal* (Summer), 464.
Kainer, Jan Melanie (1996). *Cashing in on Pay Equity? Negotiating Equal Pay in Ontario's Food Retail Sector*. Ph. D. Dissertation. York University (Canada) 0267.
King, Gary, Keohane, Robert & Verba, Sidney (KKV) (1994). *Designing Social Inquiry*. Princeton: Princeton University Press.

King, Mary C. (Ed.) (2001). *Squaring Up: Policy Strategies to Raise Women's Incomes in the United States*. Ann Arbor: University of Michigan Press.

Kingsbury, Benedict (1998). "The Concept of Compliance as a Function of Competing Conceptions of International Law", *Michigan Journal of International Law* 19: 345.

Kirschner, R., et al. (1986). "Narrowing the Gap: The Progress Toward Pay Equity", *Florida State University Law Review* 14: 657–683.

Knapp, Kiyoko Kamio (1999). "Don't Awaken the Sleeping Child: Japan's Gender Equality Law and the Rhetoric of Gradualism". *Columbia Journal of Gender and law* 8: 143.

Knop, Karen (2000). "Here and There: International Law in Domestic Courts", *NYU Journal of International Law and Policy* 32: 501.

Koh, Harold Hongju (1997). "Why Do Nations Obey International Law?" *Yale Law Journal* 106: 2599.

——, (1996). "Transnational Legal Process", *Nebraska Law Review* 75:181.

Koskenniemi, Martii (1990). "The Pull of the Mainstream", *Michigan Law Review* 88: 1947.

Kovach, Kenneth A (1996). "Comparable Worth: The Canadian Legislation", *Business Horizons* 41–46.

Krasner, Stephen D (1993). "Sovereignty, Regimes, and Human Rights", in Volker Rittberger (Ed.), *Regime Theory and International Relations*. Oxford: Clarendon Press.

Kratochwil, Friedrich (1991). *Rules, Norms and Decisions: On the Conditions of Practical and Legal Reasoning in International Relations and Domestic Affairs*. Cambridge University Press.

Ku, Julian G. (2004). "The State of New York Does Exist: How the States Control Compliance with International Law", *North Carolina Law Review* 82: 457.

Kufigwa, Happy (2001). "The Wage Gap Between Men and Women in Botswana's Formal Labor Market", *Journal of African Economies* 10(2): 127–142.

Kumlin, Johanna (2007). "The Sex Wage Gap in Japan and Sweden: The Role of Human Capital, Workplace Sex Composition, and Family Responsibility", *European Sociological Review* 23(2): 203–221.

Labor Code of the German Democratic Republic. Gesetzblatt, Part I, 22 June 1977, No. 18. Legislative Series, 1977-Ger.D.R.1. ILO.

Labor Code. Title IV. Wages. Preliminary Chapter. Equal remuneration for men and women. Legislative Series 1981-Fr.1. ILO. France.

Labor Law in New Zealand. Vol. 2. Hughes, The Law Book Company Limited.

Labor Regulations 1969. Legislative Instrument 632. Dated 15 September 1969. Legislative Series, 1969-Ghana 1, ILO.

Labor Relations Act 1987. No. 77. New Zealand.

Labor Relations Amendment Act (No. 2) 1990. No. 138. New Zealand.

Labor Standards Law of Japan.

Lagerlöf, Nils-Petter (2003). "Gender Equality and Long-run Growth", *Journal of Economic Growth* 8(4): 403–426.

Laky, Teréz (2004). *Gender Equality in Employment in Hungary and in some other Eastern European Countries*. Geneva: UNRISD.

Lander, Deirdre & O'Neill, Graham (1991). "Pay Equity: Apples, Oranges and a Can of Worms", *Asian Pacific Journal of Human Resources* 29: 16–28.

Landy, E A (1966). *The Effectiveness of International Supervision*. London: Stevens.

Larson, C. A (1971). "Equal Pay for Women in the United Kingdom", *International Labor Review* 103(1): 1–11.

Leary, Virginia (1982). *International Labor Conventions and National Law*. Hague: Martinus Nijhoff Publishers.

——, (1997). "Nonbinding Accords in the Field of Labor", in Edith Brown Weiss Ed. *International Compliance with Nonbinding Accords: A Challenge to International Law*. Washington, DC: American Society of International Law.

Leary, Virginia & Daniel Warner (Eds.) (2006). *Social Issues, Globalization and Institutions: Labor Rights and the EU, ILO, OECD and WTO*. Martinus Nijhoff Publishers.

Lee, Young S (1989). "Shaping Judicial Response to Gender Discrimination in Employment Compensation", *Public Administration Review* 49(5): 420–430.

Levine, Linda et al. (2003). *The Male-Female Wage Gap: Background and Analyses*. New York : Novinka Books.

Levine, Marvin J (1997). *Worker Rights and Labor Standards in Asia's Four New Tigers: A Comparative Perspective*. New York: Plenum Press.

Levit, Janet Koven. "The Constitutionalization of Human Rights in Argentina: Problem or Promise?" *Columbia Journal of Transnational Law* 37: 281.

Lewis, Debra J (1988). *Just Give Us the Money: A Discussion of Wage Discrimination and Pay Equity*. Vancouver: Women's Research Centre.

Li, Peter S (1992). "Race and Gender as Bases of Class Fractions and Their Effect", *The Canadian Review of Sociology and Anthropology* 29(4): 488–510.

Liggett, Barbara S (1986). *A Study of Wage Differentials between Females and Males in Administrative Positions in a Michigan University (Compensation, Equity, Equal Pay)*. ED. D. Dissertation. Western Michigan University 0257.

Lips, Hilary M (2003). "The Gender Pay Gap: Concrete Indicator of Women's Progress Toward Equality", *Analyses of Social Issues and Public Policy* 3(1): 87–109.

Liu, A. Y. C (2004). Gender Wage Gap in Vietnam: 1993–1998. *Journal of Comparative Economics* 32(3): 586.

Lo, Vai Io (1999). *Law and Industrial Relations: China and Japan after World War II*. Boston: Kluwer Law International.

Long, Stewart & Gill, Andrew (1989). "The Gender Gap in the Wages of Illegal Aliens", *Social Science Journal* 26: 65–74.

Loudon, J. P., et al. (1986). "Applying Disparate Impact to Title VII Comparable Worth Claims: An Incomparable Task", *Indiana Law Journal* 61:165–87.

Loutfi, Martha Fetherolf (2001). *Women, Gender and Work: What is Equality and How Do We Get There?* Geneva: International Labor Office.

Lovell, Peggy A (2006). "Race, Gender, and Work in Sao Paulo, Brazil, 1960–2000", *Latin American Research Review* 41(3): 63–87.

Luna, G (1990). "Understanding Gender-based Wage Discrimination: Legal Interpretation and Trends of Pay Equity in Higher Education", *Journal of Law & Education* 19: 371–84.

Lyons, Michael & Smith, Meg "*Gender Pay Equity, Wage Fixation and Workchoices: Forward to the Past?*" from http://www.qwws.org.au/filestore/OWOL%20Papers/PDF/Lyons%20and%20Smith%20FINAL%20-%20DONE.pdf (accessed on Feb 01, 2008).

Ma, Xinxin (2007). "A Comparative Study on Occupational Segregation and Its Impact on Gender Wage Differentials: Based on Micro-data from Household Survey in Japan and China" (in Chinese), *Journal of Chinese Economic Studies* 4(1–2).

Määttä, Paula (1998). *Equal Pay Policies: International Review of Selected Developing and Developed Countries*, from http://www.ilo.org/public/english/dialogue/ifpdial/publ/infocus/equalpay/index.htm (accessed on Dec 30, 2007).

Macklem, Patrick (2002). "Labor Law beyond Borders", *Journal of International Economic Law* 5 (3): 605–645.

MacRae, Heather (2005). *Transforming Gender Policy in Germany? European Gender Directives and Challenges to the Male Breadwinner Policy Path*. Ph. D. Dissertation. Carleton University (Canada) 0040.

Madden, F. J (1986). "The Legal Status of Comparable Worth: A Review of Developments in Minnesota", *Hamline Law Review* 9: 105–137.

Madhuku, L (2001). *Gender Equality in Employment: The Legal Framework in the Case of Zimbabwe*. Harare: International Labor Office.

Madison, Allen D (1997). "The Context of Employment Discrimination in Japan". *University of Detroit Mercy law Review* 74: 187.

Magnusson, Lars etc. (2003). *Equal Pay and Gender Mainstreaming*. Brussels: European Trade Union Institute.

Mahy, Benoît et al. (Eds.) (2006). *Gender Pay Differentials: Cross-national Evidence from Micro-data*. Basingstoke, England; New York: Palgrave Macmillan.

Malarkey, R et al. (1989). "The Socio-legal Impact of Equal Pay Legislation in Ontario, 1946–1979". *Osgoode Hall Law Journal* 27: 295–336.

Malik, K. K (2002). "Equal Pay Act". *Georgetown Journal of Gender and the Law* 3(2): 719–31.

Manning, A (1996). "The Equal Pay Act as an Experiment to Test Theories of the Labor Market", *Economica* 63: 191–212.

Martikainen, Riitta (2000). "Equal Pay through Collective Bargaining? Experience from Finland", *Transfer* 6(2): 227–241.

Maschke, Karen J (Ed.) (1997). *The Employment Context*. New York: Garland Publishing.

Mason, PL (1969). "Equal Pay for Male and Female Workers in Australia", *Personnel Practice Bulletin* 25(3): 171–183.

"'Market Value' as a Factor 'Other Than Sex' in Sex-based Wage Discrimination Claims", *University of Illinois Law Review* 1985: 1027–1257.

Mathys, N. J., et al. (1993). "Is Pay Equity Equitable? A Perspective that Looks Beyond Pay", *Labor Law Journal* 44: 351–60.

Maurer-Fazio, Margaret, Rawski, Thomas G. & Zhang, Wei (1999). "Inequality in the Rewards for Holding up Half the Sky: Gender Wage Gaps in China's Urban Labor Market, 1988–1994", *The China Journal* 41: 55–88.

Mavromaras, Kostas & Rudolph, Helmut (2002). "Occupational Segregation and the Male Female Wage Gap in Germany between 1985 and 1995", *Cahiers Economiques de Bruxelles* 45(2): 71–89.

Maxwell, Joseph A (1996). *Qualitative Research Design*. Thousand Oaks: Sage Publication.

Mazey, Sonia (2001). *Gender Mainstreaming in the EU: Principles and Practice*. London: Kogan Page.

Mazur, Amy G & Zwingel, Susanne (2003). "Comparing Feminist Policy in Politics and at Work in France and Germany: Shared European Union Setting, Divergent National Contexts", *The Review of Policy Research* 20(3): 365–384.

McAdams, Richard H. & Nadler, Janice (2004). *A Third Model of Legal Compliance: Testing for Expressive Effects in a Hawk/Dove Game*. IACM 17th Annual Conference Paper No. P-107.

McCann, Michael W (1994). *Rights at Work: Pay Equity Reform and the Politics of Legal Mobilization*. Chicago, Ill.: University of Chicago Press.

McColgan, Aileen (1998). *Just Wages for Women*. Oxford: Oxford University Press.

McCorquodale, Robert & Fairbrother, Richard (1999). "Globalization and Human Rights", *Human Rights Quarterly* 21(3): 735–766.

McCrudden, C (1986). "Comparable Worth: A Common Dilemma", *The Yale Journal of International Law* 11: 396–436.

——, (1983). "Equal Pay for Work of Equal Value: the Equal Pay (Amendment) Regulations 1983", *Industrial Law Journal* 12(4).

——, (1984). "Equal Pay for Work of Equal Value", *Industrial Law Journal* 13(1): 50–56.

McDermott, P. C (1990). "Pay Equity in Ontario: A Critical Legal Analysis", *Osgoode Hall Law Journal* 28: 381–407.

Mcgavin, PA (1983). "Equal Pay for Women: A Re-assessment of the Australian Experience", *Australian Economic Papers* 22(40): 48–59.

McNally, J. & Shimmin, S. (1984). "Job Evaluation and Equal Pay for Work of Equal Value", *Personnel Review* 13(1): 27–31.

Mehmet, Ozay (1999). Towards *a Fair Global Labor Market: Avoiding a New Slave Trade*. London; New York: Routledge.
Melkas, Helina (1998). *Gender Equality and Occupational Segregation in Nordic Labor Markets*. Geneva: International Labor Office.
Meng, G. (1990). "All the Parts of Comparable Worth", *Personnel Journal* 99–104.
Michael, Robert T et al. (Eds.) (1989). *Pay Equity: Empirical Inquiries*. Washington, D. C.: National Academy Press.
Milgrom, Eva M. Meyersson et al. (2001). "Equal Pay for Equal Work? Evidence from Sweden and a Comparison with Norway and the U. S", *Scandinavian Journal of Economics* 103(4): 559–583.
Milkman, Ruth (1982). "Redefining 'Women's Work': The Sexual Division of Labor in the Auto Industry during World War II", *Feminist Studies* 8(2): 336–372.
Miller, Paul W (1987). "Gender Differences in Observed and Offered Wages in Canada, 1980", *The Canadian Journal of Economics* 20(2): 225–244.
Miller, Steven K (1992). "Remuneration Systems for Labor-intensive Investments: Lessons for Equity and Growth", *International Labor Review* 131(1): 77–94.
Millward, Neil & Woodland, Stephen (1995). "Gender Segregation and Male/Female Wage Differences", *Gender, Work and Organization* 2(3): 125–139.
Minimum Wages and Conditions of Employment (General) Order, 1990. Statutory Instrument No. 106 of 1990. Government of Zambia.
Mishra, L (2000). *Child Labor in India*. New Delhi; New York: Oxford University Press.
Miura, Takao (1999). "Breakup and Privatization of Japan's Gigantic Railway Company and thoroughgoing Discrimination in Employment in the New Companies", 25 *Rodo-Soken Journal*. From http://www.yuiyuidori.net/soken/jour/j_25.html (accessed on April 20. 2005).
Monk-Turner, E. & Turner, C (2004). "The Gender Wage Gap in South Korea: How Much Has Changed in 10 Years?" *Journal of Asian Economics* 15(2): 415.
Moore, Dahlia (1992). *Labor Market Segmentation and Its Implications: Inequality, Deprivation, and Entitlement*. New York: Garland Publishing.
Moore, David H (2003). "A Signaling Theory of Human Rights Compliance", *Northwestern University Law Review* 97: 879.
Moore, John Morton (1999). "Enhancing Compliance with International Law: A Neglected Remedy", *Virginia Journal of International Law* 39: 881.
Moore, S (1995). "'Justice Doesn't Mean a Free Lunch': The Application of the Principle of Equal Pay to Occupational Pension Schemes", *European Law Review* 19–20: 159–177.
Moravcsik, Andrew (1997). "Taking Preferences Seriously: A Liberal Theory of International Politics", *International Organization* 51: 513.
——, (2000). "The Origins of Human Rights Regimes: Democratic Delegation in Postwar Europe", *International Organization* 54: 217.
Morgenthau, Hans (1979). *Human Rights and Foreign Policy*. New York: Council on Religion and International Affairs.
——, (1960). *Politics among Nations: The Struggle for Power and Peace* (3rd ed.) New York: Alfred Knopf.
Morici, Peter (2001). *Labor Standards in the Global Trading System*. Washington, D.C.: Economic Strategy Institute.
Morrell, Judy (2001). *Gender Equality in Pay Practices*. Manchester: EOC.
Mutari, Ellen, Figart, Deborah M. & Power, Marilyn (2001). "Implicit Wage Theories in *Equal Pay* Debates in the United States", *Feminist Economics* 7: 23–52.
Nafziger, James A. R (1969). "The International Labor Organization and Social Change: The Fact-Finding and Conciliation Commission on Freedom of Association", *New York University Journal of International Law and Policy* 1:15.
Nain, Gemma Tang & Bailey, Barbara (2003). *Gender Equality in the Caribbean: Reality or Illusion*. Kingston, Jamaica: UNIFEM Caribbean.

Napier, B (1988). "Equal Value-Another Barrier Falls", *New Law Journal* 138: 500–501.

Narol, M., et al. (1998). "A New Defense to the Old Defenses? The EEOC Equal Pay Act Guidelines", *Marquette Sports Law Journal* 9(1): 175–89.

National Committee on Pay Equity (1987). *Pay Equity: an Issue of Race, Ethnicity and Sex*. Washington, D.C.: National Committee on Pay Equity.

National Research Council (1989). *Pay Equity: Empirical Inquiries*. Washington DC: national Academy Press.

National Women's Consultative Council (1990). *Pay Equity for Women In Australia*. Australian Government Publishing Service, Canberra.

National Women's Law Center (2002). *The Paycheck Fairness Act: Helping to Close the Wage Gap for Women*. See www.nwlc.org/pdf/PayCheckFairnessFeb2002.pdf (accessed on Dec 30, 2007).

Neathey, Fiona et al. (2005). *Equal Pay Reviews in Practice*. Institute for Employment Studies. Working Paper Series. No. 33. Equal Opportunities Commission. Manchester.

Nelson, R (1995). "Law, Markets, and Gender Inequality in Pay", *Berkeley Women's Law Journal* 10: 61–68.

Nelson, Robert L (1999). *Legalizing Gender Inequality: Courts, Markets, and Unequal Pay for Women in the United States*. New York: Cambridge University Press.

Nergaard, Kristine and Soumeli, Eva (2002). *Gender Equal Pay in Europe*. European Foundation for the Improvement of Living and Working Conditions. Dublin.

Nieuwenhuysen, J. P. "Equal Pay for Women in Australia", *International Journal of Social Economics* 1(1): 96–110.

Nolan, Melanie (2003). "The High Tide of a Labor Market System: The Australian Male Breadwinner Model", *Labor and Industry* 13(3): 73–92.

Nussbaum, Martha (1999). "Women and Equality: The Capabilities Approach", *International Labor Review* 138(3): 227–245.

O'Connell, Mary Ellen (1995). "Enforcement and the Success of International Environmental Law", *Indiana Journal of Global Legal Studies* 3: 47.

O'Connell, Mary Ellen (1999). "New International Legal Process", *American Journal of International Law* 93:334.

O'Neill, G., Hartnell, I. & Clark, G. (1988). "Managing Salaried Remuneration: An Overview of Trends and Issues", *Human Resources Management Australia* 26(1): 7–21.

O'Neil, Kate, Balsiger, Jorg & Vandeveer, Stacy D (2004). "Actors, Norms, and Impact: Recent International Cooperation Theory and the Influence of the Agent-Structure Debate", *Annual Review of Political Science* 7: 149–175.

OECD (2007). *Declaration on Policies for the Employment of Women*, see http://webdomino1.oecd.org/horizontal/oecdacts.nsf/Display/16C0D7AF80EB0754C125729B004DB379?OpenDocument (accessed on Sep 10, 2007).

——, (1991). *Equal Pay for Work of Comparable Worth; The Experience of Industrialized Countries*, see http://www.oecd.org/dataoecd/45/56/34806919.pdf (accessed on Dec 30, 2007).

——, (1995). *Trade and Labor Standards: a Review of the Issues*. Paris, France: Organization for Economic Co-operation and Development; Washington, D.C: OECD Publications and Information Centre, distributor.

Ogasawara, Y (1998). *Office Ladies and Salaried Men: Power Gender and Work in Japanese Companies*. Los Angeles: University of California Press.

Olney, Shauna etc (1998). *Gender Equality: A Guide to Collective Bargaining*. Geneva: International Labor Office.

Oostendorp, Remco H (2004). *Globalization and the Gender Wage Gap*. World Bank Policy Research Working Paper Series 3256.

Osborne, RJ (1976). *Equal Pay for Equal Work: A Study of Legislation in the United States, Canada, the United Kingdom, and New Zealand*. London: University Microfilms International.

Oster, Sharon M (1993). "Is There a Policy Problem? The Gender Wage Gap", *Georgetown Law Journal* 82: 109.

Paci, Peirella & Joshi, Heather (1995). "Is Pay Discrimination Against Young Women a Thing of the Past? A Tale of Two Cohorts", *International Journal of Manpower* 16(2): 60–65.

Pae, Mu-gi (1995). *Women's Wages and Employment in Korea*. Seoul, Korea: Seoul National University Press.

Panford, Kwamina (1994). *African Labor Relations and Workers' Rights: Assessing the Role of the International Labor Organization*. Westport, Conn.: Greenwood Press.

Papanek, Hanna (1975). "The Work of Women: Postscript from Mexico City", *Signs* 1(1): 215–226.

Parkinson, Loraine (1989). "Note, Japan's Equal Employment Opportunity Law: An Alternative Approach to Social Change", *Columbia Law Review* 89: 604.

Paternostro, Stefano & Sahn, David (1999). *Wage Determination and Gender Discrimination in a Transition Economy: The Case of Romania*. The World Bank, Policy Research Working Paper Series: 2113.

Patten, T. (1988). *Fair Pay: The Managerial Challenge of Comparable Worth and Job Evaluation*. San Francisco: Jossey-Bass.

Pay Equity, A New Approach to a Fundamental Right: Pay Equity Task Force Final Report (2004), from http://justice.gc.ca/en/payeqsal/6000.html (accessed on Sep 10, 2007).

Pay Equity Act 1984. Acts of the Legislature of Manitoba. Canada 1984.

Pay Equity Act 1989. Ch. P-5.01. Statutes of New Brunswick. Canada 1989.

Pay Equity Act 1988. Ch. 337. Revised Statutes of Nova Scotia. Canada 1989.

Pay Equity Act 1987. Ch. P-7. Revised Statutes of Ontario. Canada 1990.

Pay Equity Act 1988. Ch. P-2. Statutes of Prince Edward Island. Canada 1989.

"Pay Equity or Pay Up: The Inevitable Evolution of Comparable Worth into Employer Liability under Title VII". *Loyola of Los Angeles Law Review* v. 21 (November 1987) p. 305–398.

Pease, Kelly Kate and Forsythe, David P (1993). "Human Rights, Humanitarian Intervention, and World Politics," *Human Rights Quarterly*, 15(2): 290–314.

Pekkanen, Saadia (2005). *International Trade Law in US Courts*, paper presented at the seminar of Center for International Studies, USC.

Perez-Arrieta, A. M (2005). "Defenses to Sex-based Wage Discrimination Claims at Educational Institutions: Exploring 'Equal Work' and 'any Other Factor Other Than Sex' in the Faculty Context". *The Journal of College and University Law* 31(2): 393–415.

Perrons, Diane (2005). "Gender Mainstreaming and Gender Equality in the New (Market) Economy: An Analysis of Contradictions", *Social Politics* 12(3): 389–411.

——, (2000). "Living with Risk: Labor Market Transformation, Employment Policies and Social Reproduction in the UK", *Economic and Industrial Democracy* 21: 283–310.

Peters, J. S (1995). *Women's Rights, Human Rights: International Feminist Perspectives*. London and New York: Routledge.

Petersen, Trond & Saporta, Ishak (2004). "The Opportunity Structure for Discrimination1", *The American Journal of Sociology* 109(4): 852–901.

Pettinger, Mark (2006). *Are Women still Experiencing Gender Discrimination in Income and Employment Positions? Why the Equal Pay Act may not be enough to Close the Pay-gap*. M. A Thesis. Wichita State University 0260.

Pettman, B.O (1974). "Equal Pay and Low Pay in Britain", *International Journal of Social Economics* 1(3): 268–279.

Pettman, B. O (Ed.) (1977). *Equal Pay for Women: Progress and Problems in Seven Countries*. Washington: Hemisphere Pub. Corp.

Pidgeon, Mary Elizabeth (1942). *"Equal Pay" for Women in War Industries*. Washington, U.S: Government Print Office.

Pillay, David (2007). "Equity and the Scope of Judicial Activism", see www.lexisnexis.co.za/.../The%20scope%20of%20Judicial%20activism%20to%20achieve%20EQUITY%203%2007%2003.doc (accessed on Oct 30, 2007).

Pines, Burton Yale (1991). "A Primer for Conservatives", *National Interest* 23:61.

Platt, Lucinda (2006). *Pay Gaps: The Position of Ethnic Minority Women and Men: Moving on Up? -Ethnic Minority Women and Work*. Manchester: EOC.

Plender, R (1982). "Equal Pay for Men and Women: Two Recent Decisions of the European Court", *American Journal of Comparative Law* 30(4).

Pocock, Barbara (1999). "Equal Pay Thirty Years On; the Policy and Practice", *The Australian Economic Review* 32(3): 279–285.

Politakis, George P. (2006). *Protecting Labor Rights as Human Rights: Present and Future of International Supervision*. Proceedings of the International Colloquium on the 80th Anniversary of the ILO Committee of Experts on the Application of Conventions and Recommendations. Geneva: International Labor Office.

Porter, Bruce (2000). "Judging Poverty: Using International Human Rights Law to Refine the Scope of Charter Rights," *Journal of Law and Social Policy* 15:117.

Posner, Eric (2003). "A Theory of the Laws of War", *University of Chicago Law Review* 70: 297.

Posner, Richard A (2002). "Some Economics of International Law: Comment on Conference Papers", *Journal of Legal Studies* 31:321.

Posner, Michael (1994–1995). "Rally Round Human Rights", *Foreign Policy* 97:133.

Prechal, Sacha et al. (1990). *Gender Discrimination Law of the European Community*. Aldershot, Hants, England: Dartmouth; Brookfield, Vt., USA : Gower Pub. Co.

Princen, Sebastiann (2004). "EC Compliance with WTO Law: The Interplay of Law and Politics", *European Journal of International Law* 15: 555–574.

Prior, E. J (1996). "Constitutional Fairness of Fraud on the Constitution? Compensatory Discrimination in India", *Case Western Reserve Journal of International Law* 12(28): 63–99.

Purvis, Nigel (1991). "Critical Legal Studies in Public International Law", *Harvard International Law Journal* 32:81.

Qian, Jieyong (1996). *Gender Wage Differentials in Urban China in the 1990s*. PhD Dissertation. State University of New York at Binghamton 0792.

Quinn, J. M (1994). "Visibility and Value: The Role of Job Evaluation in Assuring Equal Pay for Women", *Law and Policy in International Business* 14(25): 1403–1444.

Rafferty F (1994). "Equal Pay: the Evolutionary Process 1984–1994", *Journal of Industrial Relations* 36(4): 451–490.

——, (1989). "Equal Pay, Past Experience, Future Directions: A Practitioner's Perspective", *Journal of Industrial Relations* 31(4).

——, (1991). "Pay Equity: An Industrial Relations Anomaly?" *Journal of Industrial Relations* 33(1): 3–19.

Ramseyer, J. Mark (1994). "The Puzzling (In)Dependence of Courts: A Comparative Approach", *The Journal of Legal Studies* 23(2): 721.

Ramseyer, J. Mark and Rasmusen, Eric B (2003). "Judicial Independence in a Civil Law Regime: The Evidence from Japan", *The Journal of Law, Economics, and Organization* 13(2): 259.

Ratner, Steven R (2003). "Precommitment Theory and International Law: Starting a Conversation", *Texas Law Review* 81:2055.

Raustiala, Kal (2000). "Compliance & Effectiveness in International Regulatory Cooperation," *Case Western Reserve Journal of International Law* 32: 387.

——, (2002). "The Architecture of International Cooperation: Transgovernmental Networks and the Future of International Law", *Virginia Journal of International Law* 43: 1.

Raustiala, Kal & Anne-Marie Slaughter, Anne-Marie (2002). "International Law, International Relations, and Compliance", in *Handbook of International Relations*. London: Sage.

Rees, Teresa L (1999). *Women and Work: Twenty-five Years of Gender Equality in Wales*. Cardiff: University of Wales Press.
Redmond, Gerry & Kattuman, Paul (2001). "Employment Polarisation and Inequality in the UK and Hungary", *Cambridge Journal of Economics* 25: 467–480.
Reichenberg NE (1986). "Pay Equity in Review", *Public Personnel Management* 15(3): 211–231.
Reilly, Barry & Dutta, Puja Vasudeva (2005). "*The Gender Pay Gap and Trade Liberalization: Evidence for India*", PRUS Working Paper no. 32, see http://www.sussex.ac.uk/Units/PRU/wps/wp32.pdf (accessed on Dec 30, 2007).
Rendel, Margherita (1978). "Legislating for Equal Pay and Opportunity for Women in Britain", *Signs* 3(4): 897–908.
Report of the Committee on Freedom of Association (222d), 66 I. L. O. Off. Bull., Ser., B, No. 1 (1983).
Report of the Fact-Finding and Conciliation Commission on Freedom of Association Concerning Persons Employed in the Public Sector in Japan, 49 I. L. O. Off. Bull.. Spec. Supp. No. 1 (1966).
Report on the Situation of Fundamental Rights in the European Union and Its Member States in 2002. Luxembourg: Office for Official Publications of the European Communities, 2003.
Rhoads, Steven E (1993). *Incomparable Worth, Pay Equity Meets the Market*. New York: Cambridge University Press.
Riach, P.A (1969). "Equal Pay and Equal Opportunity", *Journal of Industrial Relations* 11(2): 99–110.
Ridge, Javan Bennett (1999). *Factors Associated With the Differences in Economic Return of Bachelor-level Education for Men and Women (Gender Differences)*. Ph. D. Dissertation. University of Oregon 0171.
Riggs, P. (1989). "Compensation (Pay and Benefits) in Australia: 1988 in Review", *Asia Pacific HRM*, 27(2): 6–25.
Risse, Thomas & Sikkink, Kathryn (1999). "The Socialization of International Human Rights Norms into Domestic Practices: Introduction", in Thomas Risse et al. (eds). *The Power of Human Rights: International Norms and Domestic Changes*, pp. 1–39. Cambridge, UK: Cambridge University Press.
Risse-Kappen, Thomas (1994). "Ideas Do Not Float Freely: Transnational Coalitions, Domestic Structures, and the End of the Cold War", *International Organization* 48: 185–214.
Roback, Jennifer (1993). "Beyond Equality", *Georgetown Law Journal* 82: 121.
Robinson, Derek (1998). "Differences in Occupational Earnings by Sex", *International Labor Review* 137(1):3–31.
Robinson, Helen (2005). "Regional Evidence on the Effect of the National Minimum Wage on the Gender Pay Gap", *Regional Studies* 39(7): 855–872.
——, (2002). "Wrong Side of the Track? The Impact of the Minimum Wage on Gender Pay Gaps in Britain", *Oxford Bulletin of Economics and Statistics* 64(5): 417–448.
Robinson, O (1975). "Equal Pay and Equality of Opportunity", *International Journal of Social Economics* 2(2): 87–105.
Rodgers, Yana van der Meulen (1999). *A Reversal of Fortune for Korean Women: Explaining 1983's Upward Turn in Relative Earnings*. The World Bank, Policy Research Working Paper Series: 1764.
Rogowski, Ralf et al. (Eds.) (1994). *Reflexive Labor Law: Studies in Industrial Relations and Employment Regulation*. Deventer; Boston: Kluwer Law and Taxation Publishing.
Rood, Max G (1986). *Fifty Years of Labor Law and Social Security: Studies at the Occasion of the Fiftiest Anniversary of the Chair in sociaal recht at the Rijksuniversiteit Leiden, the Netherlands*. Deventer; Boston: Kluwer Law and Taxation Publishers.
Roozendaal, Gerda Van (2002). *Trade Unions and Global Governance: The Debate on a Social Clause*. London; New York: Continuum.

Rosen, Benson (1983). "Compensation, Jobs, and Gender (Attitudes toward Equal Pay for Comparable Work Proposals; Based on a Survey of 900 Harvard Business Review Readers)", *Harvard Business Review* 61: 170.

Rosenberg, Gerald N (1991). *The Hollow Hope*. Chicago: University of Chicago Press.

Rosenfeld, Rachel A & Kalleberg, Arne L (1990). "A Cross-National Comparison of the Gender Gap in Income", *The American Journal of Sociology* 96(1): 69–106.

Rosholm, Michael & Smith, Nina (1996). "The Danish Gender Wage Gap in the 1980s: A Panel Data Study", *Oxford Economic Papers* 48: 254–279.

Roth, Louise Marie (2004). "Engendering Inequality: Processes of Sex-Segregation on Wall Street", *Sociological Forum* 19(2): 203–228.

Rubenstein, Michael (2001). *Equal Pay for Work of Equal Value: The New Regulations and Their Implications*. Salem House Publishers.

Rubery, Jill (1994). "Decentralisation and Individualisation: The Implications for Equal Pay", *Economies et Societes* 28(8): 79–97.

—, (1993). "The Economics of Equal Value", *Labor* 7(3): 117–31.

—, (1998). *Equal Pay in Europe? : Closing the Gender Wage Gap*. New York: St. Martin's Press.

—, (2003). *Pay Equity, Minimum Wage and Equality at Work*. Geneva: International Labor Office.

—, (1992). "Pay, Gender and the Social Dimension to Europe", *British Journal of Industrial Relations* 30(4): 605–21.

Rubery, Jill & Colette Fagen, Colette (1994). "Equal Pay Policy and Wage Regulation Systems in Europe", *Industrial Relations Journal* 25: 281–92.

Rubery, Jill, Grimshaw, Damian & Figueiredo, Hugo (2005). "How to close the Gender Pay Gap in Europe: Towards the Gender Mainstreaming of Pay Policy", *Industrial Relation Journal* 36: 184.

Riccucci, N. M (1988). "Union Liability for Wage Disparities between Women and Men", *University of Detroit Law Review* 65: 379–401.

Rudin, Joel P & Byrd, Kimble (2003). "U.S. Pay Equality Legislation: Sheep in Wolves' Clothing", *Employee Responsibilities and Rights Journal* 15(4): 183–190.

Rummery, Sarah (1992). "The Contribution of Intermittent Labor Force Participation to the Gender Wage Differential", *The Economic Record* 68 (202): 351–364.

Rutherglen, George (1993). "The Theory of Comparable Worth as a Remedy for Discrimination", *Georgetown Law Journal* 82: 135.

Sabates-Wheeler, Rachel & Kabeer, Naila (2003). *Gender Equality and the Extension of Social Protection*. Geneva: International Labor Office.

Sagatun, Inger J (1990). "Gender Discrimination in Criminal Justice: Relevant Law and Future Trends", *Women and Criminal Justice* 2(1): 63–81.

Sallie, Tracey (2004). *Understanding Value and Its Implications for Pay Equity and the Wage Gap: A Federal Government Case Study*. M. A Thesis. Carleton University (Canada) 0040.

Sarfati, Hedva & Bonoli, Giuliano (2002). *Labor Market and Social Protection Reforms in International Perspective: Paralle or Converging Tracks*? Aldershot, England: Ashgate.

Sarver, L. A. B (1995). "Coaching Contracts Take on the Equal Pay Act: Can (and Should) Female Coaches Tie the Score?" *Creighton Law Review* 28: 885–920.

Schatzki, G (1986). "An Observation about Comparable Worth", *University of Puget Sound Law Review* 9: 491–497.

Schlafly, Phyllis (1984). Equal *Pay for Unequal Work: a Conference on Comparable Worth*. Washington, D.C: The Fund.

Schoenbaum, Thomas J. Nakagawa, Junji & Reif, Linda C (1998). *Trilateral Perspectives on International Legal Issues: From Theory into Practice*. Ardsley: Transnational Publishers.

Schwab, Donald P (1985). "Determining the Worth of Work", *Society* 22: 61–7.

Schwartz, Warren F (1993). "Foreword: The Gender Gap in Compensation", *Georgetown Law Journal* 82: 27.

Scott, Robert E, Stephan, Paul B (2004). "Self-Enforcing International Agreements and the Limits of Coercion", *Wisconsin Law Review* 2004: 551.

Semykina, Anastasia & Linz, Susan (2007). *Do Personality Differences Explain the Gender Gap? Evidence from Three Transition Economies.* IPC Working Paper Series No. 51. From http://www.internationalpolicy.umich.edu/Labor%20Conf/AKR_WageGap.pdf (accessed on Dec 30, 2007).

Setear, John K (1996). "An Iterative Perspective on Treaties: A Synthesis of International Relations Theory and International Law", *Harvard International Law Journal* 37: 139.

Servais, Jean-Michel (2005). *International Labor Law.* The Hague: Kluwer Law International ; Frederick, MD: Sold and distributed n North, Central and South America by Aspen Publishers.

Sethuraman, S.V (1998). "*Gender, Informality and Poverty: A Global Review*", see http://www.wiego.org/papers/sethcontents.html (accessed on Dec 30, 2007).

Seventy Years of the All-China Federation of Trade Unions. Beijing: China Worker's Press, July 1995.

Sex Discrimination Act 1984. No. 4 of 1984. Acts of the Parliament/Commonwealth of Australia.

Sex Discrimination Act 1975 (Chapter 65). Her Majesty's Stationery Office, London.

Sex Discrimination Act 1986 (Chapter 59). Her Majesty's Stationery Office, London.

Sex Discrimination Amendment Act 1991. Australia.

Sex Discrimination and other Legislation Amendment Act 1992. No. 179 of 1992. Australia.

Sex Discrimination (Northern Ireland) Order 1976. No. 1042 (N.I. 15).

Sex Discrimination (Northern Ireland) Order 1988. No. 1303 (N.I. 13).

Shapiro, Martin M (1981). *Courts: A Comparative and Political Analysis.* Chicago: University of Chicago Press.

Shattuck, C. A (1985). "Sex-based Wage Discrimination: A Management View", *Denver University Law Review* 62: 393–415.

Shaw, B (1987). "Comparable Worth and Its Prospects: AFSCME v. State of Washington {770 F.2d 1401}", *Labor Law Journal* 38: 100–18.

Shaw, Josephine (1991). "Recent Developments in the Field of Labor Market Equality: Sex Discrimination Law in the Federal Republic of Germany", *Comparative Labor Law Journal* 13(1): 6–14.

Shelton, Dinah (2000). *Commitment and Compliance: The Role of Non-biding Norms in the International Legal System.* Oxford: Oxford University Press.

Shen, Jianming (1999). "The Basis of International Law: Why Nations Observe", *Dickenson Journal of International Law* 17: 287.

Short, Christine (1986). "Equal Pay - What Happened?" *The Journal of Industrial Relations* 28(3): 315–335.

Sikkink, Kathryn (1993). "The Power of Principled Ideas: Human Rights Policies in the United States and Western Europe," in Judith Goldstein and Robert Keohane, (Eds.) *Ideas and Foreign Policy: Beliefs, Institutions, and Political Change.* Ithaca: Cornell University Press.

Simchak, MM (1971). "Equal Pay in the United States", *International Labor Review* 103(6).

Simmons, Beth A (1998). "Compliance with International Agreements", *Annual Review of Political Science* 1: 75–93.

——, (2000). "International Law and International Relations: Scholarship at the Intersection of Principles and Politics", *American Society of International Law Proceedings* 95: 271.

Singh, R. (1994). "Equal Pay for Work of Equal Value: Guidance from the European Court of Justice: A Research Note", *Industrial Relations Journal* 25(2): 150–154.

Slaughter, Anne-Marie (2004). *A New World Order*. Princeton, NJ: Princeton University Press.

—, (1995). "International Law in a World of Liberal States", *European Journal of International Law* 6: 503.

—, (1995). "The Liberal Agenda for Peace: International Relations Theory and the Future of the United Nations", *Transnational Law and Contemporary Problems* 4: 377.

Slaughter, Anne-Marie & Raustiala, Kal (2002). "International Law, International Relations and Compliance", in Carlsnaes and et al. (eds), *Handbook of International Relations*. London: Sage.

Sloane, Peter J (Ed.) (1980). *Women and Low Pay*. London: Macmillan.

—, (1988). "Gender, Pay Equity and Equal Value: A Solution in Search of a Rationale?" *Managerial and Decision Economics* 45–50.

Sloane, P. J & Theodossiou, Ioannis (1994). "A Generalised Lorenz Curve Approach to Explaining the Upward Movement in Women's Relative Earnings in Britain during the 1970s", *Scottish Journal of Political Economy* 41(4): 464–76.

Smeenk, Brian P (1993). "Canada's Pay Equity Experiments: A Difficult Principle to Oppose, Pay Equity Has Become an Attractive, yet Controversial, Political Policy", *HR Magazine* 38: 58–61.

Smith, Harold L (1996). "British Feminism and the Equal Pay Issue in the 1930s", *Women's History Review* 5(1): 97–110.

Smith, SP (1977). *Equal Pay in the Public Sector: Fact or Fantasy*. Princeton: Princeton University Press.

Smithson, Janet and etc. (2004). "Flexible Working and the Gender Pay Gap in the Accountancy Profession", *Work, Employment and Society* 18(1): 115–135.

Snell, M.W, Glucklich, P. & Povall, M (1981). *Equal Pay and Opportunities: A Study of the Implementation and Effects of the Equal Pay and Sex Discrimination Acts in 26 Organizations*. London: H. M. S. O.

Sorensen, Elaine Joy (1994). *Comparable Worth: Is It a Worthy Policy?* Princeton, N.J.: Princeton University Press.

—, (1984). "Equal Pay for Comparable Worth: A Policy for Eliminating the Undervaluation of Women's Work", *Journal of Economic Issues* 18(2).

—, (1991). *Exploring the Reasons behind the Narrowing Gender Gap in Earnings*. Washington, D.C.: Urban Institute Press; Lanham, MD: Distributed by University Press of America.

Soumeli, Eva & Nergaard, Kristine (2002). *Gender Pay Equity in Europe*. See http://www.eurofound.europa.eu/eiro/2002/01/study/tn0201101s.htm (accessed on Oct 30, 2007).

Spelfogel, EJ (1981). "Equal Pay for Work of Comparable Value: A New Concept", *Labor Law Journal* 32(1).

Spiegel, Fredelle Zaiman (1994). *Women's Wages, Women's Worth: Politics, Religion, and Equity*. New York: Continuum.

Spizman, Lawrence M (2001/2002). "The Economist's Role in Equal Pay Act Litigation", *Journal of Legal Economics* 11(3): 69–85.

Stackpool-Moore (1990). "From Equal Pay to Equal Value in Australia: Myth or Reality?" *Comparative Labor Law Journal* 11: 273–94.

Starich, Megan L. (2007). "The 2006 Revisions to Japan's Equal Opportunity Employment Law: A Narrow Approach to a Pervasive Problem", *Pacific Rim law and Policy* 16: 551.

State Services Commission (1991). *Equity at Work, an Approach to Gender Neutral Job Evaluation*. New Zealand.

Stelle, I (2005). "Tracing the Single Source: Choice of Comparators in Equal Pay Claims", *The Industrial Law Journal* 34(4):338–44.

Stevenson, Mary Huff (1984). *Determinants of Low Wages for Women Workers*. New York, NY: Praeger.

Stone, Christopher D (2004). "Common but Differentiated Responsibilities in International Law", *American Journal of International Law* 98: 276.
Stone, Katherine (2004). *From Widgets to Digits: Employment Regulation for the Changing Workplace*. Oxford: Cambridge University Press.
Stratigaki, Maria (2005). "*Gender* Mainstreaming vs Positive Action: An Ongoing Conflict in EU *Gender* Equality Policy", *The European Journal of Women's Studies* 12(2): 165–186.
Strober, Myra (1972). "Lower Pay for Women: A Case of Economic Discrimination", *Industrial Relations* 11(2): 279–284.
Sugeno, Kazuo (1992). *Japanese Employment and Labor Law* 161 (Leo Kanowitz trans., Carolina Academic Press, 2002).
——(1979). "Public Employee Strike Problems and Its Legal Regulation in Japan", In Witmore Gray (Ed.), *Current Studies in Japanese Law*. Ann Arbor: University of Michigan Press.
Sullerot, Evelyne (1975). "Equality of Remuneration for Men and Women in the Member States of the EEC", *International Labor Review* 112(2–3): 87–108.
Sulzner, George T. (2000). "A Pay Equity Saga: The Public Service Alliance of Canada vs. The Treasury Board of Canada Secretariat", *Journal of Collective Negotiations* 29(2): 89–122.
Suzuki, Hiromasa (1992). "Equal Pay and Equal Opportunity Issues in Japan", in Alan Gladstone et al. (Eds.), *Labor Relations in a Changing Environment*. New York: Walter de Gruyter.
Szyszczak, E. M (1985). "Pay Inequalities and Equal Value Claims", *The Modern Law Review* 48: 139–157.
Takahashi, Nobuko (1975). "Women's Wages in Japan and the Question of Equal Pay", *International Labor Review* 111: 51–68.
Tallberg, Jonas (2002). "Paths to Compliance: Enforcement, Management, and the European Union", *International Organization* 56(3): 609–643.
Thalmann-Antene, H (1971). "Equal Pay: the Position in Switzerland", *International Labor Review* 104(4).
"The Comparable Worth Dilemma: Are Apples and Oranges Ripe for Comparison?" *Baylor Law Review* (Winter 1985), 37: 227–54.
"The Future of Comparable Worth: Looking in New Directions", *Syracuse Law Review* (1987), 37: 1189–1218.
Thomas, C (1983). "Pay Equity and Comparable Worth", *Labor Law Journal* 34(1): 3–12.
——, (2003). "Information Sources and Measures of International Labor Standards on Employment Discrimination", *Comparative Labor Law and Policy Journal* 24: 365.
Thomas, Constance, Oelz, Martin & Beaudonnet, Xavier (2004). *The Use of International Labor Law in Domestic Courts: Theory, Recent Jurisprudence, and Practical Implications*. See http://training.itcilo.it/ils/ils_judges/training_materials/english/Article%20Beaudonnet,%20Oelz,%20Thomas.pdf (accessed on Dec 30, 2007).
Thompson, A (2002). "Applying Rational Theory to International Law: The Promise and Pitfalls", *Journal of Legal Studies* 31: 285.
Thomson, Suteera (1999). "Gender Equality in Thailand: Opportunities and Challenges", *Journal of the Asian and Pacific Development Center* 1(1): 65–81.
Thornton, Margaret (1981). "(Un)equal Pay for Work of Equal Value", *The Journal of Industrial Relations* 23(4): 466–481.
Todres, E. M (1990). "Women's Work in Ontario: Pay Equity and the Wage Gap", *Ottawa Law Review* 22: 555–71.
Tomaskovic-Devey, Don & Skaggs, Sheryl (2002). "Sex Segregation, Labor Process Organization, and Gender Earnings Inequality", *The American Journal of Sociology* 108(1): 102–128.
Tomei, Manuela (2003). "Discrimination and Equality at Work: A Review of the Concepts", *International Labor Review* 142 (4): 401–418.

Tonguthai, Pawadee (2002). *Gender Equality and Decent Work in Thailand*. Bangkok: International Labor Office.
Trachtman, Joel P (1999). "Bananas, Direct Effect and Compliance", *European Journal of International Law* 9.
Traxler, Franz et al. (2001). *National Labor Relations in Internationalized Markets: a Comparative Study of Institutions, Change, and Performance*. Oxford; New York: Oxford University Press.
Treiman, Donald J et al. (Eds.) (1981). *Women, Work, and Wages: Equal Pay for Jobs of Equal Value*. Washington, D.C.: National Academy Press.
Treu, T (1986). "Equal pay and Comparable Worth: A View from Europe", *Comparative Labor Law Journal* 8(1): 1–33.
Trimble, Philip. "International Law, World Order, and Critical Legal Studies", *Stanford Law Review* 42: 811.
True, Jacqui (2003). *Gender, Globalization, and Post-socialism: the Czech Republic after Communism*. New York: Columbia University Press.
Tzannatos, Z (1987). "Equal Pay in Greece and Britain", *Industrial Relations Journal* 18(4): 275–283.
UNIFEM (2005). *Progress of the World's Women 2005*. See http://wiego.org/publications/PoWW2005_eng.pdf (accessed on Sep 10, 2007).
—, (2008). *Progress of the World's Women 2008*. http://www.unifem.org/progress/2008/media/POWW08_Report_Full_Text.pdf (accessed on Sep 30, 2009).
United Nations (2005). *Gender Equality and Empowerment: ESCAP Region*. New York: United Nations Economic and Social Commission for Asia and the Pacific.
—, (2005). *Taking Action: Achieving Gender Equality and Empowering Women*. UN Millennium Project, Task Force on Education and Gender Equality. New York: United Nations.
—, (1995). *The World's Women 1995: Trends and Statistics*. New York: United Nations.
United Nations Research Institute for Social Development (2005). *Gender Equality: Striving for Justice in an Unequal World*. See http://www.unrisd.org/80256B3C005BCCF9/(httpPublications)/1FF4AC64C1894EAAC1256FA3005E7201?OpenDocument (accessed on Dec 30, 2007).
Universal Declaration of Human Rights, GA Res. 217A (III), UN Doc. A/810 (1948).
Valticos, Nicholas (1979). *International Labor Law*. Kluwer: International Law.
Vandaele, Arne (2003). *International Labor Rights and the Social Clause: Friends or Foes?* London: Cameron May.
Vangsness K. (1971). "Equal Pay in Norway", *International Labor Review* 103(4): 379–392.
Verwilghen, Michael (Ed.) (1993). *Access to Equality between Men and Women in the European Community*. Louvain-la-Neuve: Presses Universitaires de Louvain.
Vidas, Davor (2000). *Implementing the Environmental protection Regime for the Antarctic*. London: Kluwer Academic Publishers.
Vieira, Jose Antonio Cabral & Pereira, Pedro Telhado (1993). "Wage Differential and Allocation: An Application to the Azores Islands", *Economia* (Portuguese Catholic University) 17(2): 127–59.
Vieira, N (1985). "Comparable Worth and the Gunther {County of Washington v. Gunther, 101 S. Ct. 2242} Case: The New Drive for Equal Pay", *U.C. Davis Law Review* 18: 449–486.
Wahl, Angelika Von (2005). "Liberal, Conservative, Social Democratic, or…European? The European Union as Equal Employment Regime", *Social Politics* 12(1): 67–95.
Walby, Sylvia (2003). "Policy Developments for Workplace Gender Equity in a Global Era: The Importance of the EU in the UK", *Review of Policy Research* 45–64.
Waldfogel, Jane (1994). *Women Working for Less: Family Status and Women's Pay in the United States and United Kingdom*. Ph. D. Dissertation. Harvard University 0084.
—, (1998). "Understanding the 'Family Gap' in Pay for Women with Children", *The Journal of Economic Perspectives* 12(1): 137–156.

Waltz, Kenneth N (1979). *Theory of International Politics*. Reading: Addison-Wesley Pub. Co.
Warskett, Rosemary (1990). "Wage Solidarity and Equal Value: or Gender and Class in the Structuring of Work Place Hierarchies", *Studies in Political Economy* 55–83.
Weaver, Kathleen (1991). "Comparable Worth in the United States and the Canadian - Province of Ontario", *Boston College International and Comparative Law Review* 14: 137–58.
Weiler, P (1986). "The Wages of Sex: the Uses and Limits of Comparable Worth", *Harvard Law Review* 99:1728–1807.
Weiner, N. and M. Gunderson (1990). *Pay Equity: Issues, Options and Experiences*. Toronto: Butterworths.
Weil, David N (2003). *Individual Rights and Collective Agents: the Role of Old and New Workplace Institutions in the Regulation of Labor Markets?* Cambridge, Mass.: National Bureau of Economic Research.
Weisburd, A.M (1999). "Implications of International Relations Theory for the International Law of Human Rights", *Columbia Journal of Transnational Law* 38: 45.
Weiss, Brown (1997). *International Compliance with Nonbinding Accords*. Washington, DC: American Society of International Law.
Wendt, Alexander (1995). "Constructing International Politics", *International Security* 20: 71.
Whitehouse, Gillian (2003). "Gender and Pay Equity: Future Research Directions", *Asia Pacific Journal of Human Resources* 41 (1): 116–128.
——, (1992). "Legislation and Labor Market Gender Inequality: An Analysis of OECD Countries", *Work, Employment & Society* 6: 65–86.
——, (2001). "Recent Trends in Pay Equity", *the Journal of Industrial Relations* 43(1): 66–78.
Whitehouse, Gillian & Zetlin, Di (2000). "Globalization and the Pursuit of Pay Equity: Contradictory", in Paul Edwards and Tony Elger (Eds.), *The Global Economy, National States, and the Regulating of Labor*. New York: Continuum.
Whitehouse, Gillian, Zetlin, Di & Earnshaw, Jill (2001). "Prosecuting Pay Equity: Evolving Strategies in Britain and Australia", *Gender, Work and Organization* 8(4): 365–386.
Wilkinson, Rorden (2002). "Peripheralizing Labor: The ILO, WTO and the Completion of the Bretton Woods Project", in Jeffrey Harrod & Robert O'Brien (Eds.) *Global Unions? Theory and Strategies of Organized Labor in the Global Political Economy*. New York: Routledge.
Willborn, Steven L. "Equal Pay for Work of Equal Value: Comparable Worth in the United Kingdom", *American Journal of Comparative Law* 34(3): 415–457.
——, (Ed.) (1991). *Women's Wages: Stability and Change in Six Industrialized Countries: a Research Annual*. Greenwich, Conn: JAI Press.
Williams, J. P (1995). "Lower Pay for Women's Coaches: Refuting Some Common Justifications", t*he Journal of College and University Law* 21: 643–89.
Wilson, Dolly Smith (2005). *'The True Sphere of Women'? Gender, Work and Equal Pay in Britain, 1945–1975*. Ph. D. Dissertation. Boston College 0016.
Wilson, Joseph et al. (2006). *Race and Labor Matters in the New U.S. Economy*. Lanham: Rowman & Littlefield.
Wittig, M.A. & Lowe, R.H (1989). "Comparable Worth Theory and Policy", *Journal of Social Issues* 45(4).
Wolford, Karen M (1995). "Gender Discrimination in Employment: Wage Inequity for Professional and Doctoral Degree Holders in the United States and Possible Remedies", *Journal of Education Finance* 31(1): 82–100.
Women in Development and Nation Building Act. Dated 12 February 1992. Official Gazette of the Republic of the Philippines, 4 May 1992, Vol. 88, No. 12. Labor Law Documents, 1992-PHL 2, ILO.

Women's Bureau (1987). *Pay Equity: A Survey of 7 OECD Countries*, Information Paper No. 5, Australian Government Publishing Service, Canberra.
Women and Work Commission (2006). *Shaping A Fairer Future*. See www.equalities.gov.uk/publications/wwc_shaping_fairer_future06.pdf (accessed on Dec 30, 2007).
Works Constitution Act. Federal Republic of Germany. Bundesgesetzblatt, Part I, 18 Jan.1972, No. 2. Legislative Series, 1972-Ger.F.R.1. ILO.
World Bank (2003). *Gender Equality and the Millennium Development Goals*. Washington: World Bank.
——, (2006). *Gender Equality is Smart Economics: The World Bank Gender Action Plan*. See http://siteresources.worldbank.org/INTGENDER/Resources/GAPNov2.pdf. (accessed on Sep 10, 2007).
——, (2006). *Global Monitoring Report, Millennium Development Goals: strengthening Mutual Accountability, Aid, Trade and Governance*, see http://web.worldbank.org/WBSITE/EXTERNAL/EXTDEC/EXTGLOBALMONITOR/EXTGLOBALMONITOR2006/0,,menuPK:2186472~pagePK:64218926~piPK:64218953~theSitePK:2186432,00.html (accessed on Sep 10, 2007).
——, (2006). *World Development Report 2006: Equity and Development 2*, see http://econ.worldbank.org/external/default/main?pagePK=64165259&theSitePK=469372&piPK=64165421&menuPK=64166093&entityID=000112742_20050920110826 (accessed on Sep 10, 2007).
Wynn, M (1994). "Equal Pay and Gender Segregation", *The Law Quarterly Review* 110: 556–62.
Yadav, K. P (2006). *Gender Equality and Economic Development*. New Delhi: Sarup & Sons.
Young, Oran R (1979). *Compliance and Public Authority*. Baltimore: Johns Hopkins University Press.
Zeigler, Sara L (2006). "Litigating Equality: The Limits of the Equal Pay Act", *Review of Public Personnel Administration* 26(3): 199–215.
Zuleeg, M (1999). "Gender Equality and Affirmative Action under the Law of the European Union", *Columbia Journal of European Law* 5(2): 319–28.

Websites

An Information Base on Equal Employment Opportunities for Women and Men: http://www.ilo.org/public/english/employment/gems/eeo/
Commission of Pay Equity, Quebec, Canada: http://www.ces.gouv.qc.ca/fr/english/english.asp
Equal Pay Coalition, Ontario, Canada: http://www.equalpaycoalition.org
Gender Wage Gaps in the U.S and Worldwide, Center for Gender Studies: http://gstudies.asp.radford.edu/sources/wage_gaps/worldwide.htm
Human Rights Commission of New Zealand. http://www.hrc.co.nz/home/default.php
LaborWeb: http://www.lex.unict.it/eurolabor/en/default.htm
Labor and Global Change Database: http://www.ilir.umich.edu/lagn/
National Committee on Pay Equity: http://www.pay-equity.org/
Pay Equity Commission, Canada: http://www.payequity.gov.on.ca
Pay Equity Review Resources, Department of Justice, Canada: http://www.justice.gc.ca/en/payeqsal/5000.html
The U. S. Equal Employment Opportunity Commission: www.eeoc.gov
Trade Unions and Labor Relations Database: http://www.polwiss.fuberlin.de/tu/english/index.html
World Policy Institute: http://www.worldpolicy.org

APPENDIX

C100 EQUAL REMUNERATION CONVENTION, 1951

Convention concerning Equal Remuneration for Men and Women Workers for Work of Equal Value (Note: Date of coming into force: 23:05:1953.)
Convention:C100
Place:Geneva
Session of the Conference:34
Date of adoption:29:06:1951

The General Conference of the International Labour Organisation,

Having been convened at Geneva by the Governing Body of the International Labour Office, and having met in its Thirty-fourth Session on 6 June 1951, and

Having decided upon the adoption of certain proposals with regard to the principle of equal remuneration for men and women workers for work of equal value, which is the seventh item on the agenda of the session, and

Having determined that these proposals shall take the form of an international Convention,

adopts this twenty-ninth day of June of the year one thousand nine hundred and fifty-one the following Convention, which may be cited as the Equal Remuneration Convention, 1951:

Article 1

For the purpose of this Convention –

(a) the term remuneration includes the ordinary, basic or minimum wage or salary and any additional emoluments whatsoever payable directly or indirectly, whether in cash or in kind, by the employer to the worker and arising out of the worker's employment;

(b) the term equal remuneration for men and women workers for work of equal value refers to rates of remuneration established without discrimination based on sex.

Article 2

1. Each Member shall, by means appropriate to the methods in operation for determining rates of remuneration, promote and, in so far as is consistent with such methods, ensure the application to all workers of the principle of equal remuneration for men and women workers for work of equal value.
2. This principle may be applied by means of –

   (a) national laws or regulations;
   (b) legally established or recognised machinery for wage determination;
   (c) collective agreements between employers and workers; or
   (d) a combination of these various means.

Article 3

1. Where such action will assist in giving effect to the provisions of this Convention measures shall be taken to promote objective appraisal of jobs on the basis of the work to be performed.
2. The methods to be followed in this appraisal may be decided upon by the authorities responsible for the determination of rates of remuneration, or, where such rates are determined by collective agreements, by the parties thereto.
3. Differential rates between workers which correspond, without regard to sex, to differences, as determined by such objective appraisal, in the work to be performed shall not be considered as being contrary to the principle of equal remuneration for men and women workers for work of equal value.

Article 4

Each Member shall co-operate as appropriate with the employers' and workers' organisations concerned for the purpose of giving effect to the provisions of this Convention.

Article 5

The formal ratifications of this Convention shall be communicated to the Director-General of the International Labour Office for registration.

Article 6

1. This Convention shall be binding only upon those Members of the International Labour Organisation whose ratifications have been registered with the Director-General.
2. It shall come into force twelve months after the date on which the ratifications of two Members have been registered with the Director-General.
3. Thereafter, this Convention shall come into force for any Member twelve months after the date on which its ratification has been registered.

Article 7

1. Declarations communicated to the Director-General of the International Labour Office in accordance with paragraph 2 of Article 35 of the Constitution of the International Labour Organisation shall indicate –

   a) the territories in respect of which the Member concerned undertakes that the provisions of the Convention shall be applied without modification;
   b) the territories in respect of which it undertakes that the provisions of the Convention shall be applied subject to modifications, together with details of the said modifications;
   c) the territories in respect of which the Convention is inapplicable and in such cases the grounds on which it is inapplicable;
   d) the territories in respect of which it reserves its decision pending further consideration of the position.

2. The undertakings referred to in subparagraphs (a) and (b) of paragraph 1 of this Article shall be deemed to be an integral part of the ratification and shall have the force of ratification.

3. Any Member may at any time by a subsequent declaration cancel in whole or in part any reservation made in its original declaration in virtue of subparagraph (b), (c) or (d) of paragraph 1 of this Article.
4. Any Member may, at any time at which the Convention is subject to denunciation in accordance with the provisions of Article 9, communicate to the Director-General a declaration modifying in any other respect the terms of any former declaration and stating the present position in respect of such territories as it may specify.

Article 8

1. Declarations communicated to the Director-General of the International Labour Office in accordance with paragraph 4 or 5 of Article 35 of the Constitution of the International Labour Organisation shall indicate whether the provisions of the Convention will be applied in the territory concerned without modification or subject to modifications; when the declaration indicates that the provisions of the Convention will be applied subject to modifications, it shall give details of the said modifications.
2. The Member, Members or international authority concerned may at any time by a subsequent declaration renounce in whole or in part the right to have recourse to any modification indicated in any former declaration.
3. The Member, Members or international authority concerned may, at any time at which this Convention is subject to denunciation in accordance with the provisions of Article 9, communicate to the Director-General a declaration modifying in any other respect the terms of any former declaration and stating the present position in respect of the application of the Convention.

Article 9

1. A Member which has ratified this Convention may denounce it after the expiration of ten years from the date on which the Convention first comes into force, by an act communicated to the Director-General of the International Labour Office for registration. Such denunciation shall not take effect until one year after the date on which it is registered.
2. Each Member which has ratified this Convention and which does not, within the year following the expiration of the period of ten

years mentioned in the preceding paragraph, exercise the right of denunciation provided for in this Article, will be bound for another period of ten years and, thereafter, may denounce this Convention at the expiration of each period of ten years under the terms provided for in this Article.

Article 10

1. The Director-General of the International Labour Office shall notify all Members of the International Labour Organisation of the registration of all ratifications, declarations and denunciations communicated to him by the Members of the Organisation.
2. When notifying the Members of the Organisation of the registration of the second ratification communicated to him, the Director-General shall draw the attention of the Members of the Organisation to the date upon which the Convention will come into force.

Article 11

The Director-General of the International Labour Office shall communicate to the Secretary-General of the United Nations for registration in accordance with Article 102 of the Charter of the United Nations full particulars of all ratifications, declarations and acts of denunciation registered by him in accordance with the provisions of the preceding articles.

Article 12

At such times as may consider necessary the Governing Body of the International Labour Office shall present to the General Conference a report on the working of this Convention and shall examine the desirability of placing on the agenda of the Conference the question of its revision in whole or in part.

Article 13

1. Should the Conference adopt a new Convention revising this Convention in whole or in part, then, unless the new Convention otherwise provides –

a) the ratification by a Member of the new revising Convention shall ipso jure involve the immediate denunciation of this Convention, notwithstanding the provisions of Article 9 above, if and when the new revising Convention shall have come into force;
b) as from the date when the new revising Convention comes into force this Convention shall cease to be open to ratification by the Members.

2. This Convention shall in any case remain in force in its actual form and content for those Members which have ratified it but have not ratified the revising Convention.

Article 14

The English and French versions of the text of this Convention are equally authoritative.

INDEX

Notes, tables, and figures are indicated by *n, t,* and *f* following the page number.

www.ingramcontent.com/pod-product-compliance
Lightning Source LLC
Chambersburg PA
CBHW061209240926
51846CB00006B/1157